# Lecture Notes in Computer Science     14283

The series Lecture Notes in Computer Science (LNCS), including its subseries Lecture Notes in Artificial Intelligence (LNAI) and Lecture Notes in Bioinformatics (LNBI), has established itself as a medium for the publication of new developments in computer science and information technology research, teaching, and education.

LNCS enjoys close cooperation with the computer science R & D community, the series counts many renowned academics among its volume editors and paper authors, and collaborates with prestigious societies. Its mission is to serve this international community by providing an invaluable service, mainly focused on the publication of conference and workshop proceedings and postproceedings. LNCS commenced publication in 1973.

Dalibor Klusáček · Julita Corbalán ·
Gonzalo P. Rodrigo
Editors

# Job Scheduling Strategies for Parallel Processing

26th Workshop, JSSPP 2023
St. Petersburg, FL, USA, May 19, 2023
Revised Selected Papers

*Editors*
Dalibor Klusáček ⓘ
CESNET
Prague, Czech Republic

Julita Corbalán ⓘ
Barcelona Supercomputing Center
Barcelona, Spain

Gonzalo P. Rodrigo
Apple
Cupertino, CA, USA

ISSN 0302-9743                           ISSN 1611-3349  (electronic)
Lecture Notes in Computer Science
ISBN 978-3-031-43942-1              ISBN 978-3-031-43943-8  (eBook)
https://doi.org/10.1007/978-3-031-43943-8

This Springer imprint is published by the registered company Springer Nature Switzerland AG
The registered company address is: Gewerbestrasse 11, 6330 Cham, Switzerland

Paper in this product is recyclable.

# Preface

This volume contains the papers presented at the 26th workshop on Job Scheduling Strategies for Parallel Processing (JSSPP 2023), which was held on May 19, 2023, in conjunction with the 37th IEEE International Parallel and Distributed Processing Symposium (IPDPS 2023) in St. Petersburg, Florida USA. The proceedings of previous workshops are also available from Springer as LNCS volumes 949, 1162, 1291, 1459, 1659, 1911, 2221, 2537, 2862, 3277, 3834, 4376, 4942, 5798, 6253, 7698, 8429, 8828, 10353, 10773, 11332, 12326, 12985 and 13592.

This year fourteen papers were submitted to the workshop, of which we accepted 8 regular papers and one keynote. All submitted papers went through a complete single-blind review process, with the full version being read and evaluated by an average of 3.8 reviewers. We would like to especially thank our Program Committee members and additional reviewers for their willingness to participate in this effort and their excellent, detailed and thoughtful reviews.

After three years when JSSPP was held virtually due to the worldwide COVID-19 pandemic, this year JSSPP was once again held in person in St. Petersburg, Florida USA. All talks were presented live, allowing the participants to interact with the authors of the papers. We are very thankful to the presenters of accepted papers for their participation in the live workshop session. The workshop was organized into three sessions with eight technical papers and one keynote talk.

The keynote was delivered by Morris "Moe" Jette who is the lead architect of the Slurm Workload Manager, providing resource management on about 60% of the Top 500 systems. After a 30-year career at Lawrence Livermore National Laboratory focused primarily on system software and distributed computing, he co-founded SchedMD LLC in 2010 to further develop Slurm. In his talk, Moe presented several key features of the open-source, fault tolerant and scalable Slurm Workload Manager. These include the description of Slurm entities, daemons and plugins. Next, the capabilities of Slurm to manage access to resources were thoroughly presented, describing queues, job prioritization, typical configurations and available scheduling algorithms. Also, compute node management capabilities were addressed including advanced features such as power management, cloud bursting and container support. Last but not least, future development was presented, e.g., the support for integration with external orchestrator systems like Kubernetes.

Eight papers accepted for this year's JSSPP covered several interesting problems within the resource management and scheduling domains. The first technical paper was presented by Pascuzzi et al. and investigated the requirements and properties of the asynchronous task execution of machine learning-driven high-performance computing workflows. The authors modeled the degree of asynchronicity permitted for arbitrary workflows and proposed key metrics that can be used to determine qualitative benefits when employing asynchronous execution. The paper presented results obtained through experiments on the Summit supercomputer and showed that the performance enhancements due to asynchronous execution were consistent with the presented model.

Masola et al. presented their work that aims to estimate latency induced by running concurrent kernels in partitioned GPUs. Sharing one GPU among several concurrent kernels is a good approach to improve the overall GPU utilization. However, it poses significant challenges in estimating kernel execution time latencies when kernels are dispatched to variable-sized GPU partitions. Moreover, memory interference within co-running kernels must be considered as well. In their study, Masola et al. proposed a practical and fairly accurate memory-aware latency estimation model for co-running GPU kernels.

The third paper, written by Nissim and Schwartz, studied the problem of parallel task execution where some of the tasks experience delays (stragglers). These stragglers slow down the whole computation since the slowest processor determines the runtime. In their work, Nissim and Schwartz proposed a new load-balancing solution tailored for distributed matrix multiplication. Their solution reduced latency overhead compared to existing dynamic load-balancing solutions, while also performing better compared to solutions using redundancy.

Boëzennec el al. took a detailed survey of the strengths and weaknesses of current optimization metrics used for HPC batch schedulers. The authors discussed bias and limitations of the optimization metrics most frequently found in the literature, while providing their idea on how to evaluate performance when studying HPC batch scheduling. Also, the authors proposed a new metric: the standard deviation of the utilization, which they believe can be used when the utilization reaches its limits. Importantly, the authors presented a rather deep study of the impact that the use of inaccurate walltime estimates has on these selected optimization metrics, discussing thoroughly the true meaning of these (sometimes surprising) results.

Rosa et al. did an experimental analysis of regression-obtained scheduling heuristics. Their aim was to improve our understanding of whether we gain scheduling performance by using more complex features and whether such regression-obtained heuristics provide stable scheduling performance over the evolution of HPC platforms and workloads. The authors argued that scheduling heuristics constituted by complex, large-sized polynomials are more likely to degrade the scheduling performance than simpler linear combination of the jobs' characteristics. Also, Rosa et al. showed that regression-obtained heuristics can be resilient to the long-term evolution of HPC platforms and workloads without needing to be readjusted over time.

Kishimoto and Nakamura used graph neural networks in order to predict job waiting time, e.g., in a supercomputer or a data center. Being able to provide a reasonably accurate wait time estimate is crucial for users' research planning or even for the scheduling policy itself. To address this problem, a graph neural network architecture of deep learning was employed in this study.

The last section of the workshop started with a paper written by Hall et al. In their work they analyzed the impact of coscheduling in traditional HPC systems. Frequently nowadays, systems schedule parallel jobs such that each node is allocated exclusively. However, for some HPC applications and scientific workflows such an approach may not be efficient, as it is unable to fully utilize the nodes. Coscheduling allows different jobs to use the same node, sharing its resources. The authors demonstrated that coscheduling allows for better node utilization while lowering the average job turnaround time.

Last, but not least, de la Torre and Halappanavar presented a novel strategy for the cost-efficient selection of cloud computing resources for large scientific workflows using Lagrange relaxation. Their approach is based on preselection of resources and demand decomposition to create a series of smaller sub-problems, which allow the estimation of the best cost-structures and selection of cloud computing service providers. The authors demonstrated excellent performance in relation to optimal solutions while also reducing the computational time from hours to seconds for a representative 36-month problem.

We hope you will like this year's proceedings and will be able to join us at the next JSSPP workshop, this time in San Francisco, California USA, on May 31, 2024. Enjoy your reading!

July 2023                                                          Dalibor Klusáček
                                                                    Julita Corbalán
                                                              Gonzalo P. Rodrigo

# Organization

## Program Chairs

| | |
|---|---|
| Dalibor Klusáček | CESNET, Czech Republic |
| Julita Corbalán | Barcelona Supercomputing Center, Spain |
| Gonzalo P. Rodrigo | Apple, USA |

## Program Committee

| | |
|---|---|
| Orna Agmon Ben-Yehuda | University of Haifa, Israel |
| Amaya Booker | Facebook, USA |
| Henri Casanova | University of Hawaii, USA |
| Dror Feitelson | Hebrew University, Israel |
| Eitan Frachtenberg | Facebook, USA |
| Alfredo Goldman | University of São Paulo, Brazil |
| Cristian Klein | Umeå Univeristy/Elastisys, Sweden |
| Zhiling Lan | Illinois Institute of Technology, USA |
| Priyesh Narayanan | Netflix, USA |
| Bill Nitzberg | Altair, USA |
| Nikos Parlavantzas | INSA Rennes, France |
| Lavanya Ramakrishnan | Lawrence Berkeley National Lab, USA |
| Larry Rudolph | Two Sigma, USA |
| Uwe Schwiegelshohn | TU Dortmund, Germany |
| Leonel Sousa | Universidade de Lisboa, Portugal |
| Abel Souza | University of Massachusetts Amherst, USA |
| Ramin Yahyapour | University of Göttingen, Germany |

## Additional Reviewers

| | |
|---|---|
| Ricardo Nobre | INESC-ID, Portugal |
| Sahar Moradi Cherati | INESC-ID, Portugal |
| Jiří Filipovič | Masaryk University, Czech Republic |

# Contents

# Keynote

# Architecture of the Slurm Workload Manager

Morris A. Jette$^{(\boxtimes)}$ and Tim Wickberg

SchedMD LLC, Lehi, UT 84043, USA
{jette,tim}@schedmd.com

**Abstract.** Slurm is an open source, fault-tolerant, and highly scalable workload manager used on many of the world's supercomputers and computer clusters. As a cluster workload manager, Slurm has three key functions. First, it allocates exclusive and/or non-exclusive access to resources for some duration of time. Second, it provides a framework for starting, executing, and monitoring work on the allocated resources. Finally, it arbitrates contention for resources by managing queues of pending work and enforcing administrative policies. This paper describes the current design and capabilities of Slurm.

**Keywords:** scheduling · slurm · hpc

## 1 Introduction

The development of Slurm began at Lawrence Livermore National Laboratory (LLNL) in 2002. It was originally designed as a simple resource manager[1] capable only of allocating whole nodes to jobs, then dispatching and managing those applications on their allocated resources [13]. Slurm relied upon an external scheduler such as Maui [10] to manage queues of work and schedule resources. Slurm has since evolved into a comprehensive workload scheduler capable of managing the most demanding workflows on many of the largest computers in the world. While Slurm has evolved a great deal over its two decades of existence, its original design goals have largely persisted and proven critical to its success.

- Open Source: Slurm's source code is distributed under the GNU General Public License and is freely available on Github [26]. This openness has resulted in contributions from roughly 300 individuals ranging from minor corrections to the documentation to complex added functionality.
- Portability: Slurm is written in the C language with a GNU autoconf configuration engine. Slurm can be thought of as a highly modular and generic kernel with hundreds of plugins available for customization using a building-block

---

[1] Slurm was originally an acronym for "Simple Linux Utility for Resource Management", and stylized as "SLURM". The acronym was dropped in 2012 and the preferred capitalization changed to "Slurm".

D. Klusáček et al. (Eds.): JSSPP 2023, LNCS 14283, pp. 3–23, 2023.
https://doi.org/10.1007/978-3-031-43943-8_1

approach in order to support a wide variety of hardware types, software environments, and scheduling capabilities. Site-specific plugins and scripts can easily be integrated for even greater customization. This flexibility allows Slurm to operate effectively in virtually any environment.

- Scalability: Slurm daemons are highly concurrent—with locking on a set of core data-structures—in order to support the largest computers with tens of thousands of jobs. As system sizes have increased through time, only relatively minor changes to Slurm have been required. The first exascale system—Frontier at Oak Ridge National Laboratory (ORNL)—runs Slurm, and required no system- or scale-specific modifications to the code at installation [4]. A full system application on Frontier from job submission to termination of all processes and release of its resources can be completed in under 13 s.
- Fault tolerance: Slurm has no single point of failure. Backup daemons and cached information insure effective utilization of even the most failure prone systems. Applications can continue execution through failure of allocated compute nodes.
- Security: Slurm authenticates all communication between processes within the cluster using MUNGE [16], ensuring that users cannot impersonate one another or Slurm's control processes. Optional support for JWT [14] allows authentication to Slurm from the REST interface to permit external systems interactions with the cluster.
- System administrator friendly: Slurm has strived to make the support of large and complex systems as simple as possible for system administrators. This includes use of "hostlists" for node name specifications, centralized configuration management, and simplified dynamic reconfiguration.

Simplicity was one of Slurm's original design goals. While that goal may have been satisfied while Slurm was only performing resource management, complexity has increased greatly with the addition of workload scheduling logic. Slurm's code base is currently over six hundred thousand lines, primarily in the C language.

The original functionality of Slurm was loosely based on Quadrics RMS [24], a closed source resource manager which only supported Quadrics proprietary networks and thus failed to satisfy the broader requirements of LLNL.

The remainder of this paper will present information about Slurm's overall design and capabilities as of the 23.02 release (February 2023). Detailed information about its configuration, daemons, commands and operation currently spans many hundreds of pages [29] and is outside the scope of this paper.

## 2   Slurm Entities

A **job** in Slurm is a resource allocation request. It can either be in the form of a batch script to be queued for later execution, or an interactive job for which the user awaits resource allocation and then makes real time use of it. Job information includes a numeric ID, name, time limit (minimum and/or maximum), size specifications (a minimum and/or maximum count of nodes, CPUs, sockets, cores and/or threads), names of specific nodes to include or exclude in its allocation, node features—both required (e.g., specific processor type, this specification can include AND, OR, exclusive OR, and count specifications) and preferred (e.g., faster clock speed desired), required licenses, account name, job dependency specifications (to control the order of job execution), Quality Of Service (QOS), relative priority, and queues/partitions to use. The minimum time limit and size specifications are valuable if the user is willing to sacrifice run time and/or resources in order that the job be initiated as soon as possible. Slurm's backfill scheduler will take advantage of this flexibility to allocate such a job with the maximum run time and resources possible within it's specified range without delaying the initiation time of higher priority jobs. The ability for a job to explicitly exclude specific nodes from its allocation is valuable if the user has doubts as to the integrity of specific nodes.

A **job step** in Slurm is a set of parallel tasks, typically an MPI application. A job can initiate an arbitrary number of steps serially and/or in parallel, with Slurm providing the queuing and resource management for those steps within the job's existing resource allocation. Use cases in which jobs execute thousands of steps are not uncommon, particularly when jobs may need to wait lengthy periods of time for their initial resource allocation request to be satisfied. Job step state information maintained by Slurm include its ID expressed as a job ID followed by a period and step ID (e.g., "123.45"), name, time limit (maximum), size specification (minimum and/or maximum count of nodes, CPUs, sockets, cores and/or threads), specific node names to include or exclude from its allocation, and node features required in its allocation. The job step management is lighter than job management. If currently available resources within a job allocation are insufficient for a step to be initiated then it is queued until resources are available. Slurm does not support dependencies between job steps—that functionality can be provided by the job script managing the job step workflow if necessary.

A **cluster** typically consists of a collection of nodes sharing a common network. A Slurm cluster can be on premises, in the cloud, or spread across both. A Slurm **federation** is a collection of clusters sharing a common configuration database. By default, a job is submitted to the local cluster, and user commands to gather information about jobs and queues report information about the local cluster. However, all clusters in a federation may be configured to operate as a single system from the perspective of the users. Jobs can be submitted to any individual cluster in the federation or any set of clusters (e.g., clusters from the same manufacturer or having the same architecture), and may be eligible for execution on any of the federated systems.

**Node** configuration includes a wide variety of information, most of which is collected directly from the compute node when Slurm's slurmd daemon is started. Information collected from a compute node and maintained by Slurm includes: count of boards, sockets, cores and threads, a count of CPUs (usually defined as $boards \times sockets \times cores \times threads$, but may vary depending upon configuration), memory size, generic resources (GRES) including names, types and counts (used for GPUs, network bandwidth, scratch disk space, etc.). Information not collected from a compute node but maintained by Slurm include a scheduling preference weight (used to administratively steer jobs towards specific nodes), features (an arbitrary string typically used to record operating system version, CPU type, etc.), node state (up, down, draining, etc.), and a reason for the current node state including the user ID of the individual modifying the node state and the time when state changed. For ease of use with larger clusters, node names may be specified using comma separated numbers and/or ranges (e.g., "node[00,08]", "node[0–15]", "rack[0–7]_blade[0–63]"). **NodeSets** can also be used as a shorthand for collections of nodes, and defined either by an explicit list of nodes, or automatically established on a set of common features. Nodes can be dynamically added and removed from a system, which is generally required for dynamic cluster configurations such as cloud bursting (supplementing an on premises cluster with resources from the cloud on an as needed basis).

Slurm supports the concept of **specialized cores**, which are one or more specific cores on a node reserved for system use and not allocated to jobs. This ensures an application's access to compute resources are never blocked by system overhead and optimal application parallelism can be achieved [23].

A Slurm **partition** is the name given to a job queue[2]. These queues have a wide range of available limits and access controls. Each partition may be associated with a specific set of compute nodes, although each node can be in more than one partition. Alternatively a "floating" partition may be assigned a size, but no specific nodes. When a floating partition's workload is insufficient to fully utilize it's allocated nodes, those resources are made available to other partitions. If the workload exceeds physical resources, the available resources will be distributed per partition scheduling priority, job scheduling priority and applicable limits. Each partition has an access control list, state information (up, down, draining, etc.), scheduling priority, billing weight (higher priority or otherwise more capable partitions may charge jobs at a higher rate), and rules for preemption, over-subscription, gang scheduling [11] and a wide variety of limits. A partition can include a heterogeneous variety of node types. In this case, a resource allocation request can specify the partition(s) to use along with required node features, memory size, etc. A simple example of Slurm entities is shown in Fig. 1.

In order to support a series of closely related jobs, Slurm provides the concept of a **job array**. A job array is a batch job in which a single script is executed multiple times. Typically, input and output files for the batch script differ for each execution. The user can then monitor and manage the entire job array as a single entity. Internally Slurm manages the entire job array as a single record in its job table until execution of an element in the array is ready to begin. At that time, a new job record is created for the element. This minimizes both the memory footprint and management overhead for job arrays. Internally, a single pair of files are used to record the batch script and environment variable for all tasks in the job array. For example:

---

[2] The "partition" term was inherited from Quadrics RMS, which required a strict partitioning of compute nodes within the environment. The requirement that nodes be in disjoint partitions was discarded very early on, but the terminology has persisted.

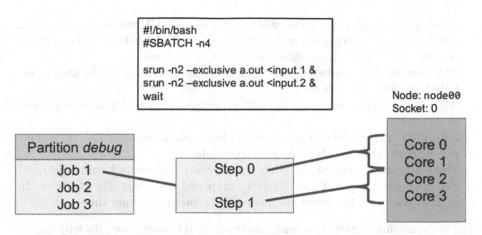

**Fig. 1.** Example partition, job and job step allocation.

$ sbatch --array=1-9000 -i my_ in_ %a -o my_ out_ %a -N1 my.bash
Submits the batch script "my.bash" to be executed 9000 times. The input and output files for each element in the job array will have a prefix of "my_in_" and "my_out_" respectively with the element number appended (e.g., "my_in_123" for the input file used by element number 123). In case some individual elements in the array fail for some reason, those specific job array element IDs may be resubmitted with those IDs identified using the command's "--array" option. For example:

$ sbatch --array=5,28 -i my_ in_ %a -o my_ out_ %a -N1 my.bash
The user can optionally specify element IDs using a range with a step count (e.g., from 1 to 50000 by 10). The user can also specify the maximum number of elements in the job array to be executing at any given time, which is valuable in managing their aggregate workload within their various resource limits. By default, each element in the job array is counted as one job for limit enforcement although limits may be configured for the maximum number of elements in any job array. Environment variables are available in the job array applications identifying the job array parameters.

Slurm supports the concept of **heterogeneous jobs**. For example, some elements of a job may require additional memory or other resources. All components of the heterogeneous job will be monitored and managed as a single entity, although each component can also be monitored and managed independently. A heterogeneous job will be allocated resources only when all components of that job can be allocated resources simultaneously, considering both resource availability and applicable limits. Heterogeneous job steps are also supported and options are available to control how applications are launched across the various components of the heterogeneous job.

In order to support complex workflows, Slurm supports a wide variety of **dependencies** as listed below:

- After: job can begin execution after the specified job IDs have begun execution
- AfterOK: job can begin execution after the specified job IDs have completed successfully (run to completion with exit code of zero)
- AfterNotOK: job can begin execution after the specified job IDs have terminated in some failed state
- AfterAny: job can begin execution after the specified job IDs have terminated in any state
- AfterCorr: an element of a job array can begin execution after the corresponding element ID in another job array completes
- Singleton: the job can begin execution after any previously initiated job with the same job name and user ID have completed (i.e., only one job owned by a given user with the same job name can be running at any time)

The system administrator can configure the desired behavior for jobs with dependencies that cannot be satisfied (e.g., a job dependent upon the successful completion of another job, but that job fails). Typically such jobs are configured to be purged.

Users can request to be notified by email when their jobs change state. This can be valuable for batch jobs in environments where long delays are possible. Job state transitions which can be used to trigger email include: begin, end, fail, requeue, and invalid dependency detected.

A Slurm **account** is used to group users into sets, independent of UNIX groups. Accounts are typically organized in a hierarchical fashion (e.g., division, group, project, etc. see Fig. 2). A user can have access to multiple accounts with a default value. Each account can have one or more account coordinators who are able to create sub-accounts, add or remove users from their account, modify limits and resource apportioning to the users and accounts under their control. The account coordinator may also be able to view accounting information normally hidden from other users, such as a record of jobs executed by other users in the accounts over which they have control.

A Slurm **association** is a combination of cluster, account, user name, and (optional) partition name. Each association can have a fair share allocation of resources and a multitude of limits. It is worth noting that these limits come in two forms. Many limits apply to individual jobs, such as the maximum time limit. Other limits apply on an aggregate basis, such as the maximum number of running jobs for an individual user or all users in some account.

A **Quality Of Service (QOS)** is used to control a job's limits, priority, and charge multiplier. A QOS may be associated with partition or independent of partitions and selected on a job by job basis. A QOS not explicitly bound to a partition can be used with any partition. The benefit in associating a QOS with a partition is in making a greater number of limits available than otherwise provided in Slurm's configuration file for a partition. A typical use case is to configure "standby", "normal", and "expedite" QOS on a system. Jobs submitted to any partition with a "standby" QOS would have very low priority and a corresponding low charge multiplier, say being charged for resource use at 20% of the normal change. Similarly, jobs submitted to any partition with a "expedite"

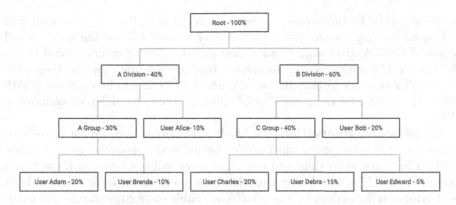

**Fig. 2.** Example account hierarchy with resource allocations.

QOS would be given a very high priority and high charge multiplier, perhaps being charged 5 times the normal rate. Access control lists can be configured to limit which accounts or users can use each QOS. QOS can also be used to define job preemption rules, so the "expedite" QOS might be configured to preempt (terminate running jobs) from the lower priority "standby" QOS. QOS limits available override the partitions and associations limits. So if a user's association has a maximum number of running jobs set to 10, but the "expedite" QOS has a limit of 20, the higher limit will apply to jobs running in the "expedite" QOS. In order to avoid confusion with the multitude of configurable limits, only a subset of limits are typically configured for associations and QOS.

The order of precedence for limits is as follows:

1. Partition QOS
2. Job QOS
3. User association
4. Account associations (ascending the hierarchy)
5. Root/Cluster association (i.e., the top of the account association hierarchy)
6. Partition configuration

If limits are defined at multiple points in this hierarchy, the point in this list where the limit is first defined will be used. Consider the following example:

- MaxJobs = 20 and MaxSubmitJobs is undefined in the partition QOS
- No limits are set in the job QOS and
- MaxJobs = 4 and MaxSubmitJobs = 50 in the user association

The limits in effect will be MaxJobs = 20 and MaxSubmitJobs = 50

A **Generic RESource (GRES)** is an arbitrary on-node resource. These can be allocated to jobs, accounted for, and have limits imposed on their use all in a generic fashion. GRES can also be managed in a hierarchical fashion. GPUs are managed in Slurm as GRES. Jobs can request a specific count of GPUs, administrators can configure GPU limits by job or user, etc. If a cluster has more than one variety of GPU, the job can request some count of GPUs using any variety of GPU available (e.g., "srun --gres=gpu:2 ...") or identify the specific varieties and counts of GPU desired (e.g., "srun --gres=gpu:rtx_5000:2,gpu:rtx_6000:1 ..."). The cgroup [20] plugin is used to enforce binding of applications to their allocated GPUs or other GRES. Resource limits for GRES can be configured with similar flexibility and the possibility of different counts for different varieties of GPU.

An **advanced reservation** is a block of resources reserved for current or future use. These resources can include specific nodes, specific cores, licenses, burst buffer space, start time, end time, and access control list (user ID or Slurm account name). The reservation can identify a count of nodes or cores without identifying specific nodes or cores, which can enable more efficient resource usage when the reservation is not regularly used, and permits any failed resources to be replaced in order to maintain the requested reservation size. The reservation can identify a start time relative to whatever the current time is (e.g., 10 min in the future), which we refer to as a "floating" reservation. Use of a relative start time can be used to ensure that privileged users or accounts can access compute resources in a timely fashion without preventing their use by the wider user community when otherwise not required. For example, one might create a floating reservation consisting of 16 arbitrary compute nodes that must be available within 30 min of the current time. This will ensure that a job requesting 16 nodes in that reservation will be able to secure those resources and begin execution within 30 min without preventing other users from making use of those resources with shorter lived jobs or jobs approaching their time limits. Reservations can be recurring (e.g., daily, weekly, etc.). A reservation can be configured so that jobs must fit entirely within its time and space constraints. Alternately a job can use resources in a partition in addition to any other available resources. Reservations can be configured as "magnetic", in which case any job that matches that reservation's access controls will be eligible to run within resources it controls when the reservation is active without explicitly requesting that use of that reservation. Another common use case for advanced reservations is to limit access to resources so that they will be idle at the time of a scheduled maintenance without the need to terminate any active jobs using those resources, but permitting jobs with lower time limits to be initiated on those resources as time permits.

## 3  Daemons

**Slurmdbd** is Slurm's database daemon, which can interface either MariaDB [15] or MySQL [17] (see Fig. 3). There is typically one slurmdbd daemon per enterprise. The slurmdbd records accounting information and manages some configuration information centrally (many limits, fair share information, QOS, licenses, etc.). When a system administrator modifies this centralized configuration information, those changes are transmitted to other Slurm daemons as needed. If the slurmdbd or its database are unavailable for some reason, the

entire Slurm enterprise will continue to operate normally, but use cached configuration information and locally store accounting information until database
access is restored. Slurmdbd is typically configured to execute as user "SlurmUser", an unprivileged user.

The **slurmctld** daemon—commonly referred to as the Slurm controller—run
as a single active daemon per cluster, although an arbitrary number of backup
daemons may be configured. The slurmctld monitors the state of resources,
decides when and where to initiate jobs and job steps, and processes almost all
user commands (except for accounting and other database related commands).
If configured for high-availability, a file system must be configured to store the
slurmctld state information such that is accessible on both the primary and all
backup controllers. Slurmctld executes as user "SlurmUser", an unprivileged user.

The **slurmd** is Slurm's compute node daemon. There is typically one slurmd
daemon per compute node. The slurmd daemon is the only Slurm daemon that
needs to execute as user root in order to spawn processes as the appropriate user.
Slurmd is quiescent after launching the job step management process (slurmstepd) except for optional accounting and message forwarding. One slurmstepd
process is spawned by slurmd for each batch script and application on a compute
node. Slurmstepd is responsible for launching the batch script or user application's tasks, handling any cgroup and filesystem namespace management, managing accounting, application I/O, signals, etc. It is possible to configure multiple
slurmd daemons to execute on each compute node in order to evaluate Slurm
behavior on larger systems. Moderately large clusters can be emulated on just a
single compute node or desktop. Each compute node in such an emulated cluster can be configured independently, for example with differing memory or CPU
counts, potentially with larger sizes than the compute node actually executing
the slurmd daemon.

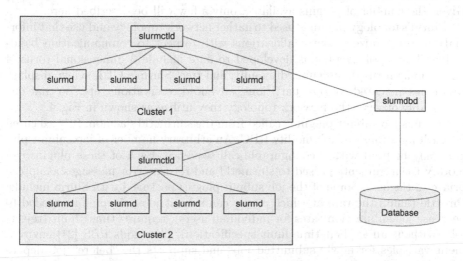

**Fig. 3.** Typical Slurm federation with two clusters.

The **slurmrestd** daemon is an interface to Slurm via REST API that translates JSON/YAML-encoded requests into Slurm Remote Procedure Calls (RPCs). Any user can initiate their own slurmrestd daemon and all remote clients are authenticated using HTTP headers. This is intended to enable use of Slurm's API outside of the cluster to web interfaces, user desktops (with appropriate security considerations), and other third-party applications.

## 4   Plugin Infrastructure

Slurm's extensive use of plugins is particularly valuable in providing portability and flexibility. Roughly 65% of Slurm's code is within its kernel including the primary data structures, system daemons, and user commands. Over 100 plugins form the remainder of the code to support a wide range of differing hardware types, software environments, and scheduling capabilities. The configured plugins are loaded when a daemon or command is started and persists throughout its lifetime. Some plugins are called from multiple daemons and commands. In some cases plugins are also called by other plugins, such as the network topology plugin being called by the scheduling plugin. Plugin infrastructure provides a level of indirection to some configurable underlying functions. One example of the value in plugins was development work performed by Hewlett-Packard (HP) in 2005 [1]. Slurm's original implementation only supported the allocation of whole compute nodes to jobs—implemented through the select/linear scheduling plugin. HP added the ability to allocate resources on a node down to the core level with a new select/cons_res plugin. Later development introduced a new select/cons_tres plugin, now the default, which extended resource scheduling support to GPUs within the nodes as well. Roughly 80% of the changes to Slurm for this enhancement were in the form of a new job scheduling plugin with the remaining changes in the kernel, much of that in the form data structure changes. Given the number of plugins available, only a few will be described here.

Slurm's topology plugin is used to gather network topology and use that information to optimize resource allocations with respect to communication bandwidth. The topology plugins developed to date include 3 dimensional torus, 4 dimensional torus, hypercube, dragonfly, and tree. Slurm's GUI, sview, displays the nodes allocated to jobs, partitions, advanced reservations, etc., so that one can readily observe the network topology they utilize as shown in Fig. 4.

Slurm's job submit plugin is called from the slurmctld daemon. It is executed for each job submit or job modify RPC. An arbitrary number of job submit plugins may be used with a configurable call sequence. Each of these plugins can modify the arguments passed to slurmctld and return error messages as appropriate to the user. Some of the job submit plugins packaged with Slurm include: throttle (limits the rate at which a user can submit jobs, sleeping as needed to decrease job submission rates for individual users), require_time_limit (rejects jobs without an explicit time limit specification), pbs (adds PBS [21] environment variables for newly submitted jobs and supports the "before" job dependency), cray (sets Cray specific generic resource parameters), and Lua (executes a customer provided Lua script with almost limitless flexibility).

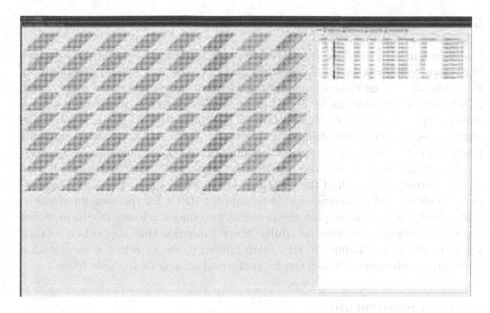

**Fig. 4.** Example of job allocations on a 4D torus interconnect. A list of jobs is shown on the right and their color coded node allocations on the left.

Four plugins are available to gather energy consumption from a node including IPMI, RAPL, and Cray. Should some new mechanism become available to gather a node's energy consumption data, one would need to develop a new Slurm plugin to gather that information and present it to the Slurm kernel in the appropriate format.

SPANK (Slurm Plugin Architecture for Node and job [K]ontrol) is a generic plugin mechanism. The plugins are written in C, but without requiring access to the Slurm source code. The plugins are executed by the Slurm daemons and the Slurm commands used for job submission. SPANK plugins can be used to add new site-specific job options, including making information about those options visible in the command's help messages. One example of SPANK use was the initial integration of Singularity containers with Slurm [25]. This plugin added new options to the Slurm job submission commands: --singularity-container, --singularity-bind and --singularity-args. It also added support for Singularity specific environment variables. The slurmstepd job step management process made use of this newly added information to initiate the application in an appropriate container environment.

The most common integration point remains through the use of site-specific scripts in the Slurm prolog and epilog interfaces. These are executed in various places (the submit host, the head node by slurmctld, or the compute node by slurmd or slurmstepd), at various times (e.g., job allocation, step startup, and task launch), by various users (SlurmUser, root or the job user). Typical use cases include establishing the environment for the job (boot nodes, node health check, configure temporary storage, etc.) or cleaning up at job completion (deleting temporary files).

## 5  Configuration

Slurm requires at least one configuration file, although some plugins require their own configuration file. These files can either be in a location readable by all daemons and user commands or the files can be replicated on every node. Alternatively, the files can be placed on the nodes where the slurmctld daemons execute (primary daemon plus backups), and the slurmctld daemon will make that configuration information available to the other daemons and commands upon request with a newer optional feature referred to as "configless" support.

A system administrator may find it difficult to upgrade the Slurm installation simultaneously across all of the enterprise. In order to support rolling upgrades, every daemon and command is able to support RPCs for three major releases, which includes its release plus the previous two major releases of Slurm. Since major releases are currently scheduled every 9 months, that supports a relaxed upgrade schedule. Changes to RPCs are limited to major releases, so upgrades between maintenance releases can be performed on a node-by-node basis.

## 6  Communications

Slurm uses a fault-tolerant hierarchical communication mechanism with configurable fanout for communications to the compute nodes. This offloads as much work as possible from the slurmctld daemon, which typically has a multitude of active threads. This also minimizes the wall time required for operations involving a large number of nodes, such as application launch and file transfer. It is typically recommended to configure a fanout value so that no more than a five level communication tree can be used to reach all compute nodes. For example, if the slurmctld needs to kill a job running on 1110 compute nodes and Slurm's fanout is configured at 10. The slurmctld daemon will take the list of 1110 compute nodes and divide it into 10 sets of 111 nodes each. The slurmctld daemon will then launch 10 threads, each communicating with a single slurmd daemon notifying it of the job to be killed along with a list of the additional 110 compute nodes that slurmd should forward the request to. Each of these 10 slurmd daemon launches 10 threads to communicate with additional slurmd daemons on other compute nodes. The process is continued until every slurmd daemon involved in the operation is reached. In this case, the process requires three levels in the communication tree. Note the communication hierarchy is created as needed and destroyed upon completion of the communications. Multiple communication hierarchies may be active at any time using different or even overlapping sets of slurmd daemons. See the example in Fig. 5.

Slurm's configurable timeout parameter is used to help detect communication failures. In the event of a failure, the daemon originating the message will send the message to another slurmd daemon in the group of compute nodes to be communicated with. Since this retry logic may result in messages being sent more than once to a slurmd daemon, the daemon retains state information to avoid duplicating operations.

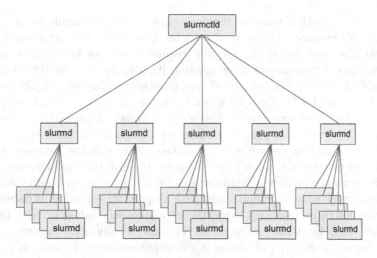

**Fig. 5.** Example hierarchical communication with fanout of 5.

The logic to spawn job steps follows a similar hierarchical communication mechanism. The srun command sends its job step launch request to the slurmctld daemon. When the slurmctld daemon satisfies the request (which might be queued pending resource availability), slurmctld returns a digitally signed step launch credential to srun. The srun command then forwards this credential with an application launch request to a set of slurmd daemons using the same fanout logic as for messages originating from the slurmctld daemon.

# 7   Job Priority

Slurm assigns a priority to each job based on a multitude of factors including age, fair share, queue/partition, QOS, size, nice value, association, and a site-managed value. The weight of each factor in determining a job's priority is configurable so that a job's priority may be based 60% on age age, 30% on fair share, etc. The age component of job priority is based upon the time when the job first becomes eligible for execution, after dependencies are satisfied, rather than its submission time. It value is proportional to that wait time with a configurable maximum time (i.e., the value could be configured to stop increasing once a job is 7 d old). Fair share is a measure of how over- or under-serviced an association is relative to its resource allocation. The window of time used in this calculation is either fixed with usage data cleared periodically (i.e., at the end of each week, month, quarter, year, etc.) or historic resource usage data is continuously decreased on an exponential basis through time. Different algorithms and parameters are available to control how fair share is computed based upon the association tree, and a plugin interface called site_factor is provided should an administrator wish to develop their own novel prioritization approach. For example, should an individual user be allowed to consume all resources allocated to his group if no other users in that group are active or should some portion of that group's resources be retained for when other users in that group become active and if so how much [2]. Job size requirements can be used to consider a job's resource requirements in computing its priority. Size in this context is configurable to consider a variety of resources with different weights for each resource (e.g., one GPU might be given the same weight as 1TB of memory in computing a job's size component of priority). A system administrator may want to increase the scheduling priority of jobs with large CPU, memory, or license requirements. This can also be reversed to favor jobs with low resource requirements. A user may specify a job's nice value to establish their relative scheduling priority in Slurm and this works similar to a process's Linux nice value, although Slurm's nice value range is much larger with a signed 32-bit value. If necessary, a system administrator may also explicitly set a job's scheduling priority in order to override the default calculated value. This is typically done to force a job to have the highest priority, and ensure it will begin execution as soon as possible.

## 8    Typical Configurations

Each site and each cluster have unique configurations and scheduling considerations. Before considering Slurm's scheduling algorithms, some typical configurations and their scheduling requirements are described below.

Roughly half of the clusters that we work with are homogeneous: every compute node has the same processors, memory size, GPUs, etc. Homogeneous clusters may be configured with a single partition for the most efficient use of resources. While every job may be in a single queue/partition, a variety of limits are typically used to prevent any single user or group of users from being allocated more resources than desired. Depending on the configuration and use case, it is not uncommon to see dozens or even hundreds of the highest priority jobs have their resource allocation deferred by one or more limit (e.g., maximum running job count by user, maximum allocated GPU count by account). In addition to the compute nodes, global resources such as licenses and burst buffer space must be managed.

The other half of the clusters we work with are heterogeneous. Such clusters may include a small number of unique compute nodes, say with GPUs or a larger memory size. Other clusters may include a dozen or more unique compute node configurations including different processor types and clock speeds. Such clusters are typically assembled over time with different organizations contributing hardware best suited for their workload and budget. For example, the physics department at a university may purchase two racks of nodes with large memory size, the chemistry department another rack of nodes with GPUs, etc. We refer to each set of resources as a "condo" or "condominium" and they are interconnected into a single cluster sharing a high speed network. Typically each condo can be accessed from two or more partitions. One partition will provide priority access to the resources with an access control list identifying the organization financing those resources (e.g., the "physics" partition will have an access control list containing the faculty and students in the physics department). A second partition might span all compute nodes in the cluster with lower priority access for any user, typically with a lower size and/or time limits. Slurm allows jobs to be submitted to multiple partitions simultaneously to take advantage of this configuration. The node "feature" parameter can be used to prevent job allocations from spanning different processor types as shown in Fig. 6.

Job throughput rate requirements also vary widely. Some workloads consist primarily of jobs that execute for days, in which case expending considerable time to optimize scheduling may be warranted. Other workloads consist primarily of jobs that execute for a few seconds and a throughput rate in the of hundreds of jobs per second may be required [30]. Slurm can support both workloads, but with different algorithms and scheduling parameters.

# 9 Scheduling Algorithm

Slurm performs a quick and simple (first-in first-out, FIFO) scheduling attempt on an event driven basis (with a configurable minimum time interval between executions): upon each job submission, job completion, or configuration change. Only the top priority jobs (a configurable count) in each partition will be evaluated for initiation and this can be useful for high throughput computing. Given the appropriate configuration and hardware, Slurm can sustain a throughput rate exceeding 100 jobs per second. Since this scheduling algorithm is FIFO, once any job in a partition is found unable to be initiated, all lower priority jobs in that partition will be left pending without further consideration.

Slurm also performs a more comprehensive FIFO scheduling attempt on a periodic basis with a configurable interval. This algorithm typically executes far less frequently than the event driven scheduling algorithm, but uses the same logic with different configuration parameters. The default configuration

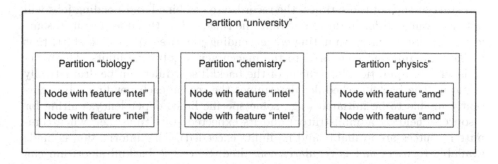

# sbatch --nodes=2 --partition=university,physics --constraint="[amd|intel]" ...

**Fig. 6.** Example heterogeneous cluster with job submission request for any two nodes with the same architecture. Plugins can be used to set default partitions and node features as appropriate.

parameters will typically enable this algorithm to evaluate jobs in every partition from the highest priority until a job unable to be initiated is identified.

Except for some high throughput computing configurations, backfill scheduling plugin is used to initiate most jobs. Without the backfill plugin, jobs in each queue are scheduled strictly in priority order as described above. The backfill scheduling plugin will initiate lower priority jobs only if doing so does not delay the expected start time of any higher priority job, although reservation of resources for higher priority jobs can be limited to jobs which have been pending for over some configurable period time or the highest priority jobs in each partition within a configurable queue depth. The expected start time of pending jobs is dependent on the expected completion time of running jobs based solely upon the job's time limit. Approximately 20 configuration parameters are available for tuning backfill scheduling such as: how far in the future to consider, what is the time resolution for scheduling, how many jobs to consider for each user, how many jobs to consider from each partition, etc. The backfill scheduler builds a table of expected resource availability through time, tracing the expected initiation and termination time of running and pending jobs. All resource limits are enforced by the backfill scheduler as it builds this table. For example, sufficient compute resources may be available to initiate the highest priority job in some partition one hour in the future, but job initiation prevented by the maximum number of CPU hours of running jobs for the job's association. In this case a lower priority job may be initiated. Since a cluster may have thousands of executing jobs and tens of thousands of pending jobs, backfill scheduling overhead is kept more manageable by the time resolution configuration parameter cited above. Say the time resolution is configured to 300 s. The resources that become available in any 300 s interval are recorded in a single record rather than one record per job completion, which might number in the tens or even hundreds of jobs for any 300 s interval. For example, consider a job expected to end in 600 s and another job expected to end in 610 s. Rather than creating records of expected system state at those two times and determining which pending jobs can start at each of those times, the records are combined and pending jobs will only be evaluated for initiation at that one time. While this does result in some loss of precision when evaluating when pending jobs are expected to start, that is likely insignificant compared to the inaccuracy in job time limits. The benefit is that computational overhead of the backfill scheduler can be dramatically reduced. The backfill scheduler determines the reason each pending job is currently unable to be initiated (e.g., some specific limit, dependency, waiting for resources, held by administrator) and its expected start time (i.e., when compute resources are available and no limits exceeded). This information is made available to users and is regularly consulted. Since the backfill algorithm can require multiple minutes to complete with large workloads, it is performed in a piecemeal manner. It acquires the appropriate locks, executes for a configurable time interval (typically a couple of seconds), releases locks for a configurable time interval (typically less than one second) in order to perform other outstanding operations (e.g., accept newly submitted jobs, process newly completed jobs, provide users with status information, etc.), and repeats the process until all pending jobs have been considered.

Slurm supports burst buffers via a plugin mechanism. Slurm will allocate burst buffer space for a job when it approaches its expected initiation time and stage-in any required data. The job will not be allocated compute resources until data stage-in has completed. When the job's computation has completed, data will be staged-out and the burst buffer space released. The burst buffers supported by Slurm plugins include Cray's DataWarp [8] and a generic Lua script based plugin.

Slurm has the ability to support a cluster that grows and shrinks on demand, typically relying upon a service such as Amazon Elastic Computing Cloud (Amazon EC2), Google Cloud Platform or Microsoft Azure for resources. These resources can be combined with an existing cluster to process excess workload (cloud bursting) or it can operate as an independent self-contained cluster. Good responsiveness and throughput can be achieved while only paying for the resources needed.

Slurm has dozens of available scheduling parameters available to control the number of jobs considered for scheduling in each partition, maximum scheduling frequency, etc. [27] Slurm also maintains detailed information about scheduling performance and makes that information available to system administrators for tuning purposes [32]. Detailed information about anticipated resource availability in the future and expected resource allocations and initiation times of pending jobs are also available.

## 10   License Scheduling

In addition to node-centric resources, Slurm supports scheduling for **licenses**. Licenses can be used to represent any resource available on a global basis such as network bandwidth or global scratch disk space; although, as implied by the name, they are most commonly used to track software licenses.

Licenses are requested as part of the job submission, and will be allocated to the job alongside the compute resources. Backfill scheduling management for these licenses is a recent optional addition, and can be enabled by the administrator. Preemption support, in which lower priority jobs can be preempted to free up sufficient licenses for higher priority ones, has also been recently added.

## 11   Application Layout

The job has control over its resource allocation with respect to sockets, cores, and threads using options at job submit time, for example threads per core, cores per socket, and sockets per node. Similarly the job step allocation can specify the number of tasks to launch per core, socket and/or core. The job step has complete control over how tasks are distributed over the allocated resources by specifying layout patterns across nodes, sockets, and/or cores. Binding tasks to allocated resources can be performed using CPU affinity and/or Linux cgroups [20]. Linux cgroups are essential for configurations where more than one job can be active at the same time on a compute node. Besides limiting each job to its allocated CPUs, cgroups can also ensure that each job is constrained to its allocated memory and not interfere with another job's memory allocation. Linux cgroups can constrain each job's RAM, kernel memory, swap space and allocated generic resources such as GPUs. There are a variety of options available to control how each task/rank of the application are bound to the job step's allocated CPUs. Cgroups are also used to collect usage data for allocated resources.

Some topology plugins support the ability for a job to specify the maximum number of leaf switches desired in its resource allocation and the maximum time to wait for such an allocation (e.g., wait up to an extra 10 min for my job's allocated nodes to be on one leaf switch). The system administrator can configure the maximum wait time for any job to secure its desired leaf count in order to limit resources idled for job layout optimization.

Jobs can increase or decrease their size per administrative controls. In the case of increasing the size of a job, the user must submit a new job to acquire the additional resources desired. Once this second job allocation has been made, the user merges the two job allocations into a single job, a process which generates a shell script the user executes in the original job in order to modify its environment variables as appropriate.

## 12  Job Profiling

Slurm has the ability to collect detailed performance information about a job step on a periodic basis. This is more information than can reasonably be recorded in Slurm's database for every job, and may involve some additional overhead to collect—therefore it is only collected when requested by the user. The user specifies what types of information are to be collected and at what frequencies (independent frequency can be configured for each data type). The types of information available for collection includes power consumption, file system usage, network interconnect usage, CPU and memory usage, and GPU utilization. At application termination the data is collected and stored into a single HDF5 [6] dataset. We recommend the HDFView [7] tool to graphically view the resulting data, which can easily identify problems such as spikes in memory usage with the timing and offending task ID (rank) identified.

## 13  Compute Node Management

Alongside traditional workload management capabilities, additional integrations have been developed to solve common HPC systems administration tasks.

Slurm has the ability to limit the power consumption of a cluster [12]. It does this by monitoring each node's power consumption and periodically adjusting its available power. Nodes consuming less than their available power will have their power availability reduced and that power will be redistributed to the other nodes in the cluster. Special mechanisms exist to manage power limits uniformly across all nodes allocated to a job as well as job startup and termination[3].

Container support for OCI images [19,28] is supported and allows for the launch of compatible containers without any external tooling on the compute nodes. Management for these container images is a direct extension of existing support for Linux subsystems such as cgroups and filesystem namespaces, and required only minimal changes to the slurmd daemon. A newly added command, scrun, allows for use of Slurm as the underpinning for common tools such as Docker [3] and Podman [22].

**slurm_pam_adopt** is a PAM [5] module that intercepts user SSH connections, and confines them to the resources that were allocated to their job. For connections initiated from other compute nodes (common with SSH-based MPI launchers), it will interrogate the originating compute node for which job that network connection originated from, and can perfectly match that to the allocated resources on that node. (If the job has not been allocated resources, the connection is usually denied depending on configuration.) For connections initiated from login nodes or other external machines, the connection will usually be permitted under resources allocated to the first job running under that user account. Besides confining these processes to resources already allocated to the job, these processes have an accounting record created for them, which details their resource usage.

**nss_slurm** is an NSS [18,31] module that allows Slurm to centrally propagate the user and group information corresponding to each jobs' owner. This mitigates issues when compute nodes, which are usually connected to LDAP, all simultaneously try to resolve user and group information when the job is initiated. In addition, certain cluster deployment approaches can preclude the need to either synchronize /etc/passwd and /etc/group files to the compute nodes, or connect the compute node to LDAP or NIS.

The **sbcast** command, and the associated --bcast option to the srun command, allow for Slurm to distribute files through its built-in tree hierarchical communication systems. Optional compression can further improve performance. This can be used for large-scale job launches to avoid performance issues from large-scale job launches on common network filesystems by moving executables into local scratch (possibly tmpfs) space. An optional mode, enabled through the --send-libs argument, allows for dynamic libraries to be identified and transmitted alongside an executable image, further improving performance for large-scale job launches.

The **scrontab** command allows for users to register a number of periodic compute jobs with a crontab compatible syntax. This is designed to mitigate a common HPC user request for cron access on login nodes, and instead launches compute jobs on designated intervals (while ensuring that only one copy of the

---

[3] This capability was successfully used at King Abdullah University of Science and Technology (KAUST) for a period when a power availability was limited. We are unaware of any other organization currently using of this capability.

process / Slurm job is launched concurrently, a feature that cron itself lacks), and avoids reliance on specific login nodes remaining online continously.

## 14   Conclusion

This paper presents an overview of Slurm's design and functionality. Slurm provides an open source tool that can effectively manage a wide variety of workloads on computers of any size. It is also highly modular in order to provide excellent flexibility and extensibility. Motivated researchers can experiment with alternative scheduling algorithms, network topologies, etc. by developing their own plugin while leveraging Slurm's extensive and stable framework.

Slurm continues to evolve with the help of numerous dedicated engineers. Areas under current development include improved integration with external orchestration systems such as Kubernetes, full adoption of an internal extensible HMAC authentication scheme [9], further improvements to the "cloud bursting" modes of operation, performance improvements in job throughput and user command interaction, and integration with external interfaces such as PMIx. Future directions, subject to community interest, may also involve improved support for energy-centric computing, ways to improve job step performance and workflow capabilities by divorcing responsibility from the central slurmctld process, and refactoring the core scheduling system to allow for different compute node hierarchies than the traditional board/socket/core/CPU model that is embedded in the existing scheduler subsystems.

## References

1. Balle, S.M., Palermo, D.J.: Enhancing an open source resource manager with multi-core/multi-threaded support. In: Frachtenberg, E., Schwiegelshohn, U. (eds.) JSSPP 2007. LNCS, vol. 4942, pp. 37–50. Springer, Heidelberg (2008). https://doi.org/10.1007/978-3-540-78699-3_3
2. Cox, R., Morrison, L.: Fair tree: fairshare algorithm for slurm. In: Proceedings of the Slurm User Group Meeting (2014). https://slurm.schedmd.com/SC14/BYU_Fair_Tree.pdf. Accessed 28 Mar 2023
3. Docker home page. https://www.docker.com/. Accessed 28 Mar 2023
4. Frontier user guide. https://docs.olcf.ornl.gov/systems/frontier_user_guide.html. Accessed 3 Feb 2023
5. Garfinkel, S., Spafford, G., Schwartz, A.: Practical UNIX and internet security, pp. 94–96. SO'Reilly (2003)
6. Hdf5 download page from the hdf group. https://www.hdfgroup.org/downloads/hdf5. Accessed 25 Mar 2023
7. Hdfview download page from the hdf group. https://www.hdfgroup.org/downloads/hdfview. Accessed 25 Mar 2023
8. Henseler, D., Landsteiner, B., Petesch, D., Wright, C., Wright, N.: Architecture and design of cray datawarp. In: Proceedings of the Cray User Group (2016). https://cug.org/proceedings/cug2016_proceedings/includes/files/pap105s2-file1.pdf. Accessed 28 Mar 2023

9. Hmac description. https://en.wikipedia.org/wiki/HMAC. Accessed 1 May 2023
10. Jackson, D., Snell, Q., Clement, M.: Core algorithms of the maui scheduler. In: Feitelson, D.G., Rudolph, L. (eds.) JSSPP 2001. LNCS, vol. 2221, pp. 87–102. Springer, Heidelberg (2001). https://doi.org/10.1007/3-540-45540-X_6
11. Jette, M.A.: Expanding symmetric multiprocessor capability through gang scheduling. In: Feitelson, D.G., Rudolph, L. (eds.) JSSPP 1998. LNCS, vol. 1459, pp. 199–216. Springer, Heidelberg (1998). https://doi.org/10.1007/BFb0053988
12. Jette, M.: Slurm power management support. In: Proceedings of the Slurm User Group (2015). https://slurm.schedmd.com/SLUG15/Power_mgmt.pdf. Accessed 26 Mar 2023
13. Yoo, A.B., Jette, M.A., Grondona, M.: SLURM: simple linux utility for resource management. In: Feitelson, D., Rudolph, L., Schwiegelshohn, U. (eds.) JSSPP 2003. LNCS, vol. 2862, pp. 44–60. Springer, Heidelberg (2003). https://doi.org/10.1007/10968987_3
14. Jwt home page. https://jwt.io/. Accessed 1 May 2023
15. Mariadb foundation home page. https://mariadb.org/. Accessed 23 Mar 2023
16. Munge home page. https://dun.github.io/munge/. Accessed 26 Apr 2023
17. Mysql home page. https://www.mysql.com/. Accessed 23 Mar 2023
18. Name service switch description. https://guix.gnu.org/manual/en/html_node/Name-Service-Switch.html. Accessed 3 Feb 2023
19. Open container initiative organization home page. https://opencontainers.org. Accessed 28 Mar 2023
20. Ondrejka, P., Majorsinova, E., Prpic, M., Landmann, R., Silas, D.: Resource management guide. https://access.redhat.com/documentation/en-us/red_hat_enterprise_linux/6/html/resource_management_guide/index. Accessed 23 Mar 2023
21. Openpbs home page. https://www.openpbs.org/. Accessed 28 Mar 2023
22. Podman home page. https://podman.io/. Accessed 28 Mar 2023
23. Pritchard, H., Roweth, D., Henseler, D., Cassella, P.: Leveraging the cray linux environment core specialization feature to realize mpi asynchronous progress on cray xe systems. In: Proceedings of the Cray User Group (2012)
24. Quadrics in linux clusters (presentation). https://hsi.web.cern.ch/HNF-Europe/sem3_2001/hnf.pdf. Accessed 3 Feb 2023
25. Singularity plugin for slurm. https://github.com/sol-eng/singularity-rstudio/blob/main/slurm-singularity-exec.md. Accessed 4 Feb 2023
26. Slurm code repository. https://github.com/SchedMD/slurm.git. Accessed 3 Feb 2023
27. Slurm scheduling configuration guide. https://slurm.schedmd.com/sched_config.html. Accessed 31 Mar 2023
28. Slurm container guide. https://slurm.schedmd.com/containers.html. Accessed 4 Feb 2023
29. Slurm documentation. https://slurm.schedmd.com/. Accessed 4 Feb 2023
30. Slurm high throughput computing administration guide. https://slurm.schedmd.com/high_throughput.html. Accessed 30 Mar 2023
31. Name service switch implementation for slurm. https://slurm.schedmd.com/nss_slurm.html. Accessed 3 Feb 2023
32. Slurm scheduling diagnostic documentation. https://slurm.schedmd.com/sdiag.html. Accessed 31 Mar 2023

# Technical Papers

# Asynchronous Execution of Heterogeneous Tasks in ML-Driven HPC Workflows

Vincent R. Pascuzzi[1] , Ozgur O. Kilic[2(✉)] , Matteo Turilli[2,3] ,
and Shantenu Jha[2,3]

[1] IBM Thomas J. Watson Research Center, Yorktown Heights, NY 10598, USA
vrpascuzzi@ibm.com
[2] Brookhaven National Laboratory, Upton, NY 11973, USA
{okilic,mturilli}@bnl.gov
[3] Rutgers, the State University of New Jersey, Piscataway, NJ 08854, USA
shantenu.jha@rutgers.edu

**Abstract.** Heterogeneous scientific workflows consist of numerous types of tasks that require execution on heterogeneous resources. Asynchronous execution of those tasks is crucial to improve resource utilization, task throughput and reduce workflows' makespan. Therefore, middleware capable of scheduling and executing different task types across heterogeneous resources must enable asynchronous execution of tasks. In this paper, we investigate the requirements and properties of the asynchronous task execution of machine learning (ML)-driven high-performance computing (HPC) workflows. We model the degree of asynchronicity permitted for arbitrary workflows and propose key metrics that can be used to determine qualitative benefits when employing asynchronous execution. Our experiments represent relevant scientific drivers, we perform them at scale on Summit, and we show that the performance enhancements due to asynchronous execution are consistent with our model.

**Keywords:** hpc · workflow · adaptability · machine learning · artificial intelligence

## 1 Introduction

Scientific discovery increasingly requires sophisticated and scalable workflows. Introducing machine learning (ML) models into traditional high performance computing (HPC) workflows have been an enabler of highly accurate modeling and a promising approach for significant scientific advances [10]. Those workflows often comprise hundreds to thousands of heterogeneous tasks [12] with diverse dimensions of heterogeneity: **implementation** (*e.g.*, executables or functions/methods in an arbitrary programming language), **resource requirements**

---

V. R. Pascuzzi—Work done while at Brookhaven National Laboratory.

D. Klusáček et al. (Eds.): JSSPP 2023, LNCS 14283, pp. 27–45, 2023.
https://doi.org/10.1007/978-3-031-43943-8_2

(*e.g.*, executing on central processing units (CPUs) and/or graphics processing units (GPUs), computational or data-intensive operations), **duration** (*e.g.*, from less than a second to many hours), and **size** (*e.g.*, from a core to many cores over one or more compute nodes). Specifically for ML-driven HPC workflows, task heterogeneity increases with GPU and multi-node message passing interface (MPI) [13] tasks alongside traditional CPU tasks. ML tasks usually require the execution of high-throughput function calls, often implemented in an interpreted language such as Python.

Typically, in ML-driven HPC workflows, a simulation phase generates data and a ML phase uses that data for training or inference. Inference results are used to guide the next set of simulations [9,24], creating a dependence between the two phases. Often, naïve bulk-synchronous parallel (BSP) executions with a hard temporal separation of simulation and ML phases lead to poor resource utilization. For example, running all the simulations before ML tasks or pausing simulations while running ML tasks let a large amount of the allocated HPC resource idle. Asynchronous executions can improve resource utilization, especially considering the increasing relevance of continuous learning, surrogate re-training, and optimal execution of multi-workflow campaigns.

Asynchronous execution is possible and should be supported at workflow-, workload- and task-level. At the workflow level, workflows are executed independently while preserving dependencies within each workflow. For example, in Ref. [21], different workflows can be executed without waiting for all instances of one workflow to finish. At the workload level, sets of heterogeneous tasks, possibly derived from multiple workflows and whose dependencies have been resolved, are executed asynchronously. Finally, at task level, each independent task is executed asynchronously.

As a consequence, middleware that manages the execution of workflows has to be able to asynchronously schedule, place, and execute heterogeneous (set of) tasks on heterogeneous resources, maximizing resource utilization while minimizing the workflow makespan. For example, that middleware has to manage the execution of MPI simulations alongside ML Python functions, each with varying resource requirements and execution lifetimes, hours for simulations, and less than a second for the ML functions. Resource utilization and efficiency depend upon the specifics of each workflow, workload mix (type of tasks and their individual properties), and how effectively the task execution middleware manages the heterogeneity of the tasks and resources.

In this paper, we focus on the resource management challenges of executing tasks with diverse resource requirements. We discuss conditions for asynchronous execution and offer a quantitative basis and experimental characterization of the improvements it can bring in terms of resource utilization and task throughput, and thus makespan. We focus on the asynchronous execution of ML-driven heterogeneous HPC workflows, offering four main contributions: (1) an asynchronous implementation of DeepDriveMD [9,16]—a framework to execute ML-driven molecular-dynamics workflows on HPC platforms at scale; (2) a performance evaluation of asynchronous DeepDriveMD; (3) a model of asynchronous behavior; and (4) a general performance evaluation of that model for workflows with a varying degrees of asynchronous execution.

In Sect. 2, we discuss several ML-driven HPC workflows and workflow systems, as generalized motivation and the importance of asynchronous execution. In Sect. 4, we define asynchronous execution and its relationship with data and control flow when designing a workflow application. In Sect. 5, we present conditions and motivations for workload-level asynchronicity alongside the concept of task execution time masking. In Sect. 6, we formalize the notion of asynchronous execution by modeling its behavior and performance for task throughput and resource utilization metrics. In Sect. 7, we compare synchronous and asynchronous executions of DeepDriveMD, measuring the latter's benefits. We then generalize those results, offering an experimental characterization of the performance gains provided by different degrees of heterogeneity for a given workflow. Finally, in Sect. 8, we discuss the implications of our model and performance analysis for the design of workflow applications with heterogeneous tasks when executed on HPC resources.

## 2   Related Work

Asynchronicity spans multiple levels of an HPC stack and affects many areas of a distributed execution. Asynchronous execution, communication, and coordination are implemented and leveraged in many runtime systems, to distribute workload among executors and/or coordinate the messaging among executing processes. Uintah [17], Charm++ [15], HPX [14], Legion [5], and PaRSEC [8] are all examples of runtime using asynchronicity to coordinate execution.

Contrary to the runtime system listed above, in this paper, we focus on asynchronous execution for ML-driven HPC workflows which consist of tasks with diverse dimensions of heterogeneity, *e.g.*, implementation, resource requirements, duration, or size. We assume tasks to be black boxes. Therefore, in our modeling, we abstract away the details of asynchronous communication as data dependencies are assumed to be satisfied either before or during execution.

PATHWAYS [4] focuses on the asynchronous distribution of dataflow to enable parallel execution of ML tasks via a gang-scheduling approach. PATHWAYS overlap computation with data coordination by dispatching data asynchronously, showing how that increases resource utilization while reducing makespan. Our work differs from PATHWAYS as we focus on the asynchronous execution of heterogeneous tasks instead of asynchronous data distribution.

DeepHyper [1] shows how asynchronous execution can benefit the hyperparameter search for deep neural networks (DNN). They implement task-level asynchronicity by evaluating partial results instead of waiting for the complete results to be ready, showing how that helps to increase resource utilization. While specialized task execution models could benefit hyper-parameter search in DNN, many dimensions of heterogeneity need to be considered to improve the performance of ML-driven heterogeneous HPC workflows. For this reason, we are focusing on generalized asynchronous modeling and execution of heterogeneous HPC workflows.

Significant examples of ML-driven HPC workflow solutions include Colmena [24], Mummi/Merlin [7,11,20], and Proxima [25]. Those solutions and the applications they support involve running a time-varying heterogeneous mix of HPC and ML tasks. As such, they could benefit from programmatic asynchronous execution, but they lack specific constructs and tools to assess the performance improvement that an asynchronous implementation would offer.

Further examples of ML-driven HPC workflow can be found in Refs. [21,22], both of which use DeepDriveMD [9,16] to couple ML and molecular dynamic simulations. The performance characterization of DeepDriveMD established that, when feasible, asynchronous execution of ML and simulation tasks can improve both resource utilization and task throughput. Those improvements are possible due to the heterogeneity of ML and simulation tasks in all dimensions mentioned in Sect. 1. Nonetheless, the implementation of asynchronous execution depends on the requirements of the task utilized and cannot be applied to all task types executed via DeepDriveMD.

# 3   Motivation

Increasing heterogeneity in scientific workflows makes asynchronous execution of heterogeneous workloads unavoidable. We can use the different ML-driven workflow implementations for neutron scattering data analysis presented in Ref. [23] as a road map for achieving higher resource utilization and lower makespan with increased degrees of asynchronicity. Their synchronous baseline, where the entire simulation executes before ML execution starts, suffers from memory bottlenecks due to the volume of data produced. Serial workflow reduces memory pressure by partitioning those tasks (simulation and ML) into so-called 'phases'; however, its synchronous execution of heterogeneous workloads could not get maximum resource utilization. Asynchronous execution ('parallel workflow') improves resource utilization while reducing the makespan. As mentioned in their future work, the next step will be to use an adaptive execution to reduce their makespan further. It is important to understand that we need an asynchronous execution model and framework to run the increasingly heterogeneous scientific workflow efficiently.

We investigate asynchronous execution of ML-driven HPC workflows, i.e., workflows with heterogeneous tasks. In this context, we define asynchronous execution as one in which multiple heterogeneous tasks execute independently. Those independent tasks can execute asynchronously either at the same time or back-to-back, depending on resource availability. For this reason, we argue there exist two conditions for workload-level asynchronicity (WLA): (1) inter-task dependencies, and (2) resource availability.

Our main objective is to understand how to reduce the workflow makespan and improve resource utilization, utilizing asynchronous execution. We need asynchronicity because of the characteristics of ML-driven HPC workflows: (1) their multiple dimensions of heterogeneity (implementation, duration, size, and resource requirements); and (2) their adaptive, dynamic, and changing workloads. WLA alone does not guarantee better resource utilization and/or makespan as the realized asynchronicity of the execution depends on task and dependency graph properties; *e.g.*, task execution time (TX) and the number of independent branches in the graph. Thus, we explain the effect of the asynchronous execution of heterogeneous workflow tasks on the makespan of the entire workflow and its correlation with resource utilization.

## 4    Design and Implementation

Computationally, HPC workflows often require the adoption of two task execution paradigms: control-flow and data-flow. In the control-flow paradigm, executing a workflow requires explicit control over distinct task instances. Each task launches with an input data set, performs a fixed amount of computation on that input, and exits execution. In the data-flow paradigm, workflow execution is defined in terms of data dependencies among tasks, establishing what data each task has to share with another task.

Design-wise, control-flow and data-flow paradigms are not mutually exclusive. Workflow engines can independently manage data staging, inter-task communication, task execution, and task processing. Task data requirements, *i.e.*, that a task can start processing only when specific input data are available, can be equally satisfied by diverse designs: (1) staging input data before executing a task; or (2) communicating (*e.g.*, streaming or sending a message with a data location) the input data to the task when that task is already executing. Note that executing a task is different from having that task start to process input data: a task can be executing but also idle.

Workflows can benefit from the concurrent use of both control and data flows when they require executing heterogeneous tasks. Some of those tasks may have to communicate their input data to each other or may idle while waiting for input data to be available. Other tasks may instead be launched only when data are already available and terminated after those data have been processed. For example, a certain type of task (*e.g.*, MPI simulations) may occupy so many resources that it would be too costly to keep them executing while idling. Conversely, some other types of tasks (*e.g.*, ML inference) may require limited and specialized resources like GPUs, execute frequently and for only a few seconds and thus being too costly to launch and terminate every time they need to run.

We explore the design space of control and data flows by modeling the asynchronous execution of ML-driven HPC workflows. Workflow execution is asynchronous when multiple **heterogeneous tasks execute independently** on the available resources. A task executes independently when it does not need to coordinate with other tasks to proceed with its execution. Note that independence here pertains to tasks that are executing, not to the dependency among tasks before their execution. For example, a task may depend on data produced by another task but, when executing, those data are already available and thus their availability does not require coordination among executing tasks. In this context, it is crucial to distinguish between tasks that are *running* and those that are *executing*. When running, a task is not necessarily performing any useful calculation as it may be idling (*i.e.*, wasting resources) until triggered to do so. Instead, an executing task is necessarily performing useful work that advances the workflow to its goal.

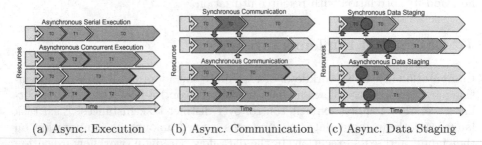

(a) Async. Execution    (b) Async. Communication    (c) Async. Data Staging

**Fig. 1.** Types of asynchronicity. Figure 1a shows two asynchronous executions: Top, T0 and T1 execute asynchronously and serially; bottom, T0 and T1 execute asynchronously and concurrently and T0 and T2 execute synchronously. Note that we used DG in Fig. 2c, assuming that T0 and T1 do not have any dependencies and T2 depends on T0. Figure 1b shows asynchronous and synchronous communication: red arrows are sent messages and green arrows are received messages; red bars indicate synchronous tasks that are waiting for their messages to be exchanged before resuming execution, and dark green bars are the time taken to execute incoming request before replying. Figure 1c shows asynchronous and synchronous data staging: red arrows show when data staging started and green arrows show when data is ready; red bars indicate synchronous tasks that cannot be executed before data become available. (Color figure online)

Figure 1 shows different types of asynchronicity. Asynchronous execution, shown in Fig. 1a, should not be confused with 'asynchronous data staging', Fig. 1c, or the more common 'asynchronous communication', Fig. 1b. The former indicates that each task's input data is staged independently, while the latter that the communication between a sender and a receiver does not need to be coordinated. Independent tasks may require staged files or perform asynchronous communication but, in this paper, we abstract those details, focusing on modeling and characterizing asynchronous execution as defined above.

Exemplars in Refs. [6,22] require a general-purpose approach to asynchronous task execution in DeepDriveMD. Such an approach should not depend on the specific implementation of each task, but instead remain agnostic to the communication and data capabilities of each task, making no assumptions about streaming capabilities. DeepDriveMD must account for tasks that have to be executed sequentially, those that can concurrently execute and communicate or exchange data, and those that have no relationship and can be executed either concurrently or sequentially.

We extended DeepDriveMD [9] to implement asynchronous executions of heterogeneous workflows. DeepDriveMD can now manage an arbitrary number of task types, each requiring an arbitrary amount of CPU cores and/or GPUs. Each task can be fully independent, dependent on the output of another task, or dependent on communicating with one or more other tasks. The asynchronous execution of DeepDriveMD can be configured to execute tasks concurrently or sequentially while respecting their dependency constraints. As with the previous version, DeepDriveMD is implemented as a thin layer on top of the RADICAL-EnsembleToolkit (EnTK) workflow engine [2,3]. EnTK keeps track of task dependencies and submits them for execution to RADICAL-Pilot [18,19], a pilot system designed to execute heterogeneous workloads on HPC platforms.

# 5    Workload-Level Asynchronicity

In this section, we investigate the details of two conditions for workload-level asynchronicity (WLA): (1) inter-task dependencies and (2) resource availability. We explore the benefits of the asynchronous execution of heterogeneous workflows by focusing on makespan and resource utilization.

## 5.1    Condition I: Inter-Task Dependencies

The asynchronicity of ML-enabled workflows depends on executing independent heterogeneous tasks. We consider tasks to be black boxes; *i.e.*, we do not make assumptions about their inner workings such as stochastic inter-task communication overheads. Accordingly, we consider only data dependencies among tasks, where data are consumed and produced as tasks' inputs and outputs. Consistent with common practice, we represent task dependencies of a workflow as a directed acyclic graph (DAG), where edges are data dependencies and nodes are tasks.

Asynchronous task execution only applies to workflows with a dependency graph (DG) that contains one or more forks (branches) with diverging paths. As such, given sufficient resources, independent tasks of different types can execute asynchronously. Figure 2 shows four DGs representative of four workflows with varying levels of inter-task data dependence. Note that task set indices are ordered breadth-first and that the $y$-axis of our DG does not necessarily correlate with time.

We define the degree of asynchronicity ($DOA_{dep}$) as the number of independent execution branches minus one. To discover independent branches, we perform a depth-first search on the DG. The lower bound on ($DOA_{dep}$), permitted by task dependencies, arises when the DG is sequential—*e.g.*, a linear chain, shown in Fig. 2a—for which $DOA_{dep} = 0$. The upper bound, *i.e.*, completely asynchronous, arises with a DG whose edge set is the empty set, such as that in Fig. 2d, where $DOA_{dep} = n$. In between those bounds, asynchronicity varies as a function of the number of forks with diverging paths.

## 5.2 Condition II: Resource Availability

Given unlimited resources, inter-task dependency is, in principle, the limiting factor to the degree of asynchronicity for a given workflow. For example, the DG in Fig. 2d has $\mathrm{DOA_{dep}} = n$, so in the case of infinite resources, each of the $n+1$ task sets' tasks can execute asynchronously. In practice, however, resources are limited, and therefore an additional condition based on the available (allocated) resources must be imposed.

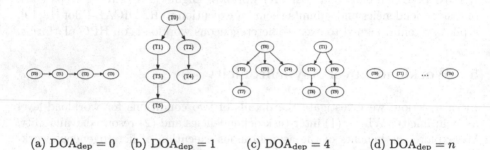

(a) $\mathrm{DOA_{dep}} = 0$    (b) $\mathrm{DOA_{dep}} = 1$    (c) $\mathrm{DOA_{dep}} = 4$    (d) $\mathrm{DOA_{dep}} = n$

**Fig. 2.** Abstract dependency graphs (DGs) and their respective task dependency degree of asynchrony, $\mathrm{DOA_{dep}}$. These DGs are abstract as only task sets (nodes), their orderings (indices) and dependencies (edges) are given; they contain no information about the number of tasks in each task set, their resource requirements, task execution time (TX), *etc.* Task set indices are ordered in a breadth-first manner.

To describe the resource-permitted degree of asynchronicity, $\mathrm{DOA_{res}}$, consider again the DG in Fig. 2d. Let $\widetilde{R}$ be the set of all allocated resources and $\cup_i R_i$ be the set resources required to asynchronously execute the $n+1$ task sets. Complete asynchronicity is achieved if and only if $\cup_i R_i \subseteq \widetilde{R}$, in which case $\mathrm{DOA_{res}} \geq \mathrm{DOA_{dep}} = n$. On the other extreme, if $R_i = \widetilde{R} \ \forall_i$, then we have two possibilities: (1) execute each task set in an arbitrary order, since the execution of the full set of tasks from any task set requires 100% of the allocated resources, or (2) execute from two or more task sets the subsets such that $\cap_i R_i = \widetilde{R}$. Despite $\mathrm{DOA_{res}} = 0$ in the first case and $\mathrm{DOA_{res}} > 0$ in the second, there exists an equivalence between the two wherein the latter effectively is the collapse of a dependency-free DG to a chain as in Fig. 2a. This scenario highlights how haphazard attempts to adopt asynchronicity into a workflow will not necessarily yield any benefit for the workflow as a whole, and instead can lead to significant loss of development time during the design and optimization process.

Richer, albeit more complex, situations lie between the two extremes. Take, for example, the workflow DG of Fig. 2c, which has $\mathrm{DOA_{dep}} = 4$. Depending on the resource requirements for each of $\{T_2\}$ through $\{T_9\}$ task sets, $0 \leq \mathrm{DOA_{res}} \leq 5$. As such, we define,

$$\mathrm{WLA} \equiv \min[\mathrm{DOA_{dep}}, \mathrm{DOA_{res}}] \tag{1}$$

to quantify the asynchronicity permitted by the workflow.

Note that asynchronous executions are not necessarily concurrent, and synchronous executions are not necessarily sequential. Tasks are asynchronous when they can execute independently of one another, while tasks are concurrent when they execute at the same time. Thus, asynchronous executions can be either sequential or concurrent, depending on resource availability. For example, two independent task sets, $\{T_0\}$ and $\{T_1\}$ from Fig. 2c, can be run one after the other if not enough resources are available to execute them concurrently. Analogously, two tasks that depend on each other (e.g., inter-task communication dependency) can execute concurrently when enough resources are available.

## 5.3   Benefits of Workflow-Level Asynchronicity

A primary motivation for asynchronous task execution is to improve resource utilization which is correlated with task throughput and thus workflow makespan. However, examples already given show how the introduction of asynchronicity does not guarantee increased task throughput, specifically when the majority of upstream tasks (ancestors) dominate resource use. When a workflow requires resources with a $\mathrm{DOA_{res}} > 0$ and it is possible to exploit TX *masking*, the overall workflow makespan can be reduced by achieving higher task throughput.

TX masking happens when longer running tasks effectively 'hide' contributions from shorter running tasks to a workflow's makespan (TTX). To illustrate masking, consider the workflow DG of Fig. 2b for which $\mathrm{DOA_{dep}} = 1$. Assume the allocated resources are such that once task set $\{T_0\}$ completes, the chains $(\{T_1\}, \{T_3\}, \{T_5\})$ and $(\{T_2\}, \{T_4\})$ can execute asynchronously; then $\mathrm{DOA_{res}} = \mathrm{DOA_{dep}} = 1$. For concreteness, further assume the following assignments:

$$t_0 = 500\mathrm{s}, \; t_1 = t_2 = 1000\mathrm{s}, \; 2t_3 = 2t_5 = t_4 = 4000\mathrm{s},$$

where $t_i \equiv t(\{T_i\})$ is the time required to execute task set $\{T_i\}$. To demonstrate the utility of masking, we begin with a purely sequential workflow using the Pipeline, Stage, and Task (PST) model [3], where the DG represents a pipeline, each rank corresponds to a stage, and each task is set to a collection of identical tasks. In the sequential model, the TTX is given simply by,

$$t^{\mathrm{Seq}} = \sum_i t_i + C, \tag{2}$$

where $i$ represents $i$th stage, $t_i$ represents TX of that stage, and $C$ is a constant representing the workflow management system's overheads such as communications. In general, $C$ is negligible with task execution times $O(10)$ minutes and larger. As such, we disregard small overheads in future calculations but consider them in later analyses. Plugging into Eq. 2 the above assigned TX values, the sequential TTX is $t^{\mathrm{Seq}} = 7500\mathrm{s}$.

We now demonstrate how the workflow TTX can be significantly reduced by exploiting the conditions for asynchronicity and the parameters of the workflow; specifically here, $\mathrm{WLA} = \min(\mathrm{DOA_{dep}}, \mathrm{DOA_{res}}) = 1$ and the TX assignments are the same as above. First, the WLA enables asynchronous execution of the chains $H_1 \equiv (\{T_1\}, \{T_3\}, \{T_5\})$ and $H_2 \equiv (\{T_2\}, \{T_4\})$. Second, the TX assignments lead to masking such that the contribution from task set $\{T_5\}$ to the workflow TTX is hidden by the execution of task set $\{T_4\}$ since $t_4 = t_3 + t_5$ and the corresponding task sets now execute asynchronously. In general, the asynchronous TTX for an asynchronous workflow is given by,

$$t^{\text{Async}} = \sum_i t_i + \max[t_{H_j}] + C$$

$$\leq t^{\text{Seq}},$$

(3)

where $t_i$ represents the sequential task sets and $t_{H_j}$ represents the TTX of chain (branch) $H_j$.

$$t_{H_j} = \sum_j t_j$$

$$\leq t^{\text{Seq}},$$

(4)

We have equality if and only if $t_{H_j} = t_{H_k} \, \forall_{j,k}$. Asynchronous execution of the workflow under discussion, therefore, has a TTX of $t_0 + t_{H_1} = 5500\text{s}$. We define the relative improvement as,

$$I \equiv 1 - \frac{t^{\text{Async}}}{t^{\text{Seq}}},$$

(5)

which, in this example, gives roughly a 26% reduction compared to the sequential execution. This example makes clear the potential gains when a workflow is designed to leverage WLA as well as TX masking.

## 6   Experiments

We design three experiments to characterize the performance of asynchronous task execution, using three heterogeneous workflows with different inter-task dependencies. We execute two implementations of a workflow for each experiment, one asynchronous and one sequential, and compare their performance. All workflows' tasks execute the stress application and, for simplicity, we omit operations such as data movement and staging which are largely platform-dependent. stress allows implementing task heterogeneity by setting arbitrary task duration (TX) and resource requirements (number of CPUs/GPUs). Further, using a synthetic task executable allows to make judicious use of shared allocations and alleviate overheads; *e.g.*, having to use application-specific input files, configurations, *etc*. As we focus on workflow asynchronicity, this approach permits analysis without loss of generality.

### 6.1   DeepDriveMD

DeepDriveMD [9] comprises four types of tasks—Simulation, Aggregation, Training, and Inference—as described earlier. All tasks but Aggregation are

**Table 1.** DeepDriveMD workflow tasks. The TX for each task was extracted from [9] and scaled down by a factor of four. A variable offset $0.05\sigma$ is added to TX of each task to mimic the stochastic behavior of actual executables.

| Task Set | CPU cores/Tasks | GPUs/Tasks | # Tasks (×3) | TX (±0.05$\sigma$) [s] |
|---|---|---|---|---|
| Simulation | 4 | 1 | 96 | 340 |
| Aggregation | 32 | 0 | 16 | 85 |
| Training | 4 | 1 | 1 | 63 |
| Inference | 16 | 1 | 96 | 38 |

heterogeneous, *i.e.*, they use both CPUs and GPUs, and the number of each type of task and their execution times vary among task sets. Table 1 details the workflow parameters which are scaled appropriately with respect to the number of nodes used for these studies.

There exist dependencies between the different task sets (similar to Fig. 2a); Simulation tasks are responsible for producing the data that is consumed by Aggregation tasks, the aggregated data is then inputted to ML model Training tasks, and lastly Inference tasks perform inference using the trained models. As such, a single iteration of this workflow necessarily needs to be sequential in terms of the execution of various tasks. In practice, however, ML training and inference typically require multiple iterations (sufficient data volumes) for convergence and to reach some level of accuracy or precision in terms of their predictions. It is therefore possible and, as will be demonstrated, advantageous to asynchronously execute tasks of different types among iterations while also ensuring that dependencies are met.

Each task set can execute concurrently, *e.g.*, all Simulation tasks run at the same time, each task set is executed sequentially, as described previously. As such, sequential execution of this workflow uses a single pipeline to orchestrate task execution, where each stage executes sequentially and spawns at least one task that receives input from a preceding one. To construct an asynchronous workflow from multiple independent chains, we use the equivalent DG shown in Fig. 3a[1], where task sets are staggered. Using the PST model, the complete DG corresponds to a single pipeline, each rank to a stage, and each task set to the tasks comprising the workload. Task specifications for this workflow are given in Table 1.

As a future work, we will remove dependencies between independent chains caused by putting each rank in a stage. In that context, we will focus on task-level dependencies to achieve adaptive asynchronicity, where: (1) tasks from different, non-converging branches can execute completely asynchronously (*e.g.* from Fig. 3a, $Aggr_0$ and $Train_1$ can run at the same time); and (2) tasks from different converging branches can still execute asynchronously as long as they don't have any dependencies between each other, *e.g.* from Fig. 3b, $\{T_1\}$ and $\{T_5\}$ could execute asynchronously and possibly concurrently.

---

[1] An alternative DG representation of this workflow is three independent chains, one for each iteration. However, this would not admit asynchronous execution as defined in Sect. 4.

## 6.2   Abstract-DG

We constructed two additional workflows from a single arbitrary abstract DG. Figure 3b shows the DG considered for these studies, which consists of eight task sets labeled {T0} through {T7} and dependencies among them.

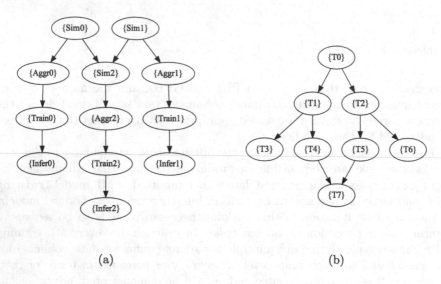

(a)                                                                (b)

**Fig. 3.** Dependency graphs corresponding to (a) DeepDriveMD and (b) arbitrary workflows.

Two concrete workflows based on the abstract DG, denoted c-DG1 and c-DG2, are considered to support the conditions for WLA, and to quantify the degree to which asynchronicity is permitted by a specific workflow instantiation. Both concrete workflows are assigned task sets with an arbitrary number of tasks, resources and TX; see Table 2.

**Table 2.** Summary of the abstract DG workflow tasks for the concrete DGs 'c-DG1' and 'c-DG2'. Similar task types are assigned the same resources and their respective task sets are grouped within braces. The task set TX values are sampled from a normal distribution $\mathcal{N}(\mu, \sigma = 0.05)$, where $\mu = $ (Mean TTX Fraction $\times$ 2000 [s]) to emulate stochastic behavior of actual executables; these fractions have been rounded to two significant figures in the table.

| Task Set | CPU cores/Task | GPUs/Task | | # Tasks (×3) | | Mean TTX Fraction | |
|---|---|---|---|---|---|---|---|
| | | c-DG1 | c-DG2 | c-DG1 | c-DG2 | c-DG1 | c-DG2 |
| {T0} | 16 | 1 | 1 | 96 | 96 | 0.38 | 0.19 |
| ({T1}, {T2}) | 40 | 0 | 0 | 32 | 32 | 0.11 | 0.08 |
| ({T3}, {T6}) | 4 | 0 | 1 | 16 | 96 | 0.06 | 0.38 |
| ({T4}, {T5}) | 32 | 1 | 1 | 16 | 16 | 0.08 | 0.12 |
| {T7} | 4 | 1 | 0 | 96 | 16 | 0.36 | 0.23 |

Task properties are chosen for each concrete workflow to explore two distinct use-cases from a single abstract DG, and how different parameters can affect the relative improvement when incorporating asynchronicity. Note that, contrary to DeepDriveMD's DG, each rank is not associated with a stage. As mentioned above, in an adaptive asynchronous execution, tasks ({T1}, {T4}) and ({T2}, {T5}) would execute asynchronously since they do not have any dependencies, but {T7} would only execute after both {T4} and {T5} are finished.

# 7     Performance Characterization

We evaluate the achievable level of asynchronicity, resource utilization, and TTX for the experimental workflows described in Sect. 6, executing them on the Oak Ridge National Laboratory's Summit supercomputer. Summit has roughly 4600 compute nodes, each with two 24-core Power9 CPUs and six NVIDIA V100 GPUs. In these studies, we use a total of 16 nodes for each experiment, giving 706 usable CPU core (62 cores are reserved by the system) and 96 GPUs.

We construct synthetic workloads representative of real-world workflow applications to characterize and evaluate the performance of our experiments. For example, we consider workloads comprising a combination of homogeneous and heterogeneous tasks, and different types of tasks with varying TX. To calculate the relative improvement $I$ (Eq. 5), for each experiment, we execute both sequential and asynchronous modes. We impose a TTX constraint on c-DG1 and c-DG2; the sequential TTX is about 2000 s for both. Results for asynchronous executions are summarized in Table 3. As part of our future work, we will test real-life workflows from different scientific domains on various HPC facilities.

## 7.1     DeepDriveMD

In principle, the DeepDriveMD workflow is sequential where the workflow follows the `Simulation` → `Aggregation` → `Training` → `Inference` flow. To implement asynchronicity, we started multiple executions of the DeepDriveMD workflow with different starting times so to run different stages asynchronously. As such,

**Table 3.** Summary of experimental results. Predicted values of $t^{Seq}$, $t^{Async}$, and $I$ include corrections accounting for overheads in EnTK (4%) and those incurred from enabling asynchronicity (2%) into the framework. While the degrees of asynchronicity ($DOA_{dep}$ and $DOA_{res}$) directly determine the workload-level asynchronicity (WLA) for a given workflow, resource utilization and task throughput, captured by the relative improvement ($I$), depend on available resources and TX masking.

| Experiment | $DOA_{dep}$ | $DOA_{res}$ | WLA | $t^{Seq}$ [s] | | $t^{Async}$ [s] | | $I$ | |
|---|---|---|---|---|---|---|---|---|---|
| | | | | Pred. | Calc. | Pred. | Calc. | Pred. | Calc |
| DeepDriveMD | 2 | 1 | 1 | 1578 | 1707 | 1399 | 1373 | 0.113 | 0.196 |
| c-DG1 | 2 | 2 | 2 | 2000 | 1945 | 1972 | 1975 | 0.014 | −0.015 |
| c-DG2 | 2 | 2 | 2 | 2000 | 1856 | 1378 | 1372 | 0.311 | 0.261 |

the workflow TTX is bounded by the level of asynchronicity permitted by the number of times, it is executed. Inspection of the DG in Fig. 3a shows that the workflow (each task set) is executed three times, and that three independent chains beginning at rank one correspond to a $DOA_{dep} = 2$. Based on task requirements in Table 1, the allocated resources give $DOA_{res} = 1$. Hence, for this workflow WLA = 1.

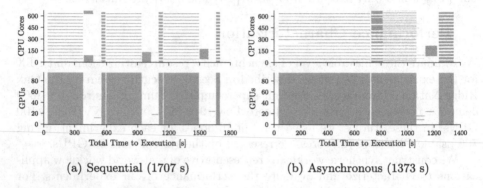

(a) Sequential (1707 s)          (b) Asynchronous (1373 s)

**Fig. 4.** Three iterations of DeepDriveMD workflow, with sequential (left) and asychronous (right) execution. The TTX improvement achieved with asynchronicity is about 20%.

Figure 4 shows the CPU and GPU resource utilization for three iterations of the DeepDriveMD workflow as a function of TTX, with white space representing resources on which there are no executing tasks and colored regions representing utilized resources. Comparing Fig. 4a and Fig. 4b, sequential and asynchronous execution, respectively, shows that the allocated resources are better utilized with asynchronicity. The improved use of resources leads to a higher task throughput, as shown by the decrease in the asynchronous workflow TTX. From Eq. 2, with the TX values from Table 1, sequential execution has a TTX of approximately $3t^{Seq} = 1578$ s, as a result of the workflow being executed three times. The independent chain in the asynchronous workflow DG with the largest combined TX is the chain with the task set {Sim2} as the top-level ancestor, giving $t_H = t^{Seq} = 526$ s. Task sets {Sim1}, {Sim2}, and the three `Inference` task sets, each requiring all 96 GPUs, are ineligible for asynchronicity due to insufficient resources. Plugging into Eq. 3 the values $2t_{Sim0} = 2t_{Sim1} = 680$ s, $3t_{Infer0} = 3t_{Infer1} = 3t_{Infer2} = 114$ s and $t_H$ returns an asynchronous workflow execution time $t^{Async} = 1320$ s, yielding $I = 0.17$.

Important to note the discrepancy of about 4% between the calculated $t^{Async}$ and the measured value of 1373 s. This can be attributed to two factors: (1) we disregard constant overheads in the EnTK framework (the constant factor $C$ in Eq. 2); and (2) Eq. 3 assumes infinite resources. Since each `Inference` task set requires all available resources, we have the scenario described in Sect. 5.2 where the otherwise independent chains collapse to a single chain dependent on the resource allocation.

In light of the TTX disagreement between theory and practice for this multi-iteration workflow, an alternative formulation for calculating $t^{\text{Async}}$ can be used:

$$t^{\text{Async}} = nt^{\text{Seq}} - (n-1)t_{\text{Aggr}} - (n-2)t_{\text{Train}}. \tag{6}$$

such that $n-1$ $(n-2)$ sets of Aggregation (Training) tasks can be executed concurrently across iterations. Equation 6 makes clear that TX-masked tasks do not contribute to the overall TTX (they are subtracted away). Thus, unlike Eq. 3, Eq. 6 correctly does not mask $t_{\text{Infer}}$ due to resource constraints. It will be useful in later analysis to generalize this equation as,

$$t^{\text{Async}} = \sum_{k=0}^{n-1} t_k(-k+n). \tag{7}$$

In the DeepDriveMD workflow, Simulation tasks have sufficiently large TX such that Aggregation and Training tasks can both be masked, $i.e.$, $t_{\text{Sim2}} > t_{\text{Aggr0}} + t_{\text{Train0}} = t_{\text{Aggr1}} + t_{\text{Train1}}$. Substituting the respective values into Eq. 6, the estimated TTX is 1345 s, a difference of 2% with respect to the measured TTX. We attribute that difference to the constant overheads of EnTK, visible in Fig. 4 as white space between task set executions (Fig. 4).

## 7.2   C-DG1

The task requirements in c-DG1 were chosen to demonstrate a case when asynchronicity has a negative impact on a workflow's TTX and task throughput. The workflow is represented by the DG in Fig. 3b, which has $\text{DOA}_{\text{dep}} = \text{DOA}_{\text{res}} = 2$ for WLA = 2. As such, the workflow permits asynchronicity but the task requirements (listed in Table 2) prevent an improvement in resource utilization and

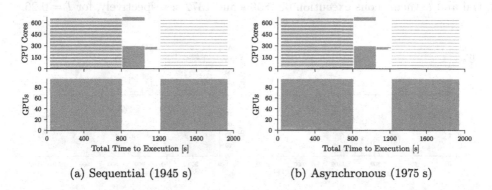

(a) Sequential (1945 s)          (b) Asynchronous (1975 s)

**Fig. 5.** Resource utilization for workflow c-DG1. Sequential (left) and asynchronous (right) execution. Due to the small TX (6% and 7%) of the task sets permitting asynchronous execution ($\{T_3\}, \{T_6\}$ and $\{\{T_4\}, \{T_5\}\}, \{T_7\}$), and additional overheads in spawning multiple workflow executions required for asynchronicity, resource utilization and task throughput improvements are negligible, ultimately resulting in a negative value of $I$.

therefore task throughput. This is due to the fact that, while it is possible to run together task sets $\{T_3\}, \{T_6\}$ and $\{\{T_4\}, \{T_5\}\}, \{T_7\}$, the relatively small TX of $\{T_3\}, \{T_6\}$ and $\{\{T_4\}, \{T_5\}\}$, as well as dependencies for $\{T_7\}$ to begin executing, offer a negligible improvement with TX masking. Indeed, the additional overheads—roughly 2% of the workflow TTX—induced by introducing asynchronicity result in a larger TTX than that of the sequential execution.

Direct application of Eq. 3 yields a predicted asynchronous TTX of 1860 s, which disagrees with the measured TTX by just under 6%: 4% of the difference is accounted for by earlier arguments made for the DeepDriveMD example, and a nearly 2% performance hit derives from the overheads of introducing asynchronicity. Accounting for this difference, Eq. 5 can be used to estimate the potential gains, giving $I = 0.01$, which does not provide motivation to adopt asynchronicity. Using the measured values of the sequential and asynchronous versions of this workflow, $I = -0.015$; asynchronicity indeed has a negative relative improvement. Therefore, workflows with similar traits to c-DG1 are preferentially sequential (Fig. 5).

## 7.3   C-DG2

Last, we show a concrete workflow from the abstract DG in Fig. 3b. Let us take the proposed approach of first predicting the relative improvement of introducing asynchronicity for this workflow, using the task requirements for c-DG2 listed in Table 2. From earlier analyses, we can anticipate an under-estimation of $4 - 6\%$ using Eq. 3. Plugging in the task execution times, the predicted TTX of this workflow is calculated to be 1300s (up to 1378 s accounting for the mentioned underestimation). From Eq. 2, the predicted TTX of the sequential execution of c-DG2 is 2000 s. The estimated relative improvement is thus $I = 0.31$, suggesting the workflow will benefit from asynchronicity. Experimentation measures sequential and asynchronous execution of 1856 s and 1372 s, respectively, for $I = 0.26$.

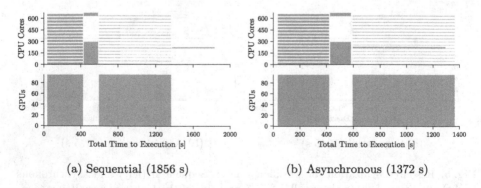

     (a) Sequential (1856 s)           (b) Asynchronous (1372 s)

**Fig. 6.** Resource utilization for workflow c-DG2. Sequential (left) and asynchronous (right) execution, with independent task sets' TTX such that $t_{T3,T6} \sim t_{T4,T5} + t_{T7}$. Exploiting TX masking and the fact that sufficient resources are available, the workflow TTX is reduced by nearly 26%.

The non-zero $DOA_{dep}$ and $DOA_{res}$, which imply a $WLA > 0$, as well as the agreement between the predicted and measured asynchronous TTX guarantee an advantage when using asynchronicity (Fig. 6).

# 8    Conclusions

We studied asynchronous execution and analyzed the performance impact that diverse degrees of asynchronicity have when executing workflows with heterogeneous tasks on HPC platforms, focusing on ML-driven workflows. This paper offers four contributions: (1) an asynchronous implementation of DeepDriveMD, a framework to execute ML-driven molecular-dynamics workflows on HPC platforms at scale; (2) a performance evaluation of asynchronous DeepDriveMD; (3) a model of asynchronous behavior; and (4) a general performance evaluation of that model for workflows with varying degrees of asynchronous execution.

By employing asynchronous execution in DeepDriveMD, a relative improvement $I = 0.196$ over the sequential mode was achieved. This improvement translates to a reduction of an experimentally measured sequential TTX of 1707 s to 1372 s with asynchronicity. Two concrete workflow realizations were defined from a single arbitrary abstract DG to demonstrate a case where the introduction of asynchronicity has a negative effect on TTX, $I = -0.015$, and another that gives a considerable asynchronous advantage, $I = 0.261$. In all experiments, our model presented in Sect. 5 accurately predicted within less than 6% the experimentally measured values, modulo framework constant overheads.

The contributions of this paper represent a first step towards the development of workflow management capabilities to execute heterogeneous tasks at scale on HPC platforms, with higher resource utilization and lower makespan. Those capabilities should be tailored to the specific requirements of ML-driven (heterogeneous) HPC workflows, and offer an asynchronous execution capability. That is a necessary precondition for the efficient and effective deployment of ML-driven workflows on HPC platforms at scale. In the future, we are looking to improve asynchronicity by using the adaptive execution of ML-driven HPC workflows. Adaptive execution will allow varying the degree of asynchronicity at runtime, based on dynamic requirements.

**Acknowledgement.** This work was supported by the ECP CANDLE and ExaWorks projects, the DOE HEP Center for Computational Excellence at BNL under B&R KA2401045, as well as NSF-1931512 (RADICAL-Cybertools). We thank Andre Merzky, Li Tan, and Ning Bao for useful discussions and support. We acknowledge Arvind Ramanathan, Austin Clyde, Rick Stevens, and Ian Foster for useful discussions and co-development of DeepDriveMD. This research used resources at OLCF ORNL, which is supported by the Office of Science of the U.S. Department of Energy under Contract No. DE-AC05-00OR22725.

# References

1. Balaprakash, P., Salim, M., Uram, T.D., Vishwanath, V., Wild, S.M.: Deephy-per: asynchronous hyperparameter search for deep neural networks. In: 2018 IEEE 25th International Conference on High Performance Computing (HiPC), pp. 42–51. IEEE (2018)
2. Balasubramanian, V., Treikalis, A., Weidner, O., Jha, S.: Ensemble toolkit: scalable and flexible execution of ensembles of tasks. In: 2016 45th International Conference on Parallel Processing (ICPP), vol. 00, pp. 458–463 (2016). https://doi.org/10.1109/ICPP.2016.59. https://doi.ieeecomputersociety.org/10.1109/ICPP.2016.59
3. Balasubramanian, V., et al.: Harnessing the power of many: extensible toolkit for scalable ensemble applications. In: International Parallel and Distributed Processing Symposium, pp. 536–545. IEEE (2018)
4. Barham, P., et al.: Pathways: asynchronous distributed dataflow for ml. Proc. Mach. Learn. Syst. **4**, 430–449 (2022)
5. Bauer, M., Treichler, S., Slaughter, E., Aiken, A.: Legion: expressing locality and independence with logical regions. In: SC 2012: Proceedings of the International Conference on High Performance Computing, Networking, Storage and Analysis, pp. 1–11. IEEE (2012)
6. Bhati, A.P., et al.: Pandemic drugs at pandemic speed: Infrastructure for accelerating covid-19 drug discovery with hybrid machine learning-and physics-based simulations on high performance computers. Interface Focus. 112021001820210018 (2021). https://doi.org/10.1098/rsfs.2021.0018
7. Bhatia, H., et al.: Generalizable coordination of large multiscale workflows: challenges and learnings at scale. In: Proceedings of the International Conference for High Performance Computing, Networking, Storage and Analysis, pp. 1–16 (2021)
8. Bosilca, G., Bouteiller, A., Danalis, A., Faverge, M., Hérault, T., Dongarra, J.J.: Parsec: exploiting heterogeneity to enhance scalability. Comput. Sci. Eng. **15**(6), 36–45 (2013)
9. Brace, A., et al.: Coupling streaming AI and hpc ensembles to achieve 100–1000× faster biomolecular simulations. In: 2022 IEEE International Parallel and Distributed Processing Symposium (IPDPS), pp. 806–816. IEEE (2022)
10. Casalino, L., et al.: Ai-driven multiscale simulations illuminate mechanisms of sars-cov-2 spike dynamics (2020). https://doi.org/10.1101/2020.11.19.390187
11. Di Natale, F., et al.: A massively parallel infrastructure for adaptive multiscale simulations: modeling ras initiation pathway for cancer. In: International Conference for High Performance Computing, Networking, Storage and Analysis, pp. 1–16 (2019)
12. Dommer, A., et al.: #covidisairborne: Ai-enabled multiscale computational microscopy of delta sars-cov-2 in a respiratory aerosol. Int. J. High-Perf. Comput. Appl. (2021). https://doi.org/10.1101/2021.11.12.468428
13. Gropp, W., Gropp, W.D., Lusk, E., Skjellum, A., Lusk, A.D.F.E.E.: Using MPI: Portable Parallel Programming with the Message-Passing Interface, vol. 1. MIT press (1999)
14. Kaiser, H., Heller, T., Adelstein-Lelbach, B., Serio, A., Fey, D.: Hpx: a task based programming model in a global address space. In: Proceedings of the 8th International Conference on Partitioned Global Address Space Programming Models, pp. 1–11 (2014)
15. Kale, L.V., Krishnan, S.: Charm++ a portable concurrent object oriented system based on c++. In: Proceedings of the Eighth Annual Conference on Object-Oriented Programming Systems, Languages, and Applications, pp. 91–108 (1993)

16. Lee, H., Turilli, M., Jha, S., Bhowmik, D., Ma, H., Ramanathan, A.: Deepdrivemd: deep-learning driven adaptive molecular simulations for protein folding. In: 2019 IEEE/ACM Third Workshop on Deep Learning on Supercomputers (DLS), pp. 12–19. IEEE (2019). https://doi.org/10.1109/DLS49591.2019.00007
17. Meng, Q., Humphrey, A., Berzins, M.: The uintah framework: a unified heterogeneous task scheduling and runtime system. In: 2012 SC Companion: High Performance Computing, Networking Storage and Analysis, pp. 2441–2448. IEEE (2012)
18. Merzky, A., Santcroos, M., Turilli, M., Jha, S.: Radical-pilot: scalable execution of heterogeneous and dynamic workloads on supercomputers. CoRR, abs/1512.08194 (2015)
19. Merzky, A., Turilli, M., Titov, M., Al-Saadi, A., Jha, S.: Design and performance characterization of radical-pilot on leadership-class platforms. IEEE Trans. Parallel Distrib. Syst. **33**(4), 818–829 (2021)
20. Peterson, J.L., et al.: Enabling machine learning-ready hpc ensembles with merlin. Future Gener. Comput. Syst. **131**, 255–268 (2022)
21. Saadi, A.A., et al.: Impeccable: integrated modeling pipeline for covid cure by assessing better leads. In: 50th International Conference on Parallel Processing, pp. 1–12 (2021)
22. Saadi, A.A., et al.: Impeccable: integrated modeling pipeline for covid cure by assessing better leads. In: 50th International Conference on Parallel Processing (ICPP 21), Lemont, IL, USA, 9–12 August 2021, p. 12. ACM, New York (2021). https://doi.org/10.1145/3472456.3473524
23. Wang, T., Seal, S.K., Kannan, R., Garcia-Cardona, C., Proffen, T., Jha, S.: A parallel machine learning workflow for neutron scattering data analysis. In: 2023 IEEE International Parallel and Distributed Processing Symposium Workshops (IPDPSW), pp. 795–798. IEEE (2023)
24. Ward, L., et al.: Colmena: scalable machine-learning-based steering of ensemble simulations for high performance computing. In: 2021 ACM Workshop on Machine Learning in High Performance Computing Environments (MLHPC), pp. 9–20. IEEE (2021)
25. Zamora, Y., Ward, L., Sivaraman, G., Foster, I., Hoffmann, H.: Proxima: accelerating the integration of machine learning in atomistic simulations. In: Proceedings of the ACM International Conference on Supercomputing, pp. 242–253 (2021)

# Memory-Aware Latency Prediction Model for Concurrent Kernels in Partitionable GPUs: Simulations and Experiments

Alessio Masola$^{(\boxtimes)}$ (iD), Nicola Capodieci, Roberto Cavicchioli,
Ignacio Sanudo Olmedo, and Benjamin Rouxel

Department of Physics, Informatics and Mathematics,
University of Modena and Reggio Emilia, Modena, Italy
{masola.alessio,capodieci.nicola,cavicchioli.roberto,
sanudo.ignacio,rouxel.benjamin}@unimore.it

**Abstract.** The current trend in recently released Graphic Processing Units (GPUs) is to exploit transistor scaling at the architectural level, hence, larger and larger GPUs in every new chip generation are released. Architecturally, this implies that the clusters count of parallel processing elements embedded within a single GPU die is constantly increasing, posing novel and interesting research challenges for performance engineering in latency-sensitive scenarios. A single GPU kernel is now likely not to scale linearly when dispatched in a GPU that features a larger cluster count. This is either due to VRAM bandwidth acting as a bottleneck or due to the inability of the kernel to saturate the massively parallel compute power available in these novel architectures. In this context, novel scheduling approaches might be derived if we consider the GPU as a partitionable compute engine in which multiple concurrent kernels can be scheduled in non-overlapping sets of clusters. While such an approach is very effective in improving the GPU overall utilization, it poses significant challenges in estimating kernel execution time latencies when kernels are dispatched to variable-sized GPU partitions. Moreover, memory interference within co-running kernels is a mandatory aspect to consider. In this work, we derive a practical yet fairly accurate memory-aware latency estimation model for co-running GPU kernels.

**Keywords:** Latency Prediction · Concurrent Kernels ·
GPGPU-Simulator · Partitionable GPU

## 1 Introduction

In the context of cyber physical systems (CPS) and related applications, in order to cope with data and compute intensive task-sets, processing platforms usually feature multi-core CPUs able to work in concert with massively parallel compute accelerators. A nowadays very common architectural solution when dealing with compute accelerators is represented by General-Purpose Graphics Processing Units (GP-GPUs or simply GPUs), as are often chosen on the account of their impressive performance per watt ratio, high availability, and the presence of fairly mature ecosystems of APIs, libraries and development kits aiming to simplify their usability. As applications complexity grows and their compute demands increase over time, novel GPU architectural blueprints must keep up with such a trend. In this sense, GPU vendors' road-maps suggest that transistor scaling enables GPU performance to continue to rise, due to higher GPU frequencies and growth in die size [21]. This latter point translates into the increasing count of clusters of parallel processing elements embedded within a single GPU die. In Layman's terms, we can say that *larger* GPUs are released generation after generation. However, compute kernels running alone are therefore not always able to exploit this new degree of parallelism offered by novel GPUs [3,18]. As a consequence of this, system engineers are researching mechanisms and methodologies to dispatch multiple kernels onto the GPU within overlapping time windows, hence assigning a variable number of GPU cores and memory resources to different kernels according to their timing and latency requirements. GPU resources to kernels assignment can be achieved in many ways: one of such mechanism has been termed *Multi-Kernel Execution* in which groups of threads belonging to different kernels might be distributed to all the GPU's compute clusters. This solution implies that blocks of threads of different kernels share the same clusters within overlapping time windows. Despite being proven to be very effective in increasing overall throughput [24], it is very difficult to control individual kernel latencies in such a scenario [17]. This is due to the fact that GPU threads are not only forced to compete for compute resources (i.e. internal cluster schedulers, ALU pipelines etc.) but also for the GPU cluster's cache hierarchy and local scratch-pad memories.

On the other hand, spatial kernel partitioning can be considered: in such a paradigm, the GPU's compute clusters are divided within non-overlapping partitions so that one or more clusters are assigned to individual kernels. In this way, the GPU last level cache (LLC, L2) is the first and most important contention point when multiple kernels are executing within overlapping time windows, which allows the system engineer to focus on a single memory contention point, once the scaling of kernels execution time as a function of assigned GPU partitions is known. Kernel execution time scaling on variable compute cluster partitions is not trivial to derive.

While ideally such a scaling function should be linear, i.e. the kernel's execution time decreases linearly as we linearly assign more GPU compute clusters, the GPU parallel capabilities might exceed the kernel degree of parallelism, hence reaching the theoretical performance peak without actually using the entire sets of GPU partitions. Moreover, memory bandwidth plays a crucial role, as highly memory-bound kernels cause L2 to VRAM memory bandwidth to act as a bottleneck so to further hinder the expected performance scaling. This latter aspect has been extensively studied and it is known as GPU roofline model [14,26].

In this work, we therefore aim to study the behaviour of GPU spatial partitioning when multiple kernels run concurrently in separated GPU partitions. More specifically, we present an intuitive, yet practical memory-interference aware performance prediction model that takes into account the individual kernels' features and memory behaviour. Compared to previous literature, our proposed methodology is able to provide reasonable accuracy when predicting kernels' execution time, and it is able to scale well when increasing the number of concurrent GPU kernels. This research is a preliminary study aimed at managing memory interference in partitions, with the future ultimate goal of assisting in the design of effective schedulers for multiple concurrent execution of kernels in a GPU.

## 2  Background

In this section, we briefly summarize the most important architectural characteristics of a GPU, the GPU programming model and the chosen simulation environment. As far as GPU terminology is concerned, without excessive loss of generality we will introduce and use throughout this paper the NVIDIA terminology in the context of the widely adopted CUDA API[1].

### 2.1  GPU Architecture

Even if the original purpose of GPUs was to accelerate graphic processing, in recent decades a GPU can be thought of as a massively parallel compute accelerator able to be deployed in a wide variety of general purpose scenarios [16]. Hardware-wise, the GPU execution model is a hybrid between a SIMT (Single Instruction Multiple Threads) and SIMD (Single Instruction Multiple Data) parallel compute engine, in which multiple instructions are executed by a large number of ALU (Arithmetical Logical Unit) pipelines in a lock-step fashion. There are evident similarities among GPUs released by different device vendors, as GPUs' ALU pipelines are always grouped into clusters of processing elements. Inside each processing cluster, both L1 cache and scratch-pad memories are shared among the ALU pipelines within the cluster. Just outside the cluster and shared among the other clusters, a last level cache (LLC) is present. This latter memory is connected to the rest of the system with an interconnection fabric. In case of a discrete GPU, this represents the connection between the LLC and the dedicated VRAM (Video Random Access Memory), or directly to system RAM in case of integrated GPUs commonly implemented in embedded System-on-Chips.

In NVIDIA terminology, ALU pipelines are named *CUDA cores* (Fig. 1), which are grouped into computing clusters named *SM, Streaming Multiprocessors*. Inside an SM, the explicitly addressable scratch-pad memory is called *shared memory*. An L1 Cache is also present.

---

[1] https://docs.nvidia.com/cuda/.

## 2.2   Programming Model and Scheduling

Software-wise, implementing a GPU application means tackling a heterogeneous programming problem. This is because the host CPU has the duty to submit copy and compute commands to the GPU and this is achieved with specific APIs designed to simplify access to the GPU compute acceleration capabilities [5]. Examples of such APIs are the NVIDIA CUDA (Compute Unified Device Architecture), which is a proprietary API, and OpenCL[2] which, in contrast, is an open-standard.

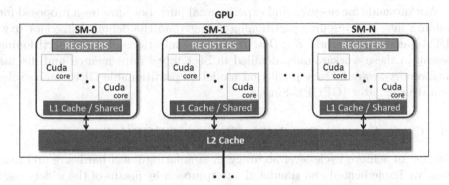

**Fig. 1.** GPU architectures are composed of a set of SMs with L2 cache shared among each SM.

In GPU APIs such as CUDA and OpenCL, commands submitted from the CPU to the GPU are related to the execution of the parallel programs onto the GPU's processing clusters. These GPU runnables are commonly referred to as *kernels*. A GPU application, therefore, has to manage data allocation, buffer movements from the CPU-only visible to the GPU-only visible memory areas (and vice versa) and kernels' dispatch calls.

The programmer has very little margin to influence the scheduling mechanisms of a GPU application. Kernels are dispatched through parallel queues of commands, that in CUDA terminology are called *streams*. In NVIDIA GPUs, commands enqueued in the same stream are executed following a FIFO order. Multiple kernels belonging to different streams might execute in parallel if the occupancy of a kernel within a stream does not saturate the compute capability of every SM. Blocks of threads of each kernel tend to be distributed among **all** the sets of SMs in a round-robin fashion: in this way, if a kernel does not saturate all the memory (i.e. shared memory and register) or compute resources (i.e. CUDA cores) of the SMs, another kernel of a different stream can execute in parallel [17].

It is important to note that the current CUDA APIs available on consumer-level GPUs do not allow programmers to control how kernels are assigned to

---

[2] https://www.khronos.org/opencl/.

*partitions* on NVIDIA GPUs. There is no publicly available method to specify which partitions should be used for a particular kernel in the CUDA programming model. As a result, the baseline CUDA stream scheduler will enforce resource sharing among blocks of threads belonging to different kernels within a single SM, which can impact the predictability of execution latencies.

The term *partition* refers to a selected subset of SMs that are, in our case, contiguous, meaning that they are ordered by their IDs. For example, if there is a GPU with 30 SMs numbered from 0 to 29, a contiguous partition of 10 SMs could include SMs with IDs ranging from 0 to 9, while a non-contiguous partition is one that includes SMs with IDs that are not ordered.

Workarounds for research and experimental purposes have been proposed for enabling inter-SM resource partitioning rather than the default behaviour (e.g. CUDA persistent threads [8]). Due to evident limitations on GPU partitioning present in these workarounds, detailed in Sect. 9, we implemented and discuss our memory-aware latency prediction model on partitionable GPUs on a cycle-accurate simulator (GPGPU-Sim).

### 2.3   Cycle Accurate Simulation Through GPGPU-Sim

In order to achieve cycle-level accuracy in simulating novel hardware architectures, we implemented and simulated our approach by means of the widely used GPGPU-Sim [13]. GPGPU-Sim is a cycle-level simulator capable of modelling arbitrary GPU architectures and executing computing workloads written using widely known APIs such as CUDA or OpenCL. As demonstrated by the research group that develops and maintains GPGPU-Sim, this simulator allows us to analyze the majority of architectures available on the market, somehow compensating for the scarce amount of documentation on low-level architectural details that are usually provided by manufacturers.

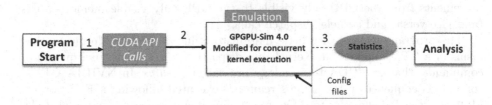

**Fig. 2.** Workflow from host to GPGPU-Sim.

In order to evaluate the correlation between the simulations and the real GPU hardware behaviour, GPGPU-Sim authors observed the Instruction Per Clock (IPC) measured through simulations and the average value obtained on real NVIDIA GPUs for a set of benchmark kernels. An impressive similarity index of 98.37% was reached. This value allows us to assume that the analysis performed with this simulator is reliable; it also enables us to modify some parts of the hardware characteristics in order to expose the limits of the existing GPU devices and to test architectural improvements for further optimization. In our work, we used GPGPU-Sim for timing analysis (emulation cycles) and measure the interference occurring at the L2 cache memory level during the concurrent execution of multiple kernels. The L2 is the point in the memory hierarchy in which we focus our attention, as this is the first contention point for GPU thread blocks of different kernels mapped in non-overlapping sets of SMs. In order to be able to define the mapping of concurrent kernels within user-defined SM partitions, we created an ad-hoc extension for GPGPU-Sim.

GPGPU-Sim produces a compiled library that allows the simulator to interpret the compiled instruction program set of CUDA device low-level source code (called PTX - Parallel Thread Execution) and simulates it within the desired hardware architecture (Fig. 2). The emulated architecture is composed of many Single Instruction Multiple Thread (SIMT) cores that model multithreaded pipelined Single Instruction Multiple Data (SIMD) execution units. Such execution units are grouped within clusters that represent what NVIDIA calls Streaming Multiprocessor (SM). Each SM contains different ALU units, application specific co-processors, and the whole memory hierarchy and interface we described in the previous section. The emulated SMs are connected to the memory partition through an interconnection network. From the interconnection network, packets that contain operations to perform are injected into a SIMT FIFO (First Input First Output) queue that manages and redirects them to the corresponding SIMT SM instruction cache. The packets contain a memory response that could be servicing an instruction fetch miss or a memory pipeline (through a Load Store unit - LDST). Instructions loaded in the instruction cache, are then fetched, decoded, and the operations to perform are eventually executed by the entire core set.

## 3   Overview

Our methodology is illustrated in Fig. 3. It details the steps taken to conduct an in-depth analysis to derive the different predictive models presented in this paper. In order to study the behaviour of a partitioned GPU, we define the concept of dynamic partition in a GPU so to be able to assign SMs to kernels and, in the following section, we describe the engineering effort that we put into GPGPU-Sim in order to modify its thread block scheduling algorithm to enable multiple concurrent kernels executions within partitioned sets of SMs.

With the necessary infrastructure in place to perform our study (Fig. 3 blocks a and b), we proceed with two profiling phases: 1. isolation profiling and, 2. parallel kernel profiling. In the isolation profiling phase, detailed in Sect. 5, we profile the kernels in a baseline scenario in which isolated kernels are potentially dispatched among the whole set of available SMs (default GPU behaviour). This allows us to collect a profile of each kernel's execution times and memory behaviour. Then, we observe how this profile evolves when the same kernel is mapped onto a subset of SMs, Fig. 3 block c. In this way, we construct the completion latency and requested memory bandwidth (BW) vs SM partition size trend for each kernel. Such profile is then used to find a predictive model that allows the system engineer to derive the kernel behaviour (Fig. 3 block d) in isolation, without the need to test all possible partition sizes for each specific kernel (Sect. 6).

In the parallel profiling phase (Sect. 7), we aim to find the interference effect of multiple kernels running concurrently. Therefore, we collect memory accesses of co-running kernels, in order to infer a predictive model able to derive the kernel completion latency including memory interference, Fig. 3 blocks e and f.

We also present a method in Sect. 8 for predicting the L2 cache BW required by a single kernel executing in isolation on varying sets of SMs, Fig. 3 block g.

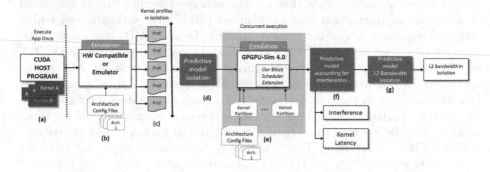

**Fig. 3.** Methodology overview.

## 4  Simulation Settings and Our GPGPU-Sim Extension

We chose to simulate an NVIDIA RTX 2060 as the target GPU for our experiments, since it is the most recent hardware that GPGPU-Sim Version 4.0.0 can emulate, and, also the one with the highest correlation index with respect to real hardware (99% [13]). Table 1 shows our configuration environment. In order to analyze our target scenarios, we modified GPGPU-Sim to enable the concept of mapping a GPU kernel to a subset of available SMs. Our modification of GPGPU-Sim implies a special configuration file given as input. During the simulator initialization phase, this configuration file is loaded by the createSIMTCluster() function, located in *gpu-sim.cc* source file.

Our configuration file contains at each line: a kernel name and a range of integer values corresponding to SMs IDs. The kernel names, retrieved after the first execution, are used in the configuration file. The ranges associated to the kernels represent the partition on which the kernel will be mapped. We assume that such partitions are contiguous and un-fragmented: each kernel will be mapped to a partition composed of contiguous SMs, and the different partitions are prevented from overlapping. The mapping is therefore stored as a data structure visible by all emulated streaming multiprocessors. It implies having a static task-set with

**Table 1.** GPGPU-Sim configuration for a NVIDIA RTX 2060.

| Name | NVIDIA RTX 2060 |
|---|---|
| Clusters | 30 |
| SM per Cluster | 1 |
| Total SM | 30 |
| L1 Cache | 4 banks, 64 KB per SM |
| L2 Cache | 24 banks, 128 KB block, total 3 MB |
| Machine ISA | sm_75 |
| Nominal BW | 348 GB/s |

which static partitions can be defined. We extended GPGPU-Sim in order to dynamically create kernel-to-SM-partition mapping during the execution of the whole simulation.

From the CPU side code (host), multiple kernels are dispatched using multiple streams. The emulated CUDA runtime divides the work belonging to the different kernels in thread blocks, also known as CTAs (Cooperative Thread Arrays) that each individual emulated SM is able to schedule. In the vanilla version of GPGPU-Sim, this is implemented by first selecting a kernel, then considering dispatching blocks belonging to that kernel, which follows the regular stream scheduling logic (see Sect. 2.2). More specifically, a method gets called for every SM instance (called SIMT cluster in GPGPU-Sim) to retrieve a kernel to execute. Once a kernel is selected, its CTAs are dispatched in a round-robin fashion among the SMs.

We modified the kernel selection method, which is called `select_kernel()` in order to restrict the eligible kernels among the ones that have been associated to the partition containing the SIMT cluster in which CTAs are going to be dispatched. This will effectively map thread blocks of specific kernels to predefined sets of SMs (Fig. 4).

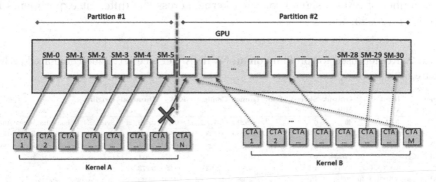

**Fig. 4.** Example of 2 kernels mapped onto 2 GPU partitions with our GPGPU-Sim extension.

We have written a host CUDA application that launches different CUDA kernels in different CUDA streams in order to perform our simulations. Such a benchmark application is used in combination with multiple settings for our added configuration files in order to be able to observe the behaviour of concurrently executing kernels in different partition sizes. We aim to understand how the performance of individual kernel scales when executed in varying partitions and by accounting for memory interference on shared memory hierarchy, i.e. the GPU L2 cache.

## 5 Memory Aware Performance Estimation

The initial profiling phase involves eight different kernels: these kernels have different computational and memory requirements and range from synthetic or very basic operations to significantly more complex kernels. Such kernels are either implemented by ourselves or taken from known benchmark suites. The group of kernels is composed of:

- *Vector add* (VADD) performs a vector addition.
- *Single Precision A X plus Y* (SAXPY) is a combination of scalar multiplication and vector addition.
- *Copy* (COPY) operates a copy between two device-side buffers.
- *Ray tracing* (RAYTRACE) performs a ray-tracing based shading on a 3D scene.
- *Direct X texture compression* (DXTC) is a texture compression algorithm.
- *Convolutional* (CONV) is a convolutional kernel over 2D matrices.
- *Matrix vector product and transpose* (MVT) realises operations on a matrix.
- *Path finder* (PF) is a path finding algorithm.

The kernels, their launch configurations, the working set size and other important information are listed in Table 2.

During this phase, we profiled the cycles required by each kernel to complete, the L2 memory BW, and the number of accesses to the GPU L2. These metrics were collected for each kernel individually while varying the SM partition size. The number of SMs assigned for each kernel across the different experiments is $\in [5, 10, 15, 20, 25, 30]$.

**Table 2.** Kernels used for profiling on an NVIDIA GeForce RTX 2060 emulated architecture.

| Kernel | Input MiB | Output MiB | Shared Mem. | Launch Config. | KIA | Duration ms | Origin |
|---|---|---|---|---|---|---|---|
| VADD | 40*2 | 40 | 0 | (81920,1,1),(128,1,1) | 0.056 | 0.379 | Synthetic/In house implementation |
| SAXPY | 40*2 | 40 | 0 | (81920,1,1),(128,1,1) | 0.059 | 0.379 | Synthetic/In house implementation |
| COPY | 40 | 40 | 0 | (81920,1,1),(128,1,1) | 0.064 | 0.271 | Synthetic/In house implementation |
| RAYTRACE | - | 1.5234 | 0 | (104,80,1),(8,8,1) | 3.575 | 2.621 | In house Implementation |
| DXTC | 0.003 + 0.5 | 0.25 | 1.5 Kb | (46,1,1),(512,1,1) | 149.265 | 3.273 | Cuda Samples |
| CONV | 0.00001 + 40 | 40 | 128 B | (327680,1,1),(32,1,1) | 0.291 | 1.089 | In house Implementation |
| MVT | 64 + 0.01*4 | 0.01*2 | 0 | (64,1,1),(64,1,1) | 0.015 | 2.878 | Polybench |
| PF | 0.5 + 255.5 | 0.5 | 2 Kb | (1024,1,1),(256,1,1) | 0.475 | 0.337 | Rodinia [6] |

## 5.1   Kernels Memory Bandwidth Analysis

First, we observe how the requested memory BW changes for each kernel as we scale up the number of SM in which they are scheduled to be executed, shown in Fig. 5. Trivially, access to the memory interface by different SMs occurs in parallel, as each SM is directly connected to different L2 banks. This implies that, as we scale down the number of SMs assigned to a kernel, its memory BW tends to decrease, as the parallelism in which the memory interface is accessed is also decreased.

Out of this first profiling phase of experiments, we can make an initial quantitative categorization of the maximum BW required by each kernel to access the L2 cache when dispatched on all the 30 SMs. We labelled the kernels in 3 different types:

- *Memory Intensive*: $\{VADD, SAXPY, COPY\}$ the BW demand ($\geq 70\%$) reaches a saturation point, and does not scale linearly, even if we increase the SM count, Fig. 5a.
- *Hybrid*: $\{CONV, MVT, PF\}$ the BW demand ($[10\%, 70\%)$) scales linearly based on the number of SMs with average utilization of compute units, Fig. 5b.
- *Computational*: $\{RAYTRACE, DXTC\}$, the BW utilization is low ($< 10\%$) while the computation requirement linearly increases with the number of SMs, Fig. 5b.

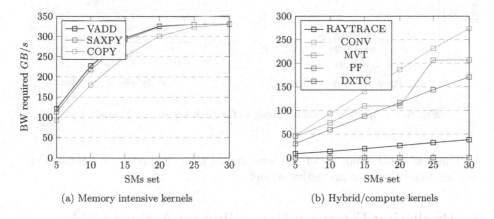

(a) Memory intensive kernels          (b) Hybrid/compute kernels

**Fig. 5.** Memory BW required by each kernel.

We performed multiple tests to understand whether there were any profiling errors on MVT, but we could not understand why MVT (Fig. 5b) has an unexpected behaviour when the set of SMs is 20 and 30 having similar near values to the previous sets. Such strange behaviour could be driven by the simulated architecture or by the kernel behaviour.

We also note that the saturation point of the BW is 330 $GB/s$ while the nominal BW of the architecture is 348 $GB/s$. This saturation point will be later referred to as the Effective Maximum Bandwidth ($EM_{BW}$).

## 5.2    Kernels Completion Latency Analysis

Second, we focus on how the latency completion time scales with the number of assigned SMs. The collected results are summarized in Fig. 6 in which execution latencies are expressed in simulation cycles. As far as memory intensive kernels are concerned, we observe a decreasing exponential behaviour of the kernel latencies that tend to stabilize as soon as the memory saturation point shown in Fig. 5 is reached. In other words, the expected behaviour of a linearly decreasing latency gets *interrupted* due to memory latencies being prevalent over instruction execution times. Such a behaviour is not exhibited in the other kernel type: while not being perfectly linear, a plateau is never reached in most of the tested kernels, instead, we observe an uninterrupted exponential decrease in the completion times.

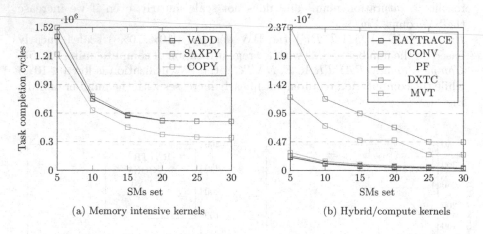

(a) Memory intensive kernels          (b) Hybrid/compute kernels

**Fig. 6.** Completion latencies analysis for each kernel (cycle analysis).

These in-depth analyses of BW and kernel latency shed some lights on the construction of further predictive models.

## 6    Predicting Latencies Depending on Assigned SMs

With the above initial results, it is trivial to understand that the number of SMs strongly influences both the memory BW and the kernel completion latency. More specifically, for non-memory intensive kernels, a linear demand on memory produces a proportional scaling on completion cycles. For memory intensive kernels, as memory requirement increases, the ability of the kernel to fully exploit the available parallelism of a larger SM count is jeopardized. Hence, our predictive model is the first to account for this kernel categorisation of memory/latency behaviour.

We first determine the BW utilisation $U_{bw}(k)$ of a kernel $k$, Eq. 1, as the ratio between the maximum nominal L2 BW ($BW_{max}$), i.e. 348 GB/s with our hardware architecture, and the effective requested BW by the kernel when executed on the maximum available SMs $N$, noted as $BW_{isolated}(k, N)$.

$$U_{bw}(k) = \frac{BW_{isolated}(k, N)}{BW_{max}} \quad (1)$$

Then, we define a *memory saturation memory* $Sat(U_{bw}(k))$, Eq. 2, based on the BW utilisation $U_{bw}(k)$, Eq. 1. By analyzing the equation (1), the more $U_{bw}(k)$ is closer to 1, the faster the memory BW saturation point is reached. Hence, the saturation function $Sat(U_{bw}(k))$ is able to capture the BW behaviour of all three kernel categories.

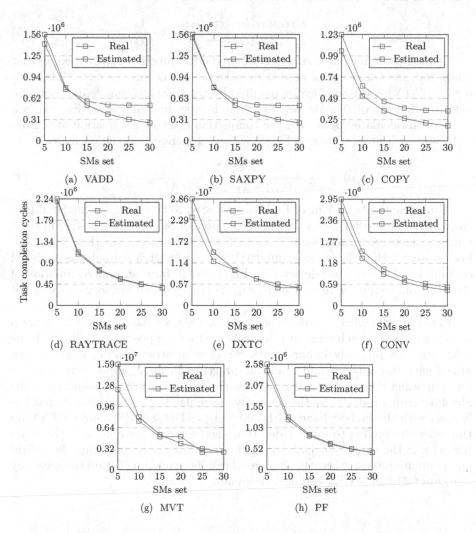

**Fig. 7.** Kernel latency prediction with varying SM size using Eq. 4.

$$Sat(U_{bw}(k)) = \frac{1}{1 + e^{-\alpha(U_{bw}(k) - S_p)}} \tag{2}$$

In Eq. (2), the term $\alpha$ is used to model the saturation function steepness. We experimentally tested several values for our predictive model and found the best results when $\alpha = 100$. The $S_p$ term represents the *saturation point*, which corresponds to a theoretical individual L2 memory bank per SM. In the GPU we are simulating, the L2 is composed of 24 banks to be accessed by 30 SMs, hence $S_p = 24/30 = 0.8$ gives us an estimation of the saturation point within the L2 cache.

We further define a *factor able to estimate the memory intensity $KAI$*, Eq. (3), as the ratio between the total number of executed instructions and the number of L2 accesses, scaled down by a factor of 1000.

$$KAI = \frac{ExecutedInstructions}{L2Accesses} \times \frac{1}{1000} \tag{3}$$

At last, we define our kernel latency prediction function $T_c(k, n)$, eq. 4, that infers *the simulation cycles* needed by a kernel $k$ to complete on $n$ SMs, with $n \leq N$. $C_k(N)$ is the total cycles required by the kernel to complete in isolation with the full set of $N$ SMs, see Fig. 6. It is easy to realize that Eq. (4) is a proportion calculated by scaling the completion time for the fraction of utilized SMs, and such proportion gets biased as kernel memory utilization increases.

$$T_c(k, n) = \frac{C_k(N)}{(Sat(U_{bw}) + 1) \cdot (N - KAI \cdot U_{bw})} \cdot \frac{N^2}{n} \tag{4}$$

Analyzing the behaviour of Eq. (4) compared to the actually simulated execution cycles in GPGPU-Sim, in Fig. 7, the prediction has a larger error in the 3 memory intensive kernels, while it works fine in the other cases. However, it has been observed that the errors committed by our predictive formula, as analyzed on individual kernels and depicted in Fig. 8, range from an underestimation of 30% to a maximum of 10% in situations where excessive memory usage is not required.

In predictive models for real-time systems, it is essential to establish a margin of correctness. This is because it is improbable that the prediction will match the reference value precisely. In our results, we set an arbitrary margin of 20%, which aligns with the industry and academic practices in many application domains for estimating the worst-case execution time (WCET) [19,20,25]. Analyzing the absolute error produced by the predictive formula (Fig. 8), we observe that the kernels with the highest bandwidth demand (VADD, SAXPY, and COPY) are the most challenging to predict due that the formula does not catch the exact behavior of the three kernels. Instead, the remaining ones, including the hybrid and compute-intensive kernels, show good results, remaining within the arbitrary margin of 20% of WCET estimation domain.

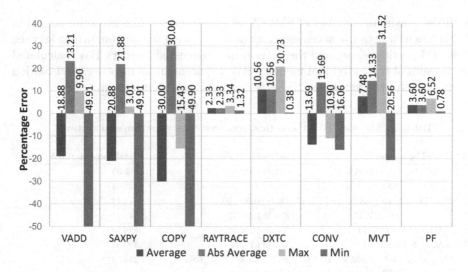

**Fig. 8.** Cycles prediction errors, using eq.(4) . Negative values are underestimations.

## 7   Modeling Memory Interference

Previous Sect. 6 defined $T_c(k, n)$ to effectively predict the number of cycles required for a kernel to complete in isolation as the number of SMs varies. When multiple kernels are concurrently executing on the same architecture, they all interfere with each other when accessing the memory, which has an impact on completion latencies.

In this section, we define a model for the amount of interference that can occur when two or more concurrent kernels are allocated to different and non-overlapping SM partitions on the GPU. This involves considering two very important aspects: 1. *modelling the decrease in the required memory BW of a kernel when mapped onto a n-sized partition, such as $n < N$*, and 2. *if m concurrent kernels run in different partitions, and each has its own memory BW requirement, then the sum of those BWs might exceed $BW_{max}$*. In this case, the latency of the running kernels will deteriorate due to interference. It is also reasonable to assume that the more the available BW limit is exceeded, the higher the magnitude of interference and related performance deterioration will be observed. Following is a series of experiments testing our assumptions.

### 7.1   Experiments and Analysis

To analyze the interference behaviour, we conducted 7 experiments with the objective of covering both critical (total required BW < max BW) and non-critical (total required BW ≥ max BW). For each experiment, labelled from 1 to 7, the number of concurrent kernels varies between 2 and 6. The kernels involved in each experiment are then mapped to non-overlapping sets of SMs, such that the sum of the size of each partition of each kernel in a single experiment coincides with the maximum number of SMs ($N = 30$). These settings are summarized in Table 3, which lists the seven experiments, indicating for all concurrent kernels: their SM partition size, and their theoretical requested memory BW, calculated as the sum of the individual memory BW requirement as measured in isolation (Sect. 5.1). All the kernels in the experiments run to completion.

**Table 3.** Memory BW theoretical requirements: experimental settings.

| ID | Kernel Name and SMs | Individual theoretical BW (GB/s) | Total theoretical BW (GB/s) |
|---|---|---|---|
| 1 | VADD 15 \| RAYTRACE 15 | 296.03 \| 19.32 | 315.35 |
| 2 | VADD 5 \| SAXPY 5 \| MVT 20 | 120.9 \| 113.19 \| 109.5 | 343.61 |
| 3 | RAYTRACE 10 \| DXTC 10 \| PF 10 | 13.39 \| 0.09 \| 59.55 | 73.14 |
| 4 | COPY 15 \| SAXPY 15 | 250.33 \| 291.77 | 542.11 |
| 5 | VADD 15 \| CONV 15 | 296.03 \| 140.37 | 436.40 |
| 6 | VADD 20 \| MVT 10 | 325.58 \| 74.33 | 399.91 |
| 7 | PF \| MVT \| RAYTRACE \| DXTC \| CONV \| COPY each with 5 | 30.04 \| 45.39 \| 8.84 \| 0.04 \| 46.96 \| 92.87 | 224.16 |

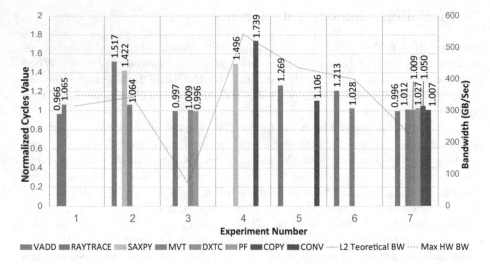

**Fig. 9.** Observed kernel latency deviation, requested BW (solid line), and nominal BW (dotted line).

Figure 9 exhibits the kernel latency deviation with the ratio $\frac{concurrent}{isolation}$ for the respective set of SM. It shows that interference exists and is likely to change depending on the memory access patterns of concurrently executing kernels and L2 cache accesses. From these experiments, we can also observe that the increase of kernel latency is dependent on the initial requested BW (solid line, right y-axis) compared to the nominal BW (dotted line). This consideration is the first pillar of our further prediction model.

Figure 10 presents the actual execution pattern, starting and completion time (in cycles) of its corresponding set of kernels. Zooming in on this execution view, we identified a set of time windows (separated by vertical dotted lines), hereafter $W$, in which the set of concurrently running kernel changes. We assume a function $K(w)$ which returns the set of kernels present in the execution window $w \in W$. For example, in the last window $w^l \in W$ only $DXTC \in K(w^l)$ executes, while in the previous one $w^{l-1} \in W$, both $\{MVT, DXTC\} = K(w^{l-1})$ are concurrently executing. Moreover, we can compute the proportion of execution $P_{overlap}(k, n, w)$ of a kernel $k$ mapped on $n$ in a window $w$, assuming $k \in K(w)$, using Eq. (5), with $C_k(n)$ from Fig. 6. This notion of execution windows is the second pillar of our predictive model.

$$P_{overlap}(k, n, w) = \frac{size(w)}{C_k(n)} \tag{5}$$

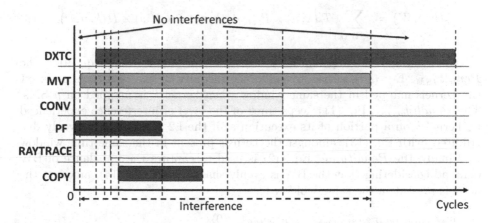

**Fig. 10.** Experiment 7 overlapping time windows of PF/MVT/RAYTRACE/DX TC/CONV/COPY, 5 SMs each.

However, to avoid the necessity to actually execute the set of kernels, we must make a set of assumptions to construct the set of execution windows $W$:

1. all kernels start at time 0, and
2. all kernels run for their worst-observed execution time in isolation on the designed set of SMs, i.e. Section 5.2.

For each overlapping time window $w \in W$, we can compute a portion of additional execution that a kernel will suffer following the two pillars applied in Eqs. (6) and (7). The former applies a penalty only if the requested BW in the time window is higher than the effective BW $EM_{BW}$, and the latter computes the interference factor $I(w)$ of the over-requested BW. If the BW requested by the set of kernels $K(w)$ exceeds the effective BW, the penalty must be increased proportionally. In Eq. (7), $S_p$, $BW_{max}$, and $BW_{isolated}(k, n)$ are identical as in Sect. 6.

$$\Pi(k,n,w) = \begin{cases} 1 & \sum_{l \in K(w)} BW_{isolated}(l,n) < EM_{BW} \\ Penalties(k,n,w) & \sum_{l \in K(w)} BW_{isolated}(l,n) \geq EM_{BW} \end{cases} \qquad (6)$$

$$I(w) = MAX(1, \frac{\sum_{l \in K(w)} BW_{isolated}(l,n)}{BW_{max} \times S_p}) \qquad (7)$$

We therefore define a function $T_c(k,n,W)$, Eq. (8), which predicts the completion latency accounting for the interference of a kernel $k$ mapped on $n$ SMs considering a set of execution window $W$. For each time window $w \in W(k)$ where $k$ is present, it sums up the execution time portion of the kernel augmented with some penalty cycles.

$$T_c(k,n,W) = \sum_{w \in W(k)} T_c(k,n) \times P_{overlap}(k,n,w) \times I(w) \times \Pi(k,n,w) \qquad (8)$$

We identified three penalties a kernel $k$ can suffer from, Eq. (9)[3]. The $Penalty_{SM}$, Eq. (10), serves to guide the inequity of the partitions amongst the kernels mapped in the same window when kernel $k$ is mapped on $n$ SMs. The $Penalty_{access}$, Eq. (11) keeps track of the level of interference experienced by kernel $k$ on a portion of its execution as if the L2 accesses were evenly distributed, with Eq. (13), amongst the kernels present in the same time window $w$. Finally, the $Penalty_{BW}$, Eq. (12) is used to capture the imbalance of BW demand considering that the BW is evenly shared, with Eq. (14), amongst the kernels present in the same window $w$.

$$\overline{Penalties} = Penalty_{SM} \times Penalty_{access} \times Penalty_{BW} \qquad (9)$$

$$Penalty_{SM} = \frac{N}{n} \times \frac{1}{size(K(w))} \qquad (10)$$

$$L2Access = \sum_{l \in K(w)} L2Access(l,w) \qquad (13)$$

$$Penalty_{access} = \frac{L2Accesses(k,w)}{L2Access(w)} \times P_{overlap} \qquad (11)$$

$$Penalty_{BW} = \frac{BW_{isolated}(k,n)}{Equity_{BW}(w)} \qquad (12)$$

$$Equity_{BW} = \frac{BW_{max}}{size(K(w))} \qquad (14)$$

However, we must bound the term $\overline{Penalties}$ to avoid unrealistic scenarios. The $\overline{Penalties}$ term represents the percentage number of cycles that needs to be added to the kernel latency to account for interference, it therefore cannot be lower than 1. On the other hand, having $\overline{Penalties}$ above 2 means that a single kernel concurrently running with another can, in the worst-case scenario, be totally stalled on L2 cache accesses, and a BW demand at 0. This case is impossible to reach with our working hardware architecture. We define $Penalties$ as in Eq. 15 and to use it in previous Eq. (6). To effectively manage the kernel

---

[3] Arguments $(k,n,w)$ in Eq. from (9) to (14) are skipped for clarity.

that addresses the majority of access requests and accommodates more requests to the memory controller, we elect a single kernel for each time window that is privileged and less penalized based on its high traffic BW demand. The elected kernel has the *Penalties* set as the scenario where the $\overline{Penalties(k,n,w)}$ is less than 1.

$$Penalties = \begin{cases} \min(Penalties_{BW}(k,n,w), I(w)) & \overline{Penalties(k,n,w)} < 1 \\ Penalty_{MPD}(k,n,w) & \overline{Penalties(k,n,w)} \geq 2 \quad (15) \\ \overline{Penalties(k,n,w)} & Otherwise \end{cases}$$

In order to leverage the $2x$ term in *Penalties*, we define a Max Penalty Density ($Penalty_{MPD}$), Eq. (16a). The concept of the request density of a kernel $k$, $DR_k$ Eq. (16b), and the maximum density value done in a certain time window $w$, is given by the term $MDA_w$, Eq. (16c).

$$Penalty_{MPD}(k,n,w) = \frac{DR(k,n,w)}{MDA(w)} \tag{16a}$$

$$DR(k,n,w) = \frac{L2Access(k,w)}{T_c(k,n)} \tag{16b}$$

$$MDA(k,n,w) = \max_{k \in K(w)} \left( \frac{L2Access(k,w)}{T_c(k,n)} \right) \tag{16c}$$

## 7.2   Comparison with a Worst-Interference Method

Most of the related works we could find aim to predict the efficiency, e.g. [28], of kernels while we aim to predict the execution time in presence of interference. We compare our method to a predictive model that considers the worst possible interference happening during concurrent executions of kernels, similarly to [28]. Then, a margin is added to the kernel latency in isolation to form a prediction of the latency accounting for interference.

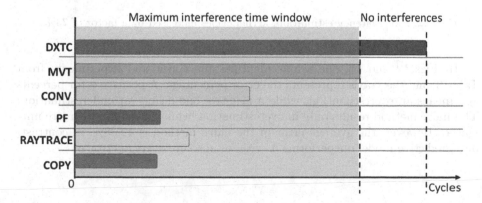

**Fig. 11.** A set of concurrent kernels with the maximum interference time interval in the light grey overlay. (Color figure online)

Let us consider a set of kernels with different in-isolation latencies. The kernel $X$ with the largest latency experiences interference from other kernels up to the completion of the second largest one. Then, the kernel $X$ executes alone and does not suffer anymore from interference. Moreover, in our naive method, the kernels with a latency shorter or equal than the second largest one suffer a maximum interference as they would never have a time interval where they execute alone on the GPU. This behaviour is exhibited in Fig. 12, where DXTC is the only kernel with a time interval without interference.

In Fig. 9, we observe that the kernel COPY from experiment 4 suffered a maximal slowdown of 73%. As an arbitrary value, the naive approach uses that value on all kernels fully present and on the portion of execution present in the maximum interference time window. We note that our 73% is a lower margin than the one presented in [28] (over 100%), however, this plays against us, as we expect that a larger margin for a naive approach generates a larger error.

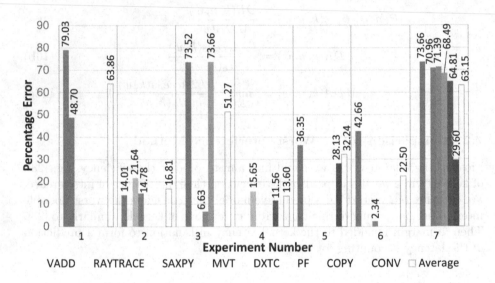

**Fig. 12.** Naive latency estimation, kernel cycles increased by a factor of 73%.

In Figs. 12 and 13, the x-axis identifies the considered experiments from Table 3, and the y-axis represents the error percentage. A positive error percentage means an overestimation, while a negative one means an underestimation. The naive method results only in overestimation, while our method is more mitigated. However, the average error of the naive method is 42.38%, in contrast, our predictive model outperforms it with an absolute average error of 5%.

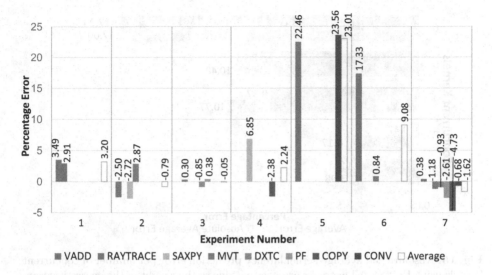

**Fig. 13.** Kernel latency estimation prediction error, using Eq. (8), on experiments from Table 3.

## 7.3 Latency and Interference Prediction Evaluations

To validate our predictive model and estimate its error, we randomly generated 100 groups of kernels, in addition to the 7 previous, with a size varying in $[2, 6]$, resulting in 107 experiments. In each group, for each kernel, we randomly decide the number of used SMs in the set $5, 10, 15, 20, 25$, with the constraints that the total number of used SM for the group must not exceed the total number of available SMs (30).

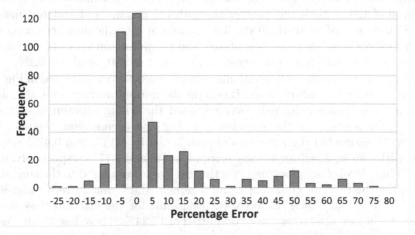

**Fig. 14.** Kernel latency prediction error, using Eq. (8), of the 107 kernel sets.

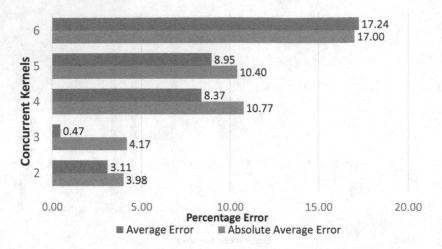

**Fig. 15.** Absolute and average kernel latency prediction error per number of concurrent kernels using Eq. (8). All averages are positive, due to the weight of the overestimation.

Figure 14 shows the error distributions of our predictive mode in Eq. (8). In order to derive general and useful information about the distribution of errors, we considered the error calculated from the difference between the emulated cycle and the one estimated by our formula. On Overall, the formula demonstrated an average error rate of 10.7% with an overestimation bias and a variance of 2.71%. As shown in Fig. 14, sporadic underestimations (negative values) and overestimations (positive values) occur during the prediction process. It is important to note that in the real-time field, particularly in the scheduling field where timing is critical, it is more favorable to overestimate rather than underestimate the execution time required by a kernel to perform its tasks. The results of our experiments, in which 2, 3, 4, 5, or 6 kernels were executed concurrently, resulted in a total of 420 single kernel predictions with 135 instances of underestimation and 285 instances of overestimation. The maximum sporadic overestimation was 76%, which occurred in 1 case out of 420, and the minimum sporadic underestimation was 20%, which also occurred in 1 case out of 420, or about 0.2%.

By also analyzing the individual different sub-classes error obtained in Fig. 15, we can recover more information. Based on the normal average (not the absolute one), the obtained formula overestimated the whole experiment's classes (Fig. 15). On average, in the sub-classes with 2 and 3 concurrent kernels, the formula overestimated the execution of each kernel by 3.11% and 0.47% respectively, with also an absolute average error of 3.98% and 4.17% respectively, indicating a high level of accuracy in predicting the cycles compared to the emulation engine. For the two sub-classes of 4 and 5 kernels, the formula overestimates on average, 8.37% and 8.95% respectively, meanwhile for the last sub-class with 6 kernels, we obtain the larger error committed of 17.24%. These last 3 sub-classes cases turn out to be the most unstable ones because more kernels require access to the same L2 banks and thus generate more interference than expected by our formula.

The results of the predictive model on different sub-classes remain well below the absolute error of 20% used in various domains for predicting the WCET, as already mentioned in Sect. 6, indicating excellent performance.

# 8   Bandwidth Prediction

In the previous sections, we successfully developed a predictive model that is able to predict the number of execution cycles required for the completion of a single kernel in both isolated and concurrent execution scenarios. To fully complete our model, we now aim to accurately predict the memory BW required by a kernel mapped on a set of SMs in isolation from an initial profile on all SMs. Hence, preventing the need to experimentally acquire the memory BW by repeatedly executing a kernel on different SM cluster sizes.

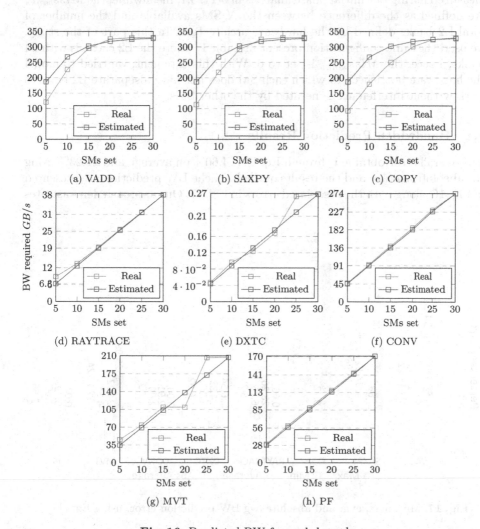

**Fig. 16.** Predicted BW for each kernel.

To achieve this goal, we model the $BW$ *measured* during the isolated execution with the full set of SMs as $BW_{isolated}(k, N)$, and the $BW_{threshold}$ as $BW_{MAX} * S_p$ (defined in Sect. 6). By utilizing the $BW_{threshold}$, we are able to switch between linear and nonlinear forms in order to adaptively change the predictor behaviour. We define the $BW(k, n)$ as the $BW$ *requirement* for a kernel $k$ when it is executed on a different set of SMs $(n)$, as outlined in Eq. (17).

$$BW(k,n) = \begin{cases} \frac{BW_{isolated}(k,N)}{N} \cdot n & BW_{isolated}(k, N) < BW_{Threshold} \\ EM_{BW} \cdot (1 - e^{(-\frac{n}{MAX(1,Miss_{banks})})}) & BW_{isolated}(k, N) \geq BW_{Threshold} \end{cases}$$
$$(17)$$

The $EM_{BW}$, with the value of 330 GB/s, is the maximum bandwidth that we measured during our initial phase analysis in Sect. 5.1, meanwhile, the $Miss_{banks}$ are defined as the difference between the $N$ SMs available and the number of total L2 banks defined by the hardware architecture. In this part of the study, we used the same configuration present in Table 1, where the L2 cache is with 24 banks, hence, the $Miss_{banks}$ is set to 6. With this exponent, we tried to model the hardware bottleneck in which each SM does not have a separate L2 bank to work without interference generated by the other SMs.

## 8.1   Bandwidth Prediction Results

The overall error obtained through Eq. 17 is 4.60% on average and 11.23% using the absolute average and the results of the L2 cache BW prediction are presented in Fig. 16, along with the associated errors in Fig. 17. Our approach demonstrates

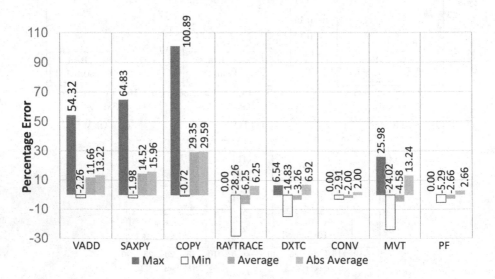

**Fig. 17.** Min, max, avg, and absolute avg BW prediction error, using Eq. (17).

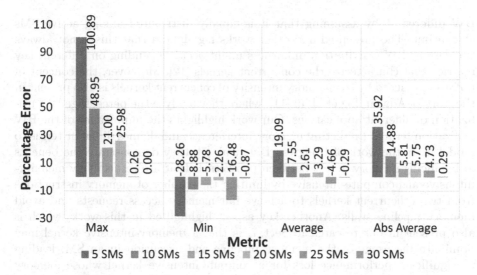

**Fig. 18.** BW avg and variance prediction error of Eq. (17) varying the SMs size.

an overestimation of the L2 BW requirement for memory-intensive kernels such as VADD, SAXPY, and COPY when a smaller set of SMs is used. In contrast, the BW demand predictions for hybrid and computational kernels are shown to be highly accurate with our formula; nevertheless, underestimations still occur.

A summary of the overall BW prediction error average and variance is presented in Fig. 18, along with the error obtained for individual SMs set (ranging from 5 to 30). On average, the error ranges from 0.3% to 19% when smaller SMs sets are chosen for kernel execution. The highest error prediction occurs when the SMs set is 5, with a prediction error of 19%.

## 9   Related Work

Not so many works found in the literature explicitly deal with performance estimation based on memory interference. The most recent one is HSM [29], in which performance decrease in co-running kernels scenarios are calculated as the ratio between instruction per cycle in isolated and shared modes in the different kernel-SM partition configurations. Another important work on this topic is the DASE (Dynamical Application Slowdown Estimation) model proposed in [10]. The authors of this work estimate the slowdowns caused by shared resources on concurrent GPGPU kernels and provide a performance estimation model for a single GPGPU application. Similarly to our work, their contribution involves a profiling phase, in which they consider cases where two kernels run concurrently. Our research takes into account different sets of concurrent kernels, potentially unlimited (tested up to six co-runners). Another related work is presented by Hong et al. in [9], in which they propose a model to estimate the execution cycles for the GPU architecture for a single kernel. They model the memory

BW differently, by assuming that it is equally distributed among active SMs at runtime. The presented and other works highlighted that this is not always the case as BW distribution unfairness might occur depending on different key metrics that characterize the concurrent kernels [12]. Moreover, the concept of unfairness caused by the memory intensity of concurrent kernels is also present in the work of Adwait Jog et al. in [11], where they analyze the percentage BW utilization of different applications. Our work highlights the importance of the BW utilization term in predicting memory interference and defines different terms to model it. In the work of Hongwen Dai et al. [7], they demonstrate the benefits of balancing memory access between two kernels that are respectively memory-intensive and compute-intensive by limiting the number of memory instructions from two concurrent kernels to achieve fair memory access requests and avoid memory pipeline stalls. Another key aspect highlighted in this work, which is also present in our research in Sect. 7, is that a memory-intensive kernel may dominate the usage of the memory pipeline and execution in an SM, leading to significant performance loss for a compute-intensive kernel whose memory requests suffer delays and cannot be timely served. Other researchers have also proposed hardware schemes and methods to better exploit concurrent kernel execution on GPUs. For example, Xu et al. [27] proposed an intra-SM slicing approach to exploit underutilized memory throughput with an improved intra-SM partitioning for the CTA of two different kernels. Additionally, Thomas et al. used the roofline model to classify applications as compute-bound or memory-bound based on their operational intensity and applied different CTA scheduling modes based on the task category and core partitioning to improve performance [22]. In this work, they also highlighted the potential performance degradation when memory-bound tasks were assigned to small SM partitions. We proposed a similar analysis by predicting and measuring the memory BW required by a kernel mapped to different GPU partitions. Adriaens et al. [1] proposed the use of spatial multitasking to group SMs into different sets that can run different kernels (up to four) in order to maximize application speedup. Ukidave et al. [23] studied the real-time support for adaptive spatial partitioning on GPUs and highlighted the importance of L2 in this process. Aguilera et al. [2] demonstrated the unfairness of spatial multitasking and proposed a fair resource allocation strategy for both performance and fairness. Emir C. Marangoz et al. [15] showed that co-running applications can have interference in L2 cache, as we also highlighted in our work, and proposed a new architecture for managing BW reservation for a single kernel during concurrent execution. Unlike most of the research efforts we summarized in this section, our goal was to provide a predictive model for memory interference in cases of GPU SM spatial partitioning. This model should then be used by a memory-aware scheduler [4] that can dynamically assign the correct SM partition to each kernel, ensuring that each kernel can meet its temporal constraints. The sequence of operations that we present for modelling the effect of interference in shared memory hierarchies can be adapted to any GPU architecture and, unlike many of the previously cited papers, does not impose constraints on the number of kernels running simultaneously on the GPU.

It is also worth mentioning the recently released NVIDIA MiG (Multi Instance GPU) technology, that is able to provide stronger isolation among GPU partitions, by allocating cache partitions. While this approach is very effective to avoid memory interference, it is only available in only a subset of highend hardware. Moreover, limitations on the dinamicity in which we can define partitions are present.

## 10  Conclusion

In this paper, we conducted a thorough examination of the performance of inter-SM partitioning of concurrent kernels using GPGPU-Sim. More specifically, we modified GPGPU-Sim in order to perform an analysis of the interference caused by concurrent kernel execution in a multi-kernel partitioning scenario. Based on the number of concurrent kernels, the cycles required for each kernel during overlap with other kernels, and the single BW required by each kernel, we developed a methodology able to predict kernel performance deterioration in the presence of memory interference caused by L2 cache sharing. In order to test the validity of our proposed approach, an extensive set of experiments has been set up. The results of these experiments indicate that, on average, our predictive model over-estimated the number of cycles required during concurrent kernel executions by 10.7% (absolute value) with a variance of 2.71%. Furthermore, when 2 or 3 kernels were competing on the GPU, our formula overestimated the cycles required by 3.11% and 0.47% respectively. Additionally, we developed a formula to predict the L2 cache BW demand by a single kernel in order to have prior knowledge of the BW requirements for individual kernels in relation to the SMs that will be assigned for their execution. Our prediction formula of the BW demand for a kernel when a smaller set of SMs is used yielded an average error range of 0.3% to 35% on different SMs sets and a total average error of 4% and 11% of absolute average error. System engineers may use our modified version of GPGPU-Sim to conduct an initial analysis of the kernels under examination, and gain insights into how the cycles required for completion and BW demand vary as the number of allocated Streaming Multiprocessors changes in an isolated scenario. By doing so, then the predictive models we presented in this paper can be easily adapted for different hardware architectures, i.e. GPUs with a different SM count and memory bank configurations. When dealing with additional kernels - that were not involved in the model construction phase - once an interference predictive model that is specific of the utilized HW is found, only a minimal, but necessary, set of profiling actions are required to be taken. These profiling phases involve measuring individual kernel performance in isolation and with no SM partitioning, as only measures about execution time, BW and compute-to-instruction ratio are needed. It is important to notice how such measures can also be easily extracted on real hardware.

In the future, the developed predictive formulas will be further tailored to different types of HW architecture, including the new Nvidia RTX 3000 series. We also plan to use our predictive model to extend state-of-the-art task models in real-time literature with the purpose of accounting for memory interference among GPU kernels.

**Acknowledgment.** This work was partly supported by ECSEL Joint Undertaking in H2020 project IMOCO4.E, grant agreement No.101007311.

# References

1. Adriaens, J.T., Compton, K., Kim, N.S., Schulte, M.J.: The case for gpgpu spatial multitasking. In: IEEE International Symposium on High-Performance Comp Architecture, pp. 1–12. IEEE (2012)
2. Aguilera, P., Morrow, K., Kim, N.S.: Fair share: Allocation of gpu resources for both performance and fairness. In: 2014 IEEE 32nd International Conference on Computer Design (ICCD), pp. 440–447. IEEE (2014)
3. et al., A.K.: Tango: A deep neural network benchmark suite for various accelerators. CoRR abs/ arXiv: 1901.04987 (2019)
4. Bak, S., Yao, G., Pellizzoni, R., Caccamo, M.: Memory-aware scheduling of multicore task sets for real-time systems. In: 2012 IEEE International Conference on Embedded and Real-Time Computing Systems and Applications, pp. 300–309. IEEE (2012)
5. Capodieci, N., Cavicchioli, R., Marongiu, A.: A taxonomy of modern gpgpu programming methods: On the benefits of a unified specification. IEEE Trans. Comput.-Aided Design Integrated Circ. Syst. (2021)
6. Che, S., et al.: Rodinia: a benchmark suite for heterogeneous computing. In: 2009 IEEE International Symposium on Workload Characterization (IISWC), pp. 44–54. IEEE (2009)
7. Dai, H., et al.: Accelerate gpu concurrent kernel execution by mitigating memory pipeline stalls. In: 2018 IEEE International Symposium on High Performance Computer Architecture (HPCA), pp. 208–220. IEEE (2018)
8. Gupta, K., Stuart, J.A., Owens, J.D.: A study of persistent threads style gpu programming for gpgpu workloads. In: 2012 Innovative Parallel Computing (InPar), pp. 1–14 (2012). https://doi.org/10.1109/InPar.2012.6339596
9. Hong, S., Kim, H.: An analytical model for a gpu architecture with memory-level and thread-level parallelism awareness. In: Proceedings of the 36th Annual International Symposium on Computer Architecture, pp. 152–163 (2009)
10. Hu, Q., Shu, J., Fan, J., Lu, Y.: Run-time performance estimation and fairness-oriented scheduling policy for concurrent gpgpu applications. In: 2016 45th International Conference on Parallel Processing (ICPP), pp. 57–66. IEEE (2016)
11. Jog, A., et al.: Application-aware memory system for fair and efficient execution of concurrent gpgpu applications. In: Proceedings of workshop on general purpose processing using GPUs, pp. 1–8 (2014)
12. Jog, A., et al.: Anatomy of gpu memory system for multi-application execution. In: Proceedings of the 2015 International Symposium on Memory System, pp. 223–234 (2015)
13. Khairy, M., Shen, Z., Aamodt, T.M., Rogers, T.G.: Accel-sim: an extensible simulation framework for validated gpu modeling. In: 2020 ACM/IEEE 47th Annual International Symposium on Computer Architecture (ISCA), pp. 473–486. IEEE (2020)
14. Konstantinidis, E., Cotronis, Y.: A quantitative roofline model for gpu kernel performance estimation using micro-benchmarks and hardware metric profiling. J. Parallel Distrib. Comput. **107**, 37–56 (2017)

15. Marangoz, E.C., Kang, K.D., Shin, S.: Designing gpu architecture for memory bandwidth reservation. In: 2021 IEEE International Symposium on Performance Analysis of Systems and Software (ISPASS), pp. 87–89. IEEE (2021)
16. Navarro, C.A., Hitschfeld-Kahler, N., Mateu, L.: A survey on parallel computing and its applications in data-parallel problems using gpu architectures. Commun. Comput. Phys. **15**(2), 285–329 (2014)
17. Olmedo, I.S., Capodieci, N., Martinez, J.L., Marongiu, A., Bertogna, M.: Dissecting the cuda scheduling hierarchy: a performance and predictability perspective. In: 2020 IEEE Real-Time and Embedded Technology and Applications Symposium (RTAS), pp. 213–225. IEEE (2020)
18. Pai, S.E.A.: Improving GPGPU concurrency with elastic kernels. In: Proceedings of the Eighteenth International Conference on Architectural Support for Programming Languages and Operating Systems, ASPLOS 2013 pp. 407–418. Association for Computing Machinery, New York (2013)
19. Rouxel, B., Skalistis, S., Derrien, S., Puaut, I.: Hiding communication delays in contention-free execution for spm-based multi-core architectures. In: 31st Euromicro Conference on Real-Time Systems (ECRTS 2019). Schloss Dagstuhl-Leibniz-Zentrum fuer Informatik (2019)
20. Silva, K.P., Arcaro, L.F., De Oliveira, R.S.: On using gev or gumbel models when applying evt for probabilistic wcet estimation. In: 2017 IEEE Real-Time Systems Symposium (RTSS), pp. 220–230. IEEE (2017)
21. Sun, Y., Agostini, N.B., Dong, S., Kaeli, D.: Summarizing cpu and gpu design trends with product data. arXiv preprint arXiv:1911.11313 (2019)
22. Thomas, W., Toraskar, S., Singh, V.: Dynamic optimizations in gpu using roofline model. In: 2021 IEEE International Symposium on Circuits and Systems (ISCAS), pp. 1–5. IEEE (2021)
23. Ukidave, Y., Kalra, C., Kaeli, D., Mistry, P., Schaa, D.: Runtime support for adaptive spatial partitioning and inter-kernel communication on gpus. In: 2014 IEEE 26th International Symposium on Computer Architecture and High Performance Computing, pp. 168–175. IEEE (2014)
24. Wang, Z., Yang, J., Melhem, R., Childers, B., Zhang, Y., Guo, M.: Simultaneous multikernel gpu: Multi-tasking throughput processors via fine-grained sharing. In: 2016 IEEE International Symposium on High Performance Computer Architecture (HPCA), pp. 358–369. IEEE (2016)
25. Wartel, F., et al.: Timing analysis of an avionics case study on complex hardware/software platforms. In: 2015 Design, Automation & Test in Europe Conference & Exhibition (DATE), pp. 397–402. IEEE (2015)
26. Williams, S., Waterman, A., Patterson, D.: Roofline: an insightful visual performance model for multicore architectures. Commun. ACM **52**(4), 65–76 (2009)
27. Xu, Q., Jeon, H., Kim, K., Ro, W.W., Annavaram, M.: Warped-slicer: efficient intra-sm slicing through dynamic resource partitioning for gpu multiprogramming. In: 2016 ACM/IEEE 43rd Annual International Symposium on Computer Architecture (ISCA), pp. 230–242. IEEE (2016)
28. Yandrofski, T., Chen, J., Otterness, N., Anderson, J.H., Smith, F.D.: Making powerful enemies on nvidia gpus. In: 2022 IEEE Real-Time Systems Symposium (RTSS), pp. 383–395. IEEE (2022)
29. Zhao, X., Jahre, M., Eeckhout, L.: Hsm: a hybrid slowdown model for multitasking gpus. In: Proceedings of the Twenty-fifth International Conference on Architectural Support for Programming Languages and Operating Systems, pp. 1371–1385 (2020)

# Stragglers in Distributed Matrix Multiplication

Roy Nissim(✉) and Oded Schwartz

The Hebrew University of Jerusalem, Jerusalem, Israel
{roynissim,odedsc}@cs.huji.ac.il

**Abstract.** A delay in a single processor may affect an entire system since the slowest processor typically determines the runtime. Problems with such stragglers are often mitigated using dynamic load balancing or redundancy solutions such as task replication. Unfortunately, the former option incurs high communication cost, and the latter significantly increases the arithmetic cost and memory footprint, making high resource overhead seem inevitable. Matrix multiplication and other numerical linear algebra kernels typically have structures that allow better straggler management. Redundancy based solutions tailored for such algorithms often combine codes in the algorithm's structure. These solutions add fixed cost overhead and may perform worse than the original algorithm when little or no delays occur. We propose a new load-balancing solution tailored for distributed matrix multiplication. Our solution reduces latency overhead by $O\,(P/\log P)$ compared to existing dynamic load-balancing solutions, where $P$ is the number of processors. Our solution overtakes redundancy-based solutions in all parameters: arithmetic cost, bandwidth cost, latency cost, memory footprint, and the number of stragglers it can tolerate. Moreover, our overhead costs depend on the severity of delays and are negligible when delays are minor. We compare our solution with previous ones and demonstrate significant improvements in asymptotic analysis and simulations: up to x4.4 and x5.3 compared to general-purpose dynamic load balancing and redundancy-based solutions, respectively.

**Keywords:** Dynamic Load Balancing · Straggler Mitigation · Distributed Computing · Numerical Linear Algebra

## 1 Introduction

Parallel programs are typically more efficient when balancing workloads across processors to minimize idle times. The increase in machine size and decrease in

This project has received funding from the European Research Council (ERC) under the European Union's Horizon 2020 research and innovation programme (grant agreement No. 818252). This work was supported by the Federmann Cyber Security Center in conjunction with the Israel national cyber directorate. This research was supported by a grant from the United States-Israel Binational Science Foundation (BSF), Jerusalem, Israel.

operation voltage tend to raise the number of errors. These errors may occur at a frequency of up to an error per second on exascale machines [5, 19, 55]. This makes it harder to balance the workload and maintain computation trustworthiness. There are three main classes of faults: i) hard faults, in which an entire processor stops working, ii) soft faults, in which a processor miscalculates, and iii) delay faults, in which the processor's average time per arithmetic operation increases. Processors' performance often varies over time due to hardware heating, shared resources, background services, and queues, among other issues [22]. The slowest processor (also known as a straggler) typically determines the running time of a parallel program. A delay in a single processor may increase the idle time of other processors, decreasing system efficiency. This paper deals with mitigating delay faults.

Two standard solutions for dealing with straggler nodes are *dynamic load balancing* (cf. [11, 14, 16, 17, 21, 23, 28, 43, 50]), and *redundancy* (cf. [3, 4, 20, 23, 25, 26, 29–31, 34–39, 41, 42, 49, 52, 57, 58, 62–65, 69]).

Dynamic load balancing solutions dynamically assign tasks to available processors to prevent idle times. These solutions are robust and easily applied to many algorithms, but tend to incur significant communication overhead. There are two sub-classes of dynamic load balancing solutions: sender-initiated, where slow processors request assistance from fast or idle processors, and receiver-initiated, where fast processors request extra work from slow processors. Sender-initiated strategies usually perform better in small and centralized systems since the resource allocation problem becomes difficult and costly in large systems. In contrast, receiver-initiated approaches (often referred to as work-stealing) do not involve central management and are more suitable for large and distributed systems due to their distributed fashion and their obliviousness to processors' speed (see [68] for a detailed survey).

Redundancy based solutions utilize redundant computations such that the output of a subset of processors suffices to construct the result. There are two main classes of redundancy based solutions: replication (cf. [3, 4, 20, 23, 26, 30, 62–64]) and code based solutions (cf. [25, 29, 31, 34–39, 41, 42, 49, 52, 57, 58, 65, 69]. Replication solutions divide computations into tasks and run them simultaneously on multiple processors. These solutions are robust and easy to employ, but incur significant resource overheads. Replication is typically preferred when no prior knowledge of the algorithm's structure is available. However, the structure of some computations, such as many numerical linear algebra kernels, permits more efficient solutions. Code based solutions divide computations into tasks and construct redundant tasks using codes. The output is then decoded when enough encoded computations are completed. These solutions involve additional costs (for the encoding and decoding phases) but reduce redundant computations and memory footprint compared to replication solutions.

## 1.1   Our Contribution

We propose Synchronized Load Balancing (*SLB*), a new dynamic load balancing solution applicable to many numerical linear algebra kernels, including matrix multiplication. Our solution requires $O\left(P/\log P\right)$ less latency than general-purpose load balancing solutions. In addition, SLB outperforms tailored redundancy solutions in all parameters: arithmetic cost, bandwidth cost, latency cost, memory footprint, and the maximal number of stragglers it can tolerate. We summarize our main results in Table 1.

**Table 1.** Straggler mitigation solutions for distributed matrix multiplication

| Algorithm | Arithmetic cost | Bandwidth cost | Latency cost | Memory footprint | Straggler tolerance |
|---|---|---|---|---|---|
| Non-mitigated | $\gamma_P \cdot F$ | $BW$ | $L$ | $M$ | $0$ |
| Lower Bound[a] | $\bar{\gamma}_a \cdot F$ | $BW$ | $L$ | $M$ | $P$ |
| Work Stealing cf. [12,15,24,33] | $\bar{\gamma}_a \cdot (1 + \frac{P}{m}) \cdot F$ | $2 \cdot BW$ | $O\left(L^2 \log L\right)$ | $M$ | $P$ |
| Replication cf. [3,4,38] | $\gamma_{P-r+1} \cdot r \cdot F$ | $r \cdot BW$ | $(1 + o(1)) \cdot L$ | $r \cdot M$ | $r - 1$ |
| MDS coding cf. [34,65,69] | $\gamma_K \cdot \frac{P}{K} \cdot F$ | $P \cdot BW$ | $O\left(L^2\right)$ | $\frac{P}{K} \cdot M$ | $P - K + 1$ |
| LT+ coding [41] | $\bar{\gamma}_a \cdot O\left(1 + \frac{\log^2 m}{\sqrt{m}}\right) \cdot F$ | $P \cdot BW$ | $O(m \cdot \log L)$ | $2 \cdot M$ | $P$ |
| Ours [here] | $\bar{\gamma}_a \cdot (1 + \frac{P}{m}) \cdot F$ | $2 \cdot BW$ | $(1 + o(1)) \cdot L$ | $M$ | $P$ |

[a] The lower bound represents a run where the load is perfectly balanced across processors in proportion to their speed. In other words, tasks are allocated so there are no idle times and no task exchanges.

$(F, BW, L, M) = \left(\frac{mnk}{P}, \frac{(n+k)m}{\sqrt{P}}, \sqrt{P}, \frac{(n+k)m}{\sqrt{P}}\right)$ are the number of arithmetic operations, bandwidth, latency, and memory costs for matrix multiplication algorithm presented in Sect. 2. $P$ is the processor count. $M$ is the memory size. $m, n, k$ are the matrices dimensions. $\gamma_i$ is the average time per arithmetic computation of the $i$'th processor (see Sect. 2). $\bar{\gamma}_a$ is the arithmetic mean of $\{\gamma_i\}$. $r \in \mathbb{N}$ and $K \in \mathbb{N}$ are parameters of the codes (see [4, 34]).

## 1.2 Related Work

Many studies have analyzed dynamic load balancing solutions for performance and scalability (cf. [12,15,24,33,47]). Acar et al. [1] proposed a work-stealing algorithm with private deques and showed similar theoretical bounds to standard algorithms (i.e., with public deques). Michael et al. [46] introduced idempotent work-stealing, which uses relaxing semantics that allows tasks to be re-computed to potentially save communication costs. Additional studies focus on optimizations for specific system structures such as heterogeneous clouds (cf. [60]), hierarchical wide-area connected clusters (cf. [61]), and dynamic cloud environments (cf. [28]), or for different optimization goals such as tasks' priority (cf. [54]), tasks' duration (cf. [66]), and energy consumption (cf. [45]).

Studies on task replication focus on general-purpose solutions (cf. [3,4,37,38, 63,64]) and multi-server systems (cf. [20,26,29,62]). Erasure based coding solutions have been proposed for matrix-vector multiplication (cf. [25,35,49,52]) and classical matrix-matrix multiplication (cf. [34,36,65,69]. Unfortunately, none of these codes utilize any partial computations performed by slower processors and therefore exhibit poor performance when there are small or no delays. Mallick et al. [41] proposed a coding solution for matrix-vector multiplication that utilizes partial computations performed by stragglers. While their solution can achieve near-ideal load balancing, it incurs high communication overhead.

### 1.3 Paper Organization

Section 2 provides preliminary information regarding machine model and collective communicators. In Sect. 3, we present and analyze our proposed solution. In Sect. 4, we compare our solution with existing ones using simulations and asymptotic analysis. Finally, Sect. 5 discusses our results and future work. Appendix A provides a detailed analysis of previous solutions for completeness.

## 2    Preliminaries

### 2.1    Models and Architecture

We assume a distributed model (cf. [6–10,13,32,51]) with $P$ identical processors, each with a local memory of size $M$. The input (resp. output) is distributed among the processors at the beginning (resp. end) of the run. Our solution works well with communication hierarchies. For simplicity, we focus on a single communication layer, i.e., peer-to-peer communication links between every pair of processors. We model algorithm run-time as the sum of arithmetic and communication costs. We denote the primary memory unit by word and a collection of words by message. Processors communicate by passing messages to each other.

We model the cost of passing a message with $w$ words by $\alpha + \beta \cdot w$, where $\alpha$ and $\beta$ are system parameters. We denote the algorithm's message (resp. word) count by $L$ (resp. $BW$). The messages (resp. words) are counted along the *critical path*, as defined in [67], i.e., simultaneously communicated messages between different pairs of processors are counted only once. This is the standard model to analyze communication costs (cf. [6–8,10,32]). To capture the effect of delays in distributed computations, we model the average time per arithmetic computation of the $i'th$ processor at time $t$ as $\gamma_i(t)$ and denote by $\gamma_i$ its average throughout the entire run. We denote the number of arithmetic operations the $i'th$ processor performs as $F_i$. With this convention, the total cost of the algorithm is $\alpha \cdot L + \beta \cdot BW + \max_i \gamma_i \cdot F_i$.[1] We denote by $\bar{\gamma}_a = \frac{1}{P}\sum_i \gamma_i$ and $\bar{\gamma}_h = \frac{P}{\sum_i \frac{1}{\gamma_i}}$ the arithmetic mean and harmonic mean of $\{\gamma_i\}_{i\in[1,\cdots,P]}$, respectively. Without loss of generality, we assume that $\gamma_1 \leq \gamma_2 \leq \cdots \leq \gamma_P$.

### 2.2    Matrix Multiplication

A matrix multiplication algorithm receives two matrices $A$ and $B$ of size $m \times n$ and $n \times k$ respectively, and outputs a matrix $C$ of size $m \times k$. We divide $A$ (resp.

---

[1] This may look similar to the standard model for analyzing the arithmetic cost of an algorithm in a heterogeneous environment (cf. [9]). However, while the heterogeneous model assumes different hardware with stable performance, our version assumes similar hardware with varying performance.

$B$) into $\sqrt{P}$ sub-matrices $A_1, \cdots, A_{\sqrt{P}}$ (resp. $B_1, \cdots, B_{\sqrt{P}}$) by its rows (resp. columns), i.e., each sub-matrix contains $\frac{n}{\sqrt{P}}$ rows (resp. columns) of $A$ (resp. $B$). We arrange the processors in a two-dimensional grid of size $\sqrt{P} \times \sqrt{P}$ and assign $A_i$ and $B_j$ to $P_{i,j}$ (the processor on the $i'th$ row and the $j'th$ column). In this setting, every output element can be computed by some processor with no additional communication. The algorithm requires $M = O\left(\frac{(m+k)\cdot n}{\sqrt{P}}\right)$ memory.

We use an inner product implementation of parallel matrix multiplication. Other parallel implementations may require less memory and communication, such as the 3D (cf. [2,44,56]) and 2.5D (cf. [44,56]). However, the inner product algorithm is exceptionally suitable for dealing with stragglers and is compatible with similar implementations in the field (cf. [3,4,12,15,24,33,34,38,65,69]). Moreover, it has equal bandwidth cost and lower latency cost compared to the 2D algorithm (cf. [18,27]).

## 2.3   Collective Communication Operations

Collective communication operations, such as broadcast and reduce, are frequently used in parallel algorithms. Sanders and Sibeyn [51] introduced the "fractional tree" algorithm, efficiently performing collective communicators such as reduce, scatter, and broadcast operations. Birnbaum and Schwartz [13] extended their results and showed how to efficiently perform $t$ simultaneous reduce operations (referred to as $t$-reduce or all-reduce when $t = P$). Their technique can easily be generalized to broadcast operation (we similarly denote $t$-broadcast and all-broadcast). We summarize the results in the following statements:

**Lemma 1. ($t$-reduce ([13]).** $t$ simultaneous reduce operations on data of size $W$ between $P$ processors cost: $F = t \cdot W$, $BW = t \cdot W$, and $L = O\left(\log P + t\right)$.

**Corollary 1. ($t$-broadcast).** $t$ simultaneous broadcast operations on data of size $W$ between $P$ processors cost: $F = 0$, $BW = t \cdot W$, and $L = O\left(\log P\right)$.

## 3   Synchronized Load Balancing

This section presents SLB, our new dynamic load-balancing solution. SLB applies to any computation that can be partitioned into independent sub-computations that run in parallel without communicating. At the beginning of the run, we divide the computation into $S$ subsets of equal size (referred to as tasks). We distribute tasks evenly among processors, so each processor holds $S/P$ tasks. At each round, the first processor to finish all its tasks initiates a synchronization phase which re-balances the tasks across *all* processors. Tasks in progress during the synchronization phase are resumed after it. Since $P$ may not always divide the number of tasks, some processors may have a single task more than others. In this case, we assign the extra tasks to the fastest processors.

The synchronization phase works as follows: an idle processor initiates an all-broadcast operation, where each processor broadcasts its number of remaining tasks. By Corollary 1, this costs: $(F, BW, L) = (O(1), O(1), O(\log P))$. Processors then locally compute an exchange scheme (detailed below), leading to an agreed task exchange scheme. The processors exchange tasks accordingly, and the computation proceeds.

**Lemma 2.** *Let $S$ denote the number of tasks at the beginning of the run. SLB performs $O(\log S)$ exchange phases.*

*Proof.* We divide the computation into rounds separated by exchange phases. We denote by $S_j$ the number of remaining tasks at the beginning of round $j$. Let $\gamma_{i_j}$ represent the average of $\gamma_i(t)$ during round $j$, i.e., the average time per arithmetic operation of the $i$'th processor during round $j$. Let $\bar\gamma_{h_j} = \frac{P}{\sum_{i=1}^{P} \frac{1}{\gamma_{i_j}}}$ denote the harmonic mean of $\gamma_{i_j}$ over all processors. Note that $\forall i, j\ \gamma_{i_j} > 0$ as $\gamma_i(t)$ represents time per arithmetic operation. Exchange phases are initiated when a processor completes its tasks. Tasks are evenly distributed at the beginning of each round, which means that each processor is assigned $\frac{S_j}{P}$ tasks at the beginning of round $j$ (for simplicity, we assume that $P$ divides $S_j$ as it has a negligible effect). Let $i^*(j) = \arg\min_i \gamma_{i_j}$ denote the fastest processor during round $j$. Thus, round $j$ is interrupted after $\frac{S_j}{P} \cdot \gamma_{i^*(j)_j}$ time units, and the $i$'th processor manages to complete only $\frac{S_j}{P} \cdot \frac{\gamma_{i^*(j)_j}}{\gamma_{i_j}}$ tasks. Overall, the number of tasks processors jointly complete is

$$\sum_{i=1}^{P} \frac{S_j}{P} \cdot \frac{\gamma_{i^*(j)_j}}{\gamma_{i_j}} = \gamma_{i^*(j)_j} \cdot \frac{\sum_{i=1}^{P} \frac{1}{\gamma_{i_j}}}{P} \cdot S_j = \frac{\gamma_{i^*(j)_j}}{\bar\gamma_{h_j}} \cdot S_j$$

Notice that $S_{j+1} = \left(1 - \frac{\gamma_{i^*(j)_j}}{\bar\gamma_{h_j}}\right) \cdot S_j$ and that $S_1 = S$. Thus,

$$S_{j+1} = \left(1 - \frac{\gamma_{i^*(j)_j}}{\bar\gamma_{h_j}}\right) \cdot S_j = \cdots = \prod_{k=1}^{j} \left(1 - \frac{\gamma_{i^*(k)_k}}{\bar\gamma_{h_k}}\right) \cdot S$$

Let $l$ denote the number of exchange phases in SLB and let $j^* = \arg\max_j \left(1 - \frac{\gamma_{i^*(j)_j}}{\bar\gamma_{h_j}}\right)$ denote the round with the least progress (in percentages). The algorithm ends after the first round with no cost overhead when there are no delays. Thus, we next assume, without loss of generality, that $\bar\gamma_{h_{j^*}} > \gamma_{i^*(j^*)_{j^*}}$, i.e., there are some delays. The algorithm ends one round after the number of remaining tasks is at most $P$. Thus,

$$P \le S_{l+1} = \prod_{k=1}^{l} \left(1 - \frac{\gamma_{i^*(k)_k}}{\bar\gamma_{h_k}}\right) \cdot S \le \left(1 - \frac{\gamma_{i^*(j^*)_{j^*}}}{\bar\gamma_{h_{j^*}}}\right)^{l} \cdot S$$

This means that

$$\frac{P}{S} \le \left(\frac{\bar\gamma_{h_{j^*}} - \gamma_{i^*(j^*)_{j^*}}}{\bar\gamma_{h_{j^*}}}\right)^{l} \rightarrow \left(\frac{\bar\gamma_{h_{j^*}}}{\bar\gamma_{h_{j^*}} - \gamma_{i^*(j^*)_{j^*}}}\right)^{l} \le \frac{S}{P}$$

and

$$l \leq \log_{\frac{\bar{\gamma}_{h_{j*}}}{\bar{\gamma}_{h_{j*}} - \gamma_{i*(j*)_{j*}}}} \left(\frac{S}{P}\right) \leq \frac{1}{\log \frac{\bar{\gamma}_{h_{j*}}}{\bar{\gamma}_{h_{j*}} - \gamma_{i*(j*)_{j*}}}} \cdot \log S = O\left(\log S\right)$$

The last equality holds since $\bar{\gamma}_{h_{j*}} > \gamma_{i*(j*)_{j*}} > 0$ are constants that do not depend on the number of tasks.

We can now prove the main theorem.

**Theorem 1.** *Let $\gamma_P \cdot F$, $BW$, $L$, and $M$ denote an algorithm's arithmetic cost, bandwidth cost, latency cost, and memory footprint, respectively. SLB costs are at most:*

$$F' = \bar{\gamma}_a \left(1 + \frac{P}{S}\right) \cdot F, \ BW' = BW + M, \ L' = L + O\left(\log^2 P\right), \ M' = M$$

*Proof.* Excluding the last round, SLB has no idle processors or redundant computations. During the last round, some processors may compute a single task while others may be idle. Thus the arithmetic cost is optimal up to a factor of $\left(1 + \frac{P}{S}\right)$, representing (potential) idle time at $P - 1$ processors for a single task. I.e., $F' = \bar{\gamma}_a \left(1 + \frac{P}{S}\right) \cdot F$. The overhead bandwidth comes from task exchanges. Since processors exchange tasks simultaneously, bandwidth cost is dominated by the data exchanged with the slowest processor. The actual cost depends on the distribution of $\{\gamma_i(t)\}_{i \in [P]}$ and is bounded by $M$. That is, when a processor does not perform any tasks, the communication cost overhead is $M$ and smaller otherwise. SLB performs $O\left(\log S\right)$ synchronization phases (Lemma 2), each uses an all-broadcast and all-reduce operation which costs $O\left(\log P\right)$ (Lemma 1, Corollary 1). By grouping tasks, we can bound $S$ with a polynomial function of $P$ and, thereby, bound the number of synchronization phases by $O\left(\log P\right)$. In total, the latency cost is $L' = L + \log^2 P$. Finally, since SLB does not require additional memory, $M' = M$.

In practice, SLB bandwidth cost overhead is expected to be significantly smaller than $M$. In addition, SLB bandwidth costs are expected to be smaller than work-stealing since randomized task transfers increase the chances of redundant transfers, such as transfers between processors above average speed.

## 3.1 Task Exchange Phase

When a processor completes its tasks, it initiates a Task Exchange Procedure. The goal is to redistribute the workload evenly among processors using minimal communication. We first address the problem where all tasks are of equal size and then show how to extend it to tasks of variable sizes.

Let $s_i$ denote the number of remaining tasks of the $i'th$ processor, and $\bar{s} = \frac{1}{P} \sum_{1=1}^{P} s_i$ be their average. We can look at an exchange program as a bipartite graph $G = (U, V, E)$, where $U$ is the set of processors that needs to transfer tasks

$(U = i|s_i > \bar{s})$, and $V$ is the set of processors that needs to receive tasks $(V = i|s_i < \bar{s})$. The edges represent the transfers, i.e., an edge $(i,j) \in E$ represents a transfer between the $i'th$ processor and the $j'th$ processor. The value of each vertex indicates the number of tasks remaining for that processor. The weight of each edge represents the number of tasks to be transferred. The post-value of each vertex in $U$ (resp. $V$) is defined by the node's value minus (resp. plus) the value of all its outgoing (resp. incoming) edges. An exchange plan is a bipartite graph where the post-values of all vertices are in the range of $[\bar{s} - 1 \ , \ \bar{s} + 1]$. Allowing greater imbalance may save communication but will not affect the algorithm's asymptotic cost. Upon calculating the exchange plan, all processors exchange tasks accordingly. Since processors exchange data simultaneously, we can use efficient collective operations to save latency costs. The maximal number of edges connecting a single vertex is at most $P - 1$. Hence, the algorithm's latency cost is $O(\log P)$. We used an all-broadcast operator to exchange processors' progress, adding $O(\log P)$ latency to the cost. Thus, reducing the latency of the task exchanging phase does not affect the algorithm's asymptotic costs.

When tasks have variable sizes, the Task Exchange Procedure should balance the workload according to the sum of tasks' sizes at each processor rather than by quantity. Let $s_i$ denote the number of remaining tasks at the $i'th$ processor and let $l_{i_1}, \cdots, l_{i_{s_i}}$ denote their sizes. Let $l_i$ denote the total task size at the $i'th$ processor $(l_i = \sum_{j=1}^{s_i} l_{i_j})$, and $\bar{l}$ the average $(\bar{l} = \frac{1}{P} \sum_{i=1}^{P} l_i)$. We can again consider an exchange program as a bipartite graph $G = (U, V, E)$, where $U$ is the set of processors that need to transfer tasks $(U = i|l_i > \bar{l})$ and $V$ is the set of processors that need to receive tasks $(V = i|l_i < \bar{l})$. The value of each vertex is $l_i$. Edges and post-values are defined similarly to the previous case (tasks of equal size). An exchange plan aims to bring the post-value of all vertices as close as possible to $\bar{l}$. We present a simple heuristic that finds the desired solution: We start with a bipartite graph $G = (U, V, E)$ (as defined earlier) with no edges $(E = \phi)$. We sort the vertices in $U$ (resp. $V$) by their values in descending (resp. ascending) order. We start with the first vertex in $U$ (highest value) and add an edge to the first processor at $V$ (the vertex with the lowest value). We set the edge's weight to the maximal value that does not violate our conditions. Notice that at least one vertex has reached the balance state and cannot connect to further edges. We look at the successive vertices in its group and repeat this procedure until we get all vertices. The algorithm runs in $O(|V| \log |V| + |U| \log |U|) = O(P \log P)$ arithmetic operations. While this algorithm may be sub-optimal, the potential communication saving is negligible.

## 3.2   Adaptive Task Exchange Procedure

The objective of the previous procedure is to re-balance the workload across the processors, which is optimal when assuming random temporary delays. In practice, various reasons cause delays, and some (like hardware malfunction, for instance) may cause long delays that affect processor performance during extensive computations. In this scenario, re-balancing the workload in each iteration is sub-optimal. As an alternative, we can employ an adaptive approach, where we deliberately cause an imbalance in the work distribution proportional to each processor's predicted speed. We can estimate the processor's speed in several ways, including based on the previous round's performance. Let $s_i^g$ (resp. $e_i^g$) denote the number of tasks the $i'th$ processor possesses at the beginning (resp. end) of the $g'th$ round. After each iteration, we want to redistribute the workload according to the processor's speed in the previous round. After the task exchange procedure, the $i'th$ processor should have $s_i^{g+1} = \sum_i e_i^g \cdot \frac{\frac{1}{s_i^g - e_i^g}}{\sum_i \frac{1}{s_i^g - e_i^g}}$ tasks. We repeat the task exchange procedure similarly to the non-adaptive case, using $\Delta_i^g = e_i^g - s_i^g$ as the value of the graph vertices. Applying the adaptive task exchange procedure does not reduce SLB's asymptotical complexity but may significantly improve its performance in practice. Moreover, an unbalanced task exchange procedure may help deal with heterogeneous systems.

# 4   Comparison

SLB and work-stealing techniques exchange tasks among processors to avoid idle times. Work-stealing randomly attempts to steal tasks from busy processors. Such attempts often receive zero or few tasks, resulting in wasteful interactions. In contrast, SLB utilizes the algorithm's structure to synchronize and optimize exchanges. Thus, SLB saves unnecessary message passing and significantly reduces latency costs (by a factor of $O\left(\frac{P}{\log P}\right)$ compared to work-stealing), which is often the bottleneck in HPC applications. Severe delays may lead to repeated synchronization phases, but they will still be more efficient than repeated random exchanges. Moreover, in such scenarios, repeated synchronization phases are still preferred over idle processors. The overhead arithmetic cost of SLB is negligible ($O\left(P \log P\right)$). That said, work-stealing is a general-purpose solution, while SLB applies to computations that can be divided into sub-computations that run in parallel on distinct processors.

We summarize the asymptotic costs of each solution in Table 1. SLB, work-stealing, and LT+ achieve near-perfect load balancing, and thus, a near-perfect arithmetic cost. However, our solution reduces the latency cost compared to the work-stealing and LT+ solutions by a factor of $O\left(L \log L\right)$ and $O\left(\frac{m \log L}{L}\right)$, respectively. Erasure-code-based solutions add significant overheads. For example, MDS and LT+ solutions require a factor of $O\left(P\right)$ more bandwidth and a factor of $O\left(L\right)$ and $O\left(\frac{m \log L}{L}\right)$ more latency, respectively. The replication solution barely adds latency, but requires significant memory, carries high overhead arithmetic costs, and has a low tolerance for stragglers.

## 4.1   Simulation

We provide in-depth large-scale simulations rather than real-world experiments. Simulations are standard practice in this line of work (cf. [20,29–31,35–37,47, 52,59,64]) although some papers provide real-world experiments (cf. [25,34]).

**Simulation Setting:** We implemented each of the six compared solutions (see Table 1) on a distributed matrix multiplication kernel, as described in Sect. 2. In addition, we implemented an optimal theoretical algorithm (referred to as the lower bound). I.e., an algorithm with no idle times that does not require exchanging tasks. The multiplication at each processor is divided into $S$ tasks by splitting the rows (resp. columns) of its portion of matrix $A$ (resp. $B$) by $\sqrt{S}$.

We ran a weak-scale simulation with exponential processor count $P = 2^i$ for $i \in [0, \cdots, 16]$. The matrices dimensions were $n \cdot 2^{\lfloor i/2 \rfloor} \times n$ and $n \times n \cdot 2^{\lceil i/2 \rceil}$. Thus, each processor multiplied two blocks of $n \times n$ for $n = 2^{12}$ (small-size, Figs. 2(a), 1(a), 3) and $n = 2^{14}$ (medium-size, Figs. 2(b),1(b), 4). We chose the matrices dimensions such that the computation will be predominantly communication bounded (for the small-size) or arithmetically bounded (for the medium-size). We ran each simulation a hundred times and calculated the average outcome. We replaced actual computation and communication with simulated times. Processors' delays are sampled from a shifted-exponential distribution. The shifted-exponential distribution is widely accepted in this line of work (cf. [1,12,15,25,26,34–36,41,42,47,49,52,62,64,68]). That said, SLB performs fewer redundant operations (arithmetic and communication) and hence is more efficient than existing solutions, regardless of the distribution. This can be seen from the analysis in Table 1.

The algorithm's runtime is computed using the model presented in Sect. 2 (the delays only affect the arithmetic costs). The arithmetic cost of each processor is the number of tasks it performs during the run multiplied by the cost of an arithmetic operation and its average delay factor. Exchanging tasks involves exchanging the associated data, i.e., $O\left(\frac{mn+nk}{\sqrt{P}\cdot\sqrt{S}}\right)$ bandwidth. We used the costs presented in Table 1 with their real constants and ignored low-order terms. The simulation was run on a personal computer. We use the constants $1e-6$, $1e-9$, and $1e-12$ for the system's performance constants $\alpha$, $\beta$, and $\gamma$, respectively. Communication-computation overlaps may save up to x2. However, we compared the solutions in communication or computation bounded scenarios. In these cases, computation hiding is expected to be negligible. Moreover, computation hiding may benefit SLB as well, and there is no reason to assume that it will have a greater effect on the compared solutions.

We used the shifted exponential distribution with a shifting parameter of 1 and a scaling parameter of 0.5, 1, or 2.5, representing large, medium, and small delays, respectively. In addition, we normalize processor delays by dividing the delay factor by the mean delay. We set the number of sub-computations $(S)$ in SLB to be $16P$. There is a small trade-off between computation and communication costs in SLB. Larger $S$ can reduce redundant arithmetic operations but may require more exchange operations. In practice, SLB is not very sensitive to $S$, for reasonable values.

**Simulation Results:** The results indicate that our solution outperforms previous solutions in all simulations for almost all $P$ values, supporting our asymptotic analysis. Figure 2(a) presents our results for medium-size matrices and medium delays. SLB and work-stealing are the closest to the lower bound in this scenario

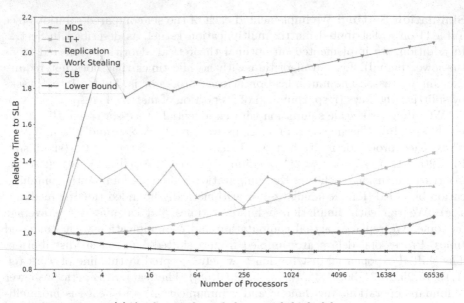

(a) Arithmetic bounded run with high delays

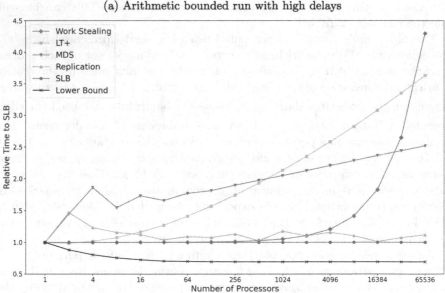

(b) Communication bounded run with high delays

**Fig. 1. Weak-scaling of straggler mitigation solutions for distributed matrix multiplication with high delays.** The x-axis denotes the number of processors in a logarithmic scale, and the y-axis denotes the running time of each solution, normalized by our solution's (SLB) running time. In sub-figure (a), each processor multiplies matrices of dimensions $2^{14} \times 2^{14}$, leading to a run that is primarily arithmetic bounded. In sub-figure (b), each processor multipy matrices of dimensions $2^{12} \times 2^{12}$, leading to a run that is primarily communication bounded. In both scenarios, SLB achieves a x1.1 - x2.1 and x1.1 - x4.4 speedup over the compared solutions, respectively.

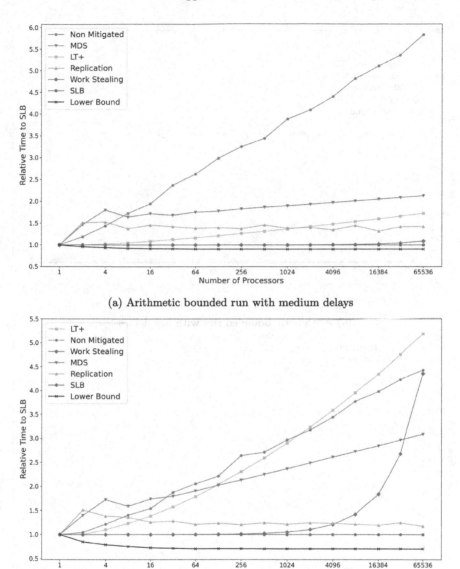

(a) Arithmetic bounded run with medium delays

(b) Communication bounded run with medium delays

**Fig. 2. Weak-scaling comparison between straggler mitigation solutions for distributed matrix multiplication with medium delays.** The delay is sampled from a shifted exponential distribution with a shifting parameter of 1 and a scale parameter of 1. The x-axis denotes the number of processors in a logarithmic scale, and the y-axis denotes the running time of each solution, normalized by our solution's (SLB) running time. In sub-figure (a), each processor multiplies matrices of dimensions $2^{14} \times 2^{14}$, leading to a run that is primarily arithmetic bounded. In sub-figure (b), each processor multiplies matrices of dimensions $2^{12} \times 2^{12}$, leading to a run that is primarily communication bounded. In both scenarios, SLB achieves a x1.05 - x5.9 and x1.1 - x5.3 speedup over the compared solutions, respectively.

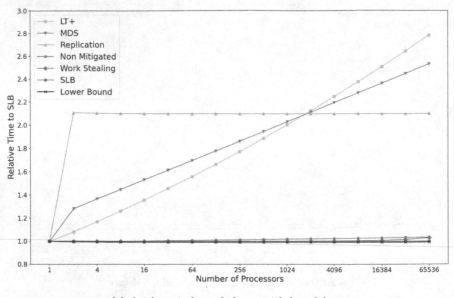

(a) Arithmetic bounded run with low delays

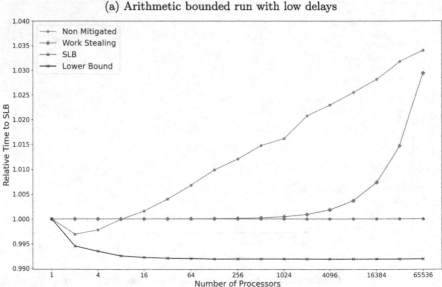

(b) Same as figure (a) above, zoom-in on the better performing solutions

**Fig. 3. Weak scaling of straggler mitigation solutions for distributed matrix multiplication with low delays.** each processor multiplies matrices of dimensions $2^{14} \times 2^{14}$, leading to a run that is primarily arithmetic bounded. The x-axis denotes the number of processors in a logarithmic scale, and the y-axis denotes the running time of each solution, normalized by our solution's (SLB) running time. SLB, work-stealing, and non-mitigated solutions perform close to optimal, while replication, MDS, and LT+ solutions perform x2.1x - x2.8 slower.

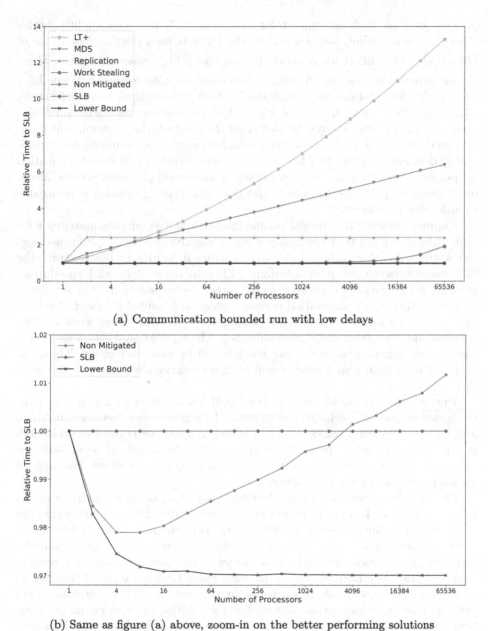

(a) Communication bounded run with low delays

(b) Same as figure (a) above, zoom-in on the better performing solutions

**Fig. 4. Weak scaling of straggler mitigation solutions for distributed matrix multiplication with low delays.** each processor multiplies matrices of dimensions $2^{12} \times 2^{12}$, leading to a run that is primarily communication bounded. The x-axis denotes the number of processors in a logarithmic scale, and the y-axis denotes the running time of each solution, normalized by our solution's (SLB) running time. SLB and the non-mitigated solutions perform close to optimal, while replication, MDS, LT+, and work-stealing solutions perform x2 - x3.4 slower.

because of their high straggler tolerance. Still, SLB performs slightly better than the work-stealing solution due to the lower latency overhead (a factor of $O\left(\frac{P}{\log P}\right)$). This difference is noticeable only for a high processor count, where the arithmetic cost does not dominate the communication overhead. While LT+ has a high tolerance for stragglers, it also has high communication overhead costs, which limit its scaling capabilities. Figure 2(b) presents our results for small-size matrices and medium delays. In this case, the computation is communication-bounded for most $P$ values, and the performances of most solutions are considerably degraded. Due to their low communication overhead, SLB and replication outperform other solutions, even for systems with small processor counts. Moreover, the discrepancy between SLB and the work-stealing solution is noticeable even for few processors.

Figure 1 presents our results on medium-size and small-size matrices with high delays. We omitted the non-mitigated algorithm since it performed significantly worse than others (x5 - x9), making it harder to demonstrate the differences between the other solutions. SLB achieves a x1.1 - x2.1 speedup on medium-sized matrices compared to the other tested solutions. On small-size matrices, where the computation is communication-bounded for most $P$ values, SLB achieved a x2.4x - x4.4 speedup compared to MDS, LT+, and work-stealing solutions due to its communication efficiency. The replication solution uses peer-to-peer communications, which are not affected by processor count. Thus, the replication solution also performs well in this scenario, shrinking the gap from SLB to x1.1.

In cases where the delays are low (Figs. 3,4), SLB, work-stealing, and the non-mitigated solution all perform close to optimal, outperforming Replication, MDS, and LT+ by a factor of x2.1x - x2.8. In addition, when the number of processors is large and the run is primarily communication bounded, SLB outperforms and scales better than work-stealing and non-mitigated solutions, reaching x2 speedup compared to work-stealing.

Overall, the performance of work-stealing solutions on small matrices significantly degrades when the processor count passes 4096, up to a point where the non-mitigated solution performs better. LT+ performance starts to deteriorate even on much smaller systems, but the efficiency decrease is slower than the work-stealing solution. Two solutions less prone to scalability issues are replication and SLB. The latter has a significantly lower latency overhead than work-stealing and LT+ solutions (logarithmic in processor count), maintaining good performances on a large scale. The replication solution involves communication between pairs of processors and is barely affected by processor count. However, it can only tolerate a limited number of stragglers, reducing its overall performance.

## 5   Discussion

Delays become more significant as the number of processors grows, thereby increasing the potential contribution of straggler mitigation solutions. However, larger machines are also associated with higher communication costs, which often degrade the performance and scalability of many solutions. Existing straggler mitigation solutions are either general-purpose (e.g., dynamic load balancing) or tailored for numerical linear algebra but can also tolerate errors (e.g., redundancy-based solutions). In both cases, existing solutions are not optimal for straggler mitigation in numerical linear algebra. Namely, they lead to unnecessary message passing or arithmetic overhead. SLB is tailored for stragglers in matrix multiplication and demonstrates significant speedups over current solutions.

We presented our proposed solution on a distributed matrix multiplication kernel. SLB applies to any computation that can be partitioned into subcomputations that run in parallel without communicating. We are currently working on extending our results to other numerical linear algebra kernels and experimenting and benchmarking on real machines. Moreover, we focused on the inner product algorithm for distributed matrix multiplication. Our algorithm can be extended to additional algorithms (such as 3D and 2.5D) with some modifications.

To the best of our knowledge, no efficient solutions are currently designed to deal simultaneously with stragglers and hard faults. Any redundancy solution that can tolerate $h$ faults can also tolerate $h'$ hard faults and $h - h'$ stragglers. However, since redundancy is not optimal for mitigating stragglers, there may still be a more efficient solution. We conjecture that the right combination of dynamic load balancing and redundancy may provide an even better method of dealing with stragglers and hard faults compared to existing solutions.

# A    Existing Solutions

In this section, we provide an analysis of existing straggler mitigation solutions.

## A.1    Dynamic Load Balancing

We review receiver-initiated load-balancing algorithms (also called work-stealing), which often perform better in decentralized models (such as ours). These solutions often share the following structure: when a target processor receives a work request, it acts in one of the following ways: if it has more than $s$ tasks, it transfers a fraction $\delta$ of the work to the processor that requested the work. If it has less than $s$ tasks, it rejects the request, which is then passed on to the next candidate. Choosing targets at random incurs the optimal asymptotic costs (see [59] for further details).

*Claim.* Let $\gamma_P \cdot F$, $BW$, $L$, and $M$ denote an algorithm's arithmetic cost, bandwidth cost, latency cost, and memory footprint, respectively. Let $F'$, $BW'$, $L'$, and $M'$ denote the costs of the algorithm applying the work-stealing solution on $C$. Then $F' = \bar{\gamma}_a \cdot (1 + \frac{P}{S}) \cdot F$, $BW' = BW + M$, $L' = L + O(P \log P)$, and $M' = M$.

*Proof.* We follow the proof of Theorem 1 with slight modifications. The main difference between SLB and work-stealing is in the number of performed task requests, which affects the latency cost. According to Theorem 2 in [59], the work-stealing technique is expected to perform $O\left(P \log S\right)$ work requests. Similarly to SLB, we bound $S$ by a polynomial function with $P$ (by grouping tasks together) so that $\log S = O\left(\log P\right)$. In total, $F' = \bar{\gamma}_a \cdot \left(1 + \frac{P}{S}\right) \cdot F$, $BW' = BW + O\left(M\right)$, $L' = L + O\left(P \log P\right)$, and $M' = M$.

## A.2    Redundancy

Here, we compare our solution to three commonly used erasure code based solutions: replication, MDS, and LT.

**Replication.** In the Replication solution, the algorithm divides the processors into $P/r$ groups of $r$ processors, where processors within the same group perform the exact same computations. The algorithm constructs the final output using the results of the fastest processor in each group.

*Claim.* Let $\gamma_P \cdot F$, $BW$, $L$, and $M$ denote an algorithm's arithmetic cost, bandwidth cost, latency cost, and memory footprint, respectively. Let $F'$, $BW'$, $L'$, and $M'$ denote the costs of the algorithm applying the replication solution on $C$. Then $F' = \gamma_{P-r+1} \cdot r \cdot F$, $BW' = BW + 2r \cdot M$, $L' = L + O\left(\log r\right)$, and $M' = r \cdot M$.

*Proof.* Since the workload is shared between $P/r$ processor (rather than $P$), each processor computes a factor of $r$ more computations and uses a factor of $r$ more memory. The algorithm uses an all-broadcast operator to share the input, and a scatter operator to share the output. This costs $2 \log r$ messages and $2r \cdot M$ words. The algorithm halts when the first processor from each set completes its tasks. In the worst-case scenario, the algorithm halts when $P - r + 1$ processors have completed their tasks. Hence, the arithmetic cost is $\gamma_{P-r+1} \cdot r \cdot F$. Summing up, we obtain $F' = \gamma_{P-r+1} \cdot r \cdot F$, $BW' = BW + 2r \cdot M$, $L' = L + O\left(\log r\right)$, and $M' = r \cdot M$.

**Erasure Codes.** An erasure code (cf. [48,53]) is a linear transformation $T$ that takes a vector $v$ of size $x1$, and outputs a vector $w$ of size $x2$, where $x1$, $x2$, and $\rho = \frac{x2}{x1}$ are called the rank, length, and rate of the code, respectively. We represent a code $T$ by a generator matrix $G$ of size $x2 \times x1$, where applying the code is equivalent to multiplying the input vector from the left with the matrix $G$. The generator matrix of a replication code is an identity matrix where each row is duplicated $r$ times. We say the code has a distance $d$ if any two code vectors differ in at least $d$ coordinates. A code with distance $d$ can recover from $d - 1$ erasures. Maximal Distance Separable codes (*MDS*) are a family of codes with maximal distance.

Random codes combine randomness in the construction of the generator matrix. Luby-Transforms codes [40] (*LT*) are a family of random codes that obey the following conditions: I) The values of its generator matrix are either one or zero. II) The density of each row (number of non-zeroes elements) is sampled randomly from some distribution. III) The locations of the non-zeroes are sampled uniformly. A popular choice for the density distribution is the Robust Soliton degree distribution [40].

**MDS.** Given an MDS code with rank $K$ and length $P$, the algorithm partitions the problem into $K$ tasks and constructs $P$ new tasks in place of the original ones. The $i'th$ processor computes the $i'th$ task, and the final output is produced from the outcomes of the first $K$ processors to finish.

*Claim.* Let $\gamma_P \cdot F$, $BW$, $L$, and $M$ denote an algorithm's arithmetic cost, bandwidth cost, latency cost, and memory footprint, respectively. Let $F'$, $BW'$, $L'$, and $M'$ denote the costs of the algorithm applying the MDS solution[2] on $C$. Then $F' = \gamma_K \cdot O\left(\frac{P}{K} \cdot F\right)$, $BW' = BW + 2P \cdot M$, $L' = L + O(P)$, and $M' = \frac{P}{K} \cdot M$.

*Proof.* Input (resp. output) redistribution involves code encoding (resp. decoding) and an all-reduce operation. By Corollary 1, this adds $2P \cdot M$ bandwidth cost, $O(P)$ latency cost, and an arithmetic cost, which is often negligible. Moreover, each processor performs a factor of $\frac{P}{K}$ more arithmetic computations (since the workload is distributed among $K$ processors instead of among $P$) and uses a factor of $\frac{P}{K}$ more memory. The algorithm halts when $K$ processors have completed their tasks. Thus, the arithmetic cost is $\gamma_K \cdot O\left(\frac{P}{K} \cdot F\right)$.

**LT.** Mallick et al. [41] proposed a new variation of the LT coding solution (denoted here as *LT+*) that utilizes partial computations performed by all processors and attains near-ideal load balancing. In the LT+ solution, each processor broadcasts an update message every time it completes a task. The algorithm generates $\rho \cdot S$ new tasks (in place of the originals) using the LT code and halts when enough tasks have been completed.

*Remark 1.* Using the Robust Soliton degree distribution [40], the encoding and decoding complexity of a code of size $x$ with probability $1 - \epsilon$ is $O(x \log \frac{x}{\epsilon})$. Any $x + \sqrt{x} \cdot \log^2 \frac{x}{\epsilon}$ symbols are sufficient to construct the output.

*Claim.* Let $\gamma_P \cdot F$, $BW$, $L$, and $M$ denote an algorithm's arithmetic cost, bandwidth cost, latency cost, and memory footprint, respectively, and let $F'$, $BW'$, $L'$, and $M'$ denote the costs of the algorithm applying the LT+ solution to $C$. Then $F' = \bar{\gamma}_a \cdot O\left(1 + \frac{\log^2 s}{\sqrt{S}}\right) \cdot F$, $BW' = BW + 2P \cdot M$, $L' = L + O(S \cdot \log P)$, and $M' = \rho \cdot M$.

---

[2] We present here the basic MDS code and the associated overhead costs. Several variations of the MDS solution incur lower overhead costs, for example, by using Systematic MDS codes or sub-classes with lower decoding complexity.

*Proof.* Input and output distribution phases are similar to the MDS solution but with different weights. Since both use an all-reduce operation, the overhead costs remain the same. The algorithm constructs the final output when processors have computed a sufficient amount of tasks globally (maintaining a near-perfect[3] load balancing. The number of completed tasks expected to be sufficient for recovery is $O\left(S + \sqrt{S}\log^2 S\right)$ (Claim 1), which means that each processor is expected to perform a factor of $O\left(1 + \frac{\log^2 S}{\sqrt{S}}\right)$ more computations compared to the non-mitigated algorithm. Notifying the processors when each task is completed adds $S \cdot P$ bandwidth and $O\left(S \cdot \log P\right)$ latency (Corollary 1). The algorithm generates a factor of $\rho$ more tasks and thus uses a factor of $\rho$ more memory. Summing up, the additional costs are: $\left(F', BW', L'\right) = \left(\bar{\gamma}_a \cdot O\left(1 + \frac{\log^2 S}{\sqrt{S}}\right) \cdot F,\ BW + 2P \cdot M,\ L + O\left(S\log P\right)\right).$

# References

1. Acar, U.A., Charguéraud, A., Rainey, M.: Scheduling parallel programs by work stealing with private deques. In: Proceedings of the 18th ACM SIGPLAN Symposium on Principles and Practice of Parallel Programming, pp. 219–228 (2013)
2. Agarwal, R.C., Balle, S.M., Gustavson, F.G., Joshi, M., Palkar, P.: A three-dimensional approach to parallel matrix multiplication. IBM J. Res. Dev. **39**(5), 575–582 (1995)
3. Ananthanarayanan, G., Ghodsi, A., Shenker, S., Stoica, I.: Effective straggler mitigation: attack of the clones. In: Proceedings of the 10th USENIX Conference on Networked Systems Design and Implementation, pp. 185–198. USENIX Association (2013)
4. Ananthanarayanan, G., et al.: Reining in the outliers in map-reduce clusters using mantri. In: Proceedings of the 9th USENIX Conference on Operating Systems Design and Implementation, pp. 265–278. USENIX Association (2010)
5. Avizienis, A., Laprie, J.C., Randell, B., Landwehr, C.: Basic concepts and taxonomy of dependable and secure computing. IEEE Trans. Dependable Secure Comput. **1**(1), 11–33 (2004)
6. Ballard, G., et al.: Communication optimal parallel multiplication of sparse random matrices. In: Proceedings of the Twenty-Fifth Annual ACM Symposium on Parallelism in Algorithms and Architectures, SPAA 2013, pp. 222–231. Association for Computing Machinery (2013)
7. Ballard, G., Carson, E., Demmel, J., Hoemmen, M., Knight, N., Schwartz, O.: Communication lower bounds and optimal algorithms for numerical linear algebra. Acta Numer **23**, 1–155 (2014)
8. Ballard, G., Demmel, J., Holtz, O., Schwartz, O.: Communication-optimal parallel and sequential cholesky decomposition. SIAM J. Sci. Comput. **32**(6), 3495–3523 (2010)
9. Ballard, G., Demmel, J., Gearhart, A.: Brief announcement: communication bounds for heterogeneous architectures. In: Proceedings of the Twenty-third Annual ACM symposium on Parallelism in Algorithms and Architectures, pp. 257–258 (2011)

---

[3] Near-perfect load balancing is only achieved when $\frac{\bar{\gamma}_a}{\gamma_1} > \rho$, otherwise processors are expected to have idle times.

10. Ballard, G., Demmel, J., Holtz, O., Schwartz, O.: Graph expansion and communication costs of fast matrix multiplication. J. ACM (JACM) **59**(6), 1–23 (2013)
11. Basermann, A., et al.: Dynamic load-balancing of finite element applications with the drama library. Appl. Math. Model. **25**(2), 83–98 (2000)
12. Berenbrink, P., Friedetzky, T., Goldberg, L.A.: The natural work-stealing algorithm is stable. SIAM J. Comput. **32**(5), 1260–1279 (2003)
13. Birnbaum, N., Schwartz, O.: Fault tolerant resource efficient matrix multiplication. In: Proceedings of the Eighth SIAM Workshop on Combinatorial Scientific Computing 2018. SIAM (2018)
14. Biswas, R., Das, S., Harvey, D., Oliker, L.: Parallel dynamic load balancing strategies for adaptive irregular applications. Appl. Math. Model. **25**(2), 109–122 (2000)
15. Blumofe, R.D., Leiserson, C.E.: Scheduling multithreaded computations by work stealing. J. ACM (JACM) **46**(5), 720–748 (1999)
16. Boneti, C., Gioiosa, R., Cazorla, F.J., Corbalan, J., Labarta, J., Valero, M.: Balancing hpc applications through smart allocation of resources in mt processors. In: 2008 IEEE International Symposium on Parallel and Distributed Processing, pp. 1–12 (2008)
17. Boneti, C., Gioiosa, R., Cazorla, F.J., Valero, M.: A dynamic scheduler for balancing hpc applications. In: SC 2008: Proceedings of the 2008 ACM/IEEE Conference on Supercomputing, pp. 1–12 (2008)
18. Cannon, L.E.: A cellular computer to implement the Kalman filter algorithm. Montana State University (1969)
19. Cappello, F., Geist, A., Gropp, W., Kale, S., Kramer, B., Snir, M.: Toward exascale resilience: 2014 update. Supercomput. Front. Innovations **1**(1), 5–28 (2014)
20. Casanova, H.: Benefits and drawbacks of redundant batch requests. J. Grid Comput. **5**(2), 235–250 (2007)
21. Clarke, D., Lastovetsky, A., Rychkov, V.: Dynamic load balancing of parallel computational iterative routines on higly heterogeneous hpc platforms. Parallel Process. Lett. **21**(02), 195–217 (2011)
22. Dean, J., Barroso, L.: The tail at scale. Commun. ACM **56**(2), 74–80 (2013)
23. Dean, J., Ghemawat, S.: Mapreduce: simplified data processing on large clusters. Commun. ACM **51**(1), 107–113 (2008)
24. Dinan, J., Larkins, D.B., Sadayappan, P., Krishnamoorthy, S., Nieplocha, J.: Scalable work stealing. In: Proceedings of the Conference on High Performance Computing Networking, Storage and Analysis, pp. 1–11 (2009)
25. Dutta, S., Cadambe, V., Grover, P.: "Short-dot": computing large linear transforms distributedly using coded short dot products. IEEE Trans. Inf. Theory **65**(10), 6171–6193 (2019)
26. Gardner, K., Zbarsky, S., Doroudi, S., Harchol-Balter, M., Hyytia, E.: Reducing latency via redundant requests: exact analysis. SIGMETRICS Perform. Eval. Rev. **43**(1), 347–360 (2015)
27. Van de Geijn, R.A., Watts, J.: Summa: scalable universal matrix multiplication algorithm. Concurrency-Pract. Exper. **9**(4), 255–274 (1997)
28. Gupta, A., Sarood, O., Kale, L.V., Milojicic, D.: Improving hpc application performance in cloud through dynamic load balancing. In: 2013 13th IEEE/ACM International Symposium on Cluster, Cloud, and Grid Computing, pp. 402–409 (2013)
29. Huang, L., Pawar, S., Zhang, H., Ramchandran, K.: Codes can reduce queueing delay in data centers. In: 2012 IEEE International Symposium on Information Theory Proceedings, pp. 2766–2770 (2012)

30. Joshi, G., Liu, Y., Soljanin, E.: On the delay-storage trade-off in content download from coded distributed storage systems. IEEE J. Sel. Areas Commun. **32**(5), 989–997 (2014)
31. Joshi, G., Soljanin, E., Wornell, G.: Efficient redundancy techniques for latency reduction in cloud systems. ACM Trans. Model. Perform. Eval. Comput. Syst. **2**(2) (2017)
32. Koanantakool, P., et al.: Communication-avoiding parallel sparse-dense matrix-matrix multiplication. In: 2016 IEEE International Parallel and Distributed Processing Symposium (IPDPS), pp. 842–853 (2016)
33. Kumar, V., Grama, A., Vempaty, N.: Scalable load balancing techniques for parallel computers. J. Parallel Distrib. Comput. **22**(1), 60–79 (1994)
34. Lee, K., Lam, M., Pedarsani, R., Papailiopoulos, D., Ramchandran, K.: Speeding up distributed machine learning using codes. IEEE Trans. Inf. Theory **64**(3), 1514–1529 (2018)
35. Lee, K., Pedarsani, R., Papailiopoulos, D., Ramchandran, K.: Coded computation for multicore setups. In: 2017 IEEE International Symposium on Information Theory (ISIT), pp. 2413–2417 (2017)
36. Lee, K., Suh, C., Ramchandran, K.: High-dimensional coded matrix multiplication. In: 2017 IEEE International Symposium on Information Theory (ISIT), pp. 2418–2422 (2017)
37. Li, S., Maddah-Ali, M.A., Avestimehr, A.S.: Coded mapreduce. In: 2015 53rd Annual Allerton Conference on Communication, Control, and Computing (Allerton), pp. 964–971 (2015)
38. Li, S., Maddah-Ali, M.A., Yu, Q., Avestimehr, A.S.: A fundamental tradeoff between computation and communication in distributed computing. IEEE Trans. Inf. Theory **64**(1), 109–128 (2018)
39. Li, S., Supittayapornpong, S., Maddah-Ali, M.A., Avestimehr, S.: Coded terasort. In: 2017 IEEE International Parallel and Distributed Processing Symposium Workshops (IPDPSW), pp. 389–398 (2017)
40. Luby, M.: Lt codes. In: Proceedings of the 43rd Annual IEEE Symposium on Foundations of Computer Science, pp. 271–280. IEEE (2002)
41. Mallick, A., Chaudhari, M., Sheth, U., Palanikumar, G., Joshi, G.: Rateless codes for near-perfect load balancing in distributed matrix-vector multiplication. Proc. ACM Meas. Anal. Comput. Syst. **3**(3) (2019)
42. Mallick, A., Chaudhari, M., Sheth, U., Palanikumar, G., Joshi, G.: Rateless codes for near-perfect load balancing in distributed matrix-vector multiplication. Commun. ACM **65**(5), 111–118 (2022)
43. Márquez, C., César, E., Sorribes, J.: Graph-based automatic dynamic load balancing for HPC agent-based simulations. In: Hunold, S., et al. (eds.) Euro-Par 2015. LNCS, vol. 9523, pp. 405–416. Springer, Cham (2015). https://doi.org/10.1007/978-3-319-27308-2_33
44. McColl, W.F., Tiskin, A.: Memory-efficient matrix multiplication in the BSP model. Algorithmica **24**(3), 287–297 (1999)
45. Menon, H., Acun, B., De Gonzalo, S.G., Sarood, O., Kalé, L.: Thermal aware automated load balancing for hpc applications. In: 2013 IEEE International Conference on Cluster Computing (CLUSTER), pp. 1–8 (2013)
46. Michael, M.M., Vechev, M.T., Saraswat, V.A.: Idempotent work stealing. In: Proceedings of the 14th ACM SIGPLAN Symposium on Principles and Practice of Parallel Programming, pp. 45–54 (2009)

47. Mitzenmacher, M.: Analyses of load stealing models based on differential equations. In Proceedings of the Tenth ACM symposium on Parallel Algorithms and Architectures, pp. 212–221 (1998)
48. Reed, I.S., Solomon, G.: Polynomial codes over certain finite fields. J. Soc. Ind. Appl. Math. **8**(2), 300–304 (1960)
49. Reisizadeh, A., Prakash, S., Pedarsani, R., Avestimehr, A.S.: Coded computation over heterogeneous clusters. IEEE Trans. Inf. Theory **65**(7), 4227–4242 (2019)
50. Said, S.A., Habashy, S.M., Salem, S.A., Saad, E.M.: An optimized straggler mitigation framework for large-scale distributed computing systems. IEEE Access **10** (2022)
51. Sanders, P., Sibeyn, J.F.: A bandwidth latency tradeoff for broadcast and reduction. Inf. Process. Lett. **86**(1), 33–38 (2003)
52. Severinson, A., Graell i Amat, A., Rosnes, E.: Block-diagonal and lt codes for distributed computing with straggling servers. IEEE Trans. Commun. **67**(3), 1739–1753 (2019)
53. Singleton, R.: Maximum distanceq-nary codes. IEEE Trans. Inf. Theory **10**(2), 116–118 (1964)
54. Sinha, A.B., Kale, L.V.: A load balancing strategy for prioritized execution of tasks. In: [1993] Proceedings Seventh International Parallel Processing Symposium, pp. 230–237 (1993)
55. Snir, M., et al.: Addressing failures in exascale computing. Inter. J. High Performance Comput. Appli. **28**(2), 129–173 (2014)
56. Solomonik, E., Demmel, J.: Communication-optimal parallel 2.5D matrix multiplication and LU factorization algorithms. In: Jeannot, E., Namyst, R., Roman, J. (eds.) Euro-Par 2011. LNCS, vol. 6853, pp. 90–109. Springer, Heidelberg (2011). https://doi.org/10.1007/978-3-642-23397-5_10
57. Son, K., Choi, W.: Distributed matrix multiplication based on frame quantization for straggler mitigation. IEEE Trans. Signal Process. **70** (2022)
58. Tandon, R., Lei, Q., Dimakis, A., Karampatziakis, N.: Gradient coding: avoiding stragglers in distributed learning. In: Proceedings of the 34th International Conference on Machine Learning. Proceedings of Machine Learning Research, vol. 70, pp. 3368–3376. PMLR (2017)
59. Tchiboukdjian, M., Gast, N., Trystram, D., Roch, J.L., Bernard, J.: A tighter analysis of work stealing. In: Cheong, O., Chwa, K.Y., Park, K. (eds.) Algorithms and Computation, pp. 291–302. Springer, Berlin (2010). https://doi.org/10.1007/978-3-642-17514-5_25
60. Tumanov, A., Cipar, J., Ganger, G.R., Kozuch, M.A.: alsched: algebraic scheduling of mixed workloads in heterogeneous clouds. In: Proceedings of the third ACM Symposium on Cloud Computing, pp. 1–7 (2012)
61. Van Nieuwpoort, R.V., Kielmann, T., Bal, H.E.: Efficient load balancing for wide-area divide-and-conquer applications. In: Proceedings of the Eighth ACM SIGPLAN Symposium on Principles and Practices of Parallel Programming, pp. 34–43 (2001)
62. Vulimiri, A., Godfrey, P., Mittal, R., Sherry, J., Ratnasamy, S., Shenker, S.: Low latency via redundancy. In: Proceedings of the Ninth ACM Conference on Emerging Networking Experiments and Technologies, CoNEXT 2013, pp. 283–294. Association for Computing Machinery (2013)
63. Wang, D., Joshi, G., Wornell, G.: Efficient task replication for fast response times in parallel computation. In: The 2014 ACM International Conference on Measurement and Modeling of Computer Systems, SIGMETRICS 2014, pp. 599–600. Association for Computing Machinery (2014)

64. Wang, D., Joshi, G., Wornell, G.: Using straggler replication to reduce latency in large-scale parallel computing. SIGMETRICS Perform. Eval. Rev. **43**(3), 7–11 (2015)
65. Wang, S., Liu, J., Shroff, N.: Coded sparse matrix multiplication. In: Proceedings of the 35th International Conference on Machine Learning. Proceedings of Machine Learning Research, vol. 80, pp. 5152–5160. PMLR (2018)
66. Wimmer, M., Cederman, D., Träff, J.L., Tsigas, P.: Work-stealing with configurable scheduling strategies. ACM SIGPLAN Notices **48**(8), 315–316 (2013)
67. Yang, C., Miller, B.P.: Critical path analysis for the execution of parallel and distributed programs. In: [1988] Proceedings. The 8th International Conference on Distributed, pp. 366–373 (1988)
68. Yang, J., He, Q.: Scheduling parallel computations by work stealing: a survey. Inter. J. Parallel Program. **46**(2) (2018)
69. Yu, Q., Maddah-Ali, M., Avestimehr, S.: Polynomial codes: an optimal design for high-dimensional coded matrix multiplication. In: Guyon, I., Luxburg, U.V., Bengio, S., Wallach, H., Fergus, R., Vishwanathan, S., Garnett, R. (eds.) Advances in Neural Information Processing Systems 30, pp. 4403–4413. Curran Associates, Inc. (2017)

# Optimization Metrics for the Evaluation of Batch Schedulers in HPC

Robin Boëzennec[1]([✉]), Fanny Dufossé[2], and Guillaume Pallez[3]

[1] Inria, Labri, University of Bordeaux, Bordeaux, France
robin.boezennec@gmail.com
[2] Univ. Grenoble Alpes, Inria, CNRS, Grenoble INP, LIG, 38000 Grenoble, France
[3] Inria, Université de Rennes, Rennes, France

**Abstract.** Machine Learning techniques are taking a prominent position in the design of system softwares. In HPC, many work are proposing to use such techniques (specifically Reinforcement Learning) to improve the performance of batch schedulers.

Their main limitation is the lack of transparency of their decision. This underlines the importance of choosing correctly the optimization criteria when evaluating these solutions. In this work, we discuss bias and limitations of the most frequent optimization metrics in the literature. We provide elements on how to evaluate performance when studying HPC batch scheduling. We also propose a new metric: the standard deviation of the utilization, which we believe can be used when the utilization reaches its limits.

We then experimentally evaluate these limitations by focusing on the use-case of runtime estimates. One of the information that HPC batch schedulers use to schedule jobs on the available resources is user runtime estimates: an estimation provided by the user of how long their job will run on the machine. These estimates are known to be inaccurate, hence many work have focused on improving runtime prediction.

**Keywords:** Metric · Online Scheduling · High Performance Computing · Runtime estimates · EASY

## 1 Introduction

In recent years, most of industrial and academic large experiments have been replaced or simultaneously simulated with large scale applications. This development corresponds to the increase of massively parallel computing platforms. The High Performance Computing (HPC) platforms are typically developed to execute such massive computing jobs. The largest platform, Frontier [2] has recently reached the exascale level, that was envisioned by parallel computing research community for decades.

Large HPC platforms encounter a high rate of submission of new jobs that lead to a percentage of utilization over 90%. This implies a capacity to allocates these jobs fast enough to avoid congestion. The scheduling techniques were studied for decades and mainly lead to a characteristic of the most efficient scheduling techniques: their simplicity. The most sophisticated methods using machine learning approach [5,9] can barely match the performance of nowadays classical scheduling methods such as EASY-BF.

EASY-BF mainly consists in a FCFS approach completed by a backfilling step. Jobs are considered in their order of submission and assigned as soon as the requested number of servers are available. This method creates some utilization *gaps* (i.e. idle nodes). To avoid such idle time, in a second step, the queue of waiting jobs is considered to find one or more jobs that can fill the gap and being executed without delaying the first come job.

Machine Learning techniques are taking a prominent position in the design of system softwares. In HPC, many work are proposing to use such techniques (specifically Reinforcement Learning) to improve the performance of batch schedulers [23,24]. To motivate the importance of these strategies, the authors often focus on a selected optimization criteria such as the mean bounded slowdown, without looking *under the hood* at what these black box algorithms do.

The question of scheduling performance is ambiguous. For each job, the objective is obviously its finish time, but the performance has to be evaluated globally. Two kind of criteria are mainly considered. The percentage of utilization or the maximum arrival rate of jobs are platform oriented objectives. The users oriented objectives use average or weighted average values of a formula that combine the waiting time and the runtime or the walltime of each job. The selection of the criteria is a critical issue in scheduling, as some criteria are associated to a priority order of jobs based on their duration or their number of nodes. For example, the objective of average completion time is minimized with ordering jobs by shortest runtime first. This is not consistent with platforms dimensioned for jobs requesting a large number of servers for a long duration.

In this work, we discuss more thoroughly the use of quantitative optimization criteria for the design of HPC Resource and Job Management Software (aka Batch Schedulers). Specifically, we precise how some criteria hide effects that could be seen as negative from an HPC perspective.

Our main contributions are the following:

1. We give a qualitative analysis of many optimization criteria used in the literature. We stress how most of the recent work that have claimed to improve the performance of EASY-BF have done so on criteria that we show to be extremely biased towards very small jobs. This is the case of many recent work that have proposed to use deep-learning for resource management and that have not proposed a qualitative analysis of their results.
2. We demonstrate the statements from this analysis by studying the classical EASY-BF algorithm on two workloads (Mira and Theta) with two runtime estimate functions: a very precise one, and the actual runtime estimate provided by users. This section confirms that without performing a qualitative analysis and by simply looking at specific performance, one cannot conclude a study.

In Sect. 2, we discuss the objective criteria that are considered in scheduling framework. We focus on their limitations for HPC systems, and provide alternatives to improve them. We then work on demonstrating experimentally our statements. Section 3.1 details the methodology of the different evaluations before presenting and analyzing the results in Sect. 3.2. Section 4 discusses related work. Finally, Sect. 5 concludes the work.

# 2  Evaluating the Quality of a Schedule

Several optimization criteria are used to evaluate the performance of a Resource and Job Management Software. In this Section, we discuss more in depth those objectives, particularly in the context of High-Performance Computing. We explain their limitations in this context.

The analysis presented in this work is targeted for High-Performance Computing: building a machine able to perform ExaFlops targets the execution of large scale applications mostly and the validation of the performance of a solution should reflect this. Extreme-scale platforms have a high operating cost and are expected to be utilized as much as possible.

Analysis of HPC system traces showed that *Users are now submitting medium-sized jobs because the wait times for larger sizes tend to be longer* [17]. To execute medium-size jobs, it is probably more efficient (cost-wise) to have multiple smaller clusters than an HPC machine with a dense interconnect.

In order to define the objective we use the following notations for job $J_i$:

| | |
|---|---|
| $r_i$ | The release time of job $J_i$ (also called submission time) |
| $C_i$ | The completion time of job $J_i$ |
| $t_i^{\text{real}}$ | The real length of job $J_i$ (also called execution time) |
| $t_i^{\text{wait}} = C_i - r_i - t_i^{\text{real}}$ | The waiting time of job $J_i$ |

## 2.1  Mean (bounded) Slowdown

The average slowdown (also called mean flow) is the main optimization criteria in many recent works on improving resource management in HPC [4,14,24]. Its goal is to provide a measure of fairness over applications.

The slowdown $S_i$ of job $J_i$ (also called the flow of the job) corresponds to the ratio of the time it spent in the system over its real execution time. Formally, it is defined as

$$S_i = \frac{t_i^{\text{real}} + t_i^{\text{wait}}}{t_i^{\text{real}}} = \frac{C_i - r_i}{t_i^{\text{real}}}$$

Note that in practice many jobs are extremely small (few seconds). In these cases their slowdown could be arbitrarily high even if their wait time is ridiculously small (a five minutes wait time for a job that dies instantly (one second) would result in a slowdown of 300).

The solution that is often used is to consider a variant of the slowdown called the *bounded slowdown*:

$$S_i^b = \max\left(\frac{C_i - r_i}{\max\left(t_i^{\text{real}}, \tau\right)}, 1\right) \qquad (1)$$

where $\tau$ is a constant that prevents the slowdown of smaller jobs from surging. Then the average bounded slowdown $\bar{S}$ is:

$$\bar{S}^b = \frac{1}{n}\sum_i S_i^b, \quad \text{where } n \text{ is the number of jobs}$$

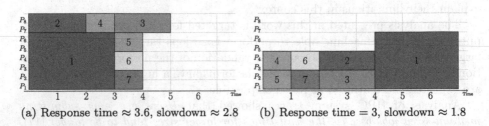

(a) Response time $\approx 3.6$, slowdown $\approx 2.8$      (b) Response time $= 3$, slowdown $\approx 1.8$

**Fig. 1.** In this example, all jobs are released at $t = 0$. Despite what appears to be a more efficient strategy, the left schedule has worse average response time and slowdown than the right schedule.

*Limits for HPC workloads* By improving the quality of service to the small jobs, one can considerably improve this objective. This is often what is actually measured when work study this objective, and is the opposite of what a system administrator of an HPC machine is looking for. This is illustrated in Fig. 1.

In Sect. 3.2, we also show that this is subject to a high variability, and hence the performance is highly dependent on the input data.

*Alternative Approach.* To understand the actual behavior of the system, some work [7] consider the bounded slowdown as a function of the size of the job. In this case, this objective is not one to optimize anymore, but more a qualitative way to measure and understand the performance of a solution. Another approach is to use a weighted version of the average slowdown where large jobs are given more weight than smaller jobs.

### 2.2  Utilization

This optimization criteria measures how fully the platform is occupied. It is a particularly important objective for an HPC platform that costs multiple-million of dollars yearly to operate. This is the main objective studied in [10–12].

If $W(t_1, t_2)$ is the total amount of work done between $t_1$ and $t_2$ on a platform with $N$ nodes, the utilization $U(t_1, t_2)$ on the interval $[t_1, t_2]$ is measured as:

$$U(t_1, t_2) = \frac{W(t_1, t_2)}{N \cdot (t_2 - t_1)}. \tag{2}$$

Note that when jobs fail to complete fully (for instance because their walltime is underestimated), it is interesting to measure the "useful utilization", i.e. the volume of computation that lead to a successful execution [7] .

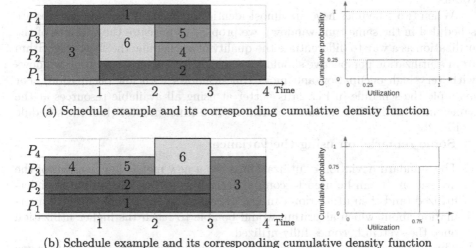

(a) Schedule example and its corresponding cumulative density function

(b) Schedule example and its corresponding cumulative density function

**Fig. 2.** Even though the global utilization is the same between the two schedules (13/16), the distribution of their utilization differ significantly.

*Limits for HPC Workloads.* One of the main limitation concerns machines with lower submission rate (i.e. that are not "packed"), then any scheduling solution has the same (low) utilization since it corresponds to executing almost all jobs during the whole window. Utilization by itself does not allow to discriminate between different schedule qualities (Fig. 2).

Another one is the fact that it is more a system administrator target: how to maximize the yield of my machine. It does not give a sense of the quality of the schedule: an easy way to maximize utilization would be to have a large queue of jobs waiting to be executed and find the one that works best at all time (often favoring smaller jobs that can fill a hole).

*Alternative Approach.* Our observations show that in some scenarios if the utilization of an HPC platform is lower than 93%, the "quality" of a scheduler has no impact on the average utilization of the schedule.

There are settings where the workload has different "modes" (such as intensive in the day; low on requests in the night), in this case it may be interesting to study utilization of these workloads separately. Having a good understanding of one's workload is important.

We found that a way to measure this is to study the density function of the utilization (see Fig. 2). Indeed intuitively, for two identical job submission schemes a "better" scheduling algorithm will have more phases at very high utilization (and hence more at lower utilization). Indeed, it can pack jobs as soon as they are available, whereas a poorer scheduling quality will delay jobs from phases of time with intensive job counts to phases with less intensive job counts.

When two schedules have an almost identical utilization (because all jobs are scheduled in the same time window), we propose to measure the variance of the utilization as a way to differentiate the quality of a schedule: the "best" algorithm from a utilization perspective should have a higher variance (more time-windows with very high occupation and more time-windows with low occupation). For example the schedule in Fig. 2a is better at using all available resources at the same time, leading to a variance of utilization 9 times greater than the schedule in Fig. 2b.

**Some remarks on using the variance:**

1. The standard deviation of utilization is not a new metric independent of the utilization. It can be used to compare schedulers when the system is under-utilized (and then utilization can not discriminate algorithms), to give information about which algorithm would be able to reach the higher utilization once the system becomes fully utilized.
2. This metric allows to qualify whether one schedule is better than another one from a utilization perspective, but it lacks interpretability: what does having a variance $x$ times greater than another one means overall? This is an open question for us.
3. It is important to note that the variance is only relevant to compare schedules with a similar utilization. If it is not the case, one can just tell which schedule is better by looking at the utilization.

## 2.3   Response Time (and Wait Time)

Mean response time (or mean wait time) is a metric often used in the literature [10,12,16,19,21,23]. The response time $\mathcal{RT}_i$ of a job $J_i$ is the duration between the submission of the job and its completion, or equivalently its wait time and its length.

$$\mathcal{RT}_i = t_i^{\text{wait}} + t_i^{\text{real}}$$

The mean response time is equivalent to the mean wait time since the difference is the mean runtime which depends on the workloads but not on the schedule. In the following, we only address the response time, but our reasoning identically apply to wait time.

*Limits for HPC Workloads.* Using this objective gives equal importance to all jobs, independently of the work they represent. In an HPC workload, this gives an advantage to the numerous "small" jobs, even if they only represent a very small portion of the workload. In Fig. 1 we can see that the scheduling on the top intuitively looks more efficient than the second, and yet it has a worst mean response time. This is because the scheduling on the bottom favors small jobs despite being less effective at densely packing jobs.

Similarly to the mean bounded slowdown, we show in Sect. 3.2 that when using a workload from a big compute center (with a high jobs sizes variability), the mean response time is mainly going to be influenced by the proportion of very small jobs which are backfilled (and then have a very low response time). In addition to not corresponding to what we want to optimize, it is also subject to a lot of variability and is quite random which is going to disturb the evaluation of performance. This is something that was confirmed by our experiments and which is covered more in depth in Sect. 3.2.

In the end, this is a limit for the response time objective because simply improving it does not necessarily mean improving the quality of the overall schedule (from an HPC perspective).

*Alternative Approach.* Goponenko et al. [13] have used the weighted mean response time, where one weights the response time by a priority (such as the total amount of work of a job, or the number of nodes that a processor uses). We argue that when computing the average response time in the context of an HPC job scheduler, one should give a higher weight to bigger jobs. For example giving a weight proportional to the area of the job would allow to transform the mean response time in a system administrator metric: as Goponenko et al. [13] underlined, using this weight would mean swapping a job with two smaller jobs of the same duration but half the resources would not change the weighted response time. This way neither small nor big jobs are favored, and what is measured is the ability of the scheduler to densely pack jobs.

Alternatively, Gainaru et al. [12] have proposed to measure only the response time of non-backfilled jobs.

## 2.4   Additional Comments

As we said, many objectives when optimized have negative side effect for large scale platform (such as improving the performance of small jobs at the detriment of large jobs).

Yet many work, particularly recent work that discuss improving batch-scheduling techniques using machine learning still optimize these objectives. As an example, recent research directions have focused on using RL-based scheduling in batch schedulers [23,24]. They show that by using RL into the batch scheduling, one can improve considerably the response time and bounded slowdown at a small cost in utilization.

By simply looking at the objective function, their analysis lacks quality elements that could show the limits of their performance as discussed in the previous section. Specifically it is very likely that their significant improvement in response time or slowdown are mostly used by the improvement of the slowdown/response time of small jobs, which may be done at the detriment of those of larger jobs.

Work by Carastan-Santos et al. [4] where the ML algorithm provides a priority function confirms this intuition and the fact that learning-based batch schedulers with the objective of bounded slowdown simply give higher priority to small jobs. Similarly, Legrand et al. [14] have realized the importance of small jobs for bounded slowdown and focus on having an oracle which guesses which job is small and which is large. This is sufficient for significant performance gains for this objective.

## 3   Use-Case: The Impact of Runtime Estimates

HPC Resource and Job Management Systems rely on user-submitted runtime estimate functions. These estimates are known to be inaccurate. Many work [3, 17] have focused on improving runtime prediction.

To demonstrate the risk of evaluating quantitatively a schedule, we propose to evaluate the performance of two notable runtime estimate functions: a perfect estimate, and the estimate provided by the users (see Sect. 3.1). The results on metrics detailed in Sect. 2 are detailed in Sect. 3.2.

### 3.1   Evaluation Methodology

We simulate the execution of EASY-BF using the batch simulator Batsim on the workloads of platforms Mira and Theta.

**Batsim.** Simulations are run in Batsim [8] (version 4.1.0), a simulator to analyze batch schedulers with the EASY-BF version of the algorithm easy_bf_fast from Batsched (version 1.4.0). easy_bf_fast is an online scheduler. Batsched is a set of Batsim-compatible algorithms implemented in C++.

Our most intense simulations (compute-wise) execute 10 000 jobs on 49 152 nodes, which corresponds to Mira's characteristics. A single simulation with this setup takes about 10 min to complete on a laptop with a processor intel i5-8350U. It has 4 cores, 8 threads, a max frequency of 3.6GHz, and 6MB of cache.

**Workloads.** We used traces from computers Mira and Theta [1] of the Argonne National Laboratory. The Mira supercomputer was launched in 2012 at the 3rd place of TOP500 [2] HPC centers. It ran 49 152 nodes (and 16 times more cores) and was maintained until 2019. The available trace covers years 2014 to 2018. It contains a total of 330k jobs.

The Theta platform was launched in 2016 and runs 4 392 nodes (and 64 times more cores) with traces from 2017 to 2022. We have not used the first year of Theta because the number of cores used was varying. Without this year, the trace contains about 420k jobs.

In both cases, system admins were giving incentives to users to request a number of nodes which is an integer power of two, that is nearly always the case [17].

For the evaluations, we create a total of 70 inputs by partitioning the traces in sets of 10k consecutive jobs (30 for Mira, 40 for Theta): we sorted traces by submission time, and we used the jobs from index 1 to 300 000 (by slice of 10 000) for Mira, and from index 1 to 400 000 (by slice of 10 000) for Theta.

These samples provide a wide variability of workloads: on Mira they span from 12 d of consecutive submissions to 110 d, with a mean duration of 59 d, while on Theta they span from 15 to 61 d with a mean of 40 d.

The workloads are then constructed as follows. Consider the jobs sorted by their release times:

1. We study the workload starting from $t_{1001}$, the release time of its $1001^{st}$ job;
2. The 1000 first jobs are used to have a non-empty queue at the beginning of the analysis, and hence all their release times are set to $t_{1001}$.

**Measuring Performance.** Since we simulate subset of the traces, we need to prune the traces for the performance evaluation in order to remove possible side-effects that may not be representative.

*Utilization Related Objectives.* The utilization and its standard deviation are measured on a given time window as presented in Equation (2). If only a part of a job is inside the window, we ignore the part of the job that is outside the window. To remove side-effects, we crop the borders of the execution window to measure performances when the scheduler is in its steady state. This is consistent with the literature [21]. The measure window is defined as

$$[t_1, t_2] = [0.15 \cdot \text{max\_submission\_time}, 0.85 \cdot \text{max\_submission\_time}].$$

*Bounded Slowdown and Response Time.* When computing these objectives, we do not include the performance of the first and last 15% jobs to measure the performance of the steady state (For details : the 10% jobs in the initial queue are included in these 15%, which mean that at the start we crop the 10% in the initial queue plus the first 5% scheduled jobs.). We use $\tau = 10s$ for the bounded slowdown (Equation (1)), following the literature [21].

*Relative Improvement for a Given Metric.* In the evaluation we discuss the *relative improvement of* EXACT *over* USER-WALLTIME *for an objective O* (which we abbreviate sometimes as *Relative Improvement*). This relative improvement $\text{RI}(O)$ is measured as:

– If $O$ is a maximization objective (e.g. utilization, utilization standard deviation), then

$$\text{RI}(O) = \frac{O_{\text{EXACT}} - O_{\text{USER-WALLTIME}}}{O_{\text{USER-WALLTIME}}} \tag{3}$$

- If $O$ is a minimization objective (e.g. response time, bounded slowdown), then

$$\text{RI}(O) = \frac{O_{\text{USER-WALLTIME}} - O_{\text{EXACT}}}{O_{\text{USER-WALLTIME}}} \qquad (4)$$

This difference allows to see clearly that when $\text{RI}(O) > 0$ then EXACT performs better than USER-WALLTIME by a factor $\text{RI}(O)$ on objective $O$, while when $\text{RI}(O) < 0$, then EXACT performs worse than USER-WALLTIME by a factor $-\text{RI}(O)$ on objective $O$.

**Runtime Estimate Functions.** The goal of this work is to evaluate the impact of the precision of runtime estimates. Hence we define several walltime functions. Given $r$ the runtime of a job (in seconds):

- EXACT : $r \mapsto r + 1$second. This simulates an almost perfect estimate (except for extremely small jobs, but this simplifies the interaction with Batsim).
- USER-WALLTIME, it corresponds to the walltime provided by the users.

### 3.2 Experimental Evaluation

In this section we simulate a study of the impact of walltime accuracy in the performance of Resource and Job Management Software in order to discuss various metrics.

**Coarse-Grain Analysis.** The two runtime estimate functions are evaluated in Fig. 3 over the various criteria discussed in Sect. 2: Bounded Slowdown (Sect. 2.1), Utilization (Sect. 2.2), Response Time and Weighted Response time (Sect. 2.3). In these figures, to discuss the performance difference between the two runtime estimates functions, we use the relative improvement of EXACT over USER-WALLTIME as computed by Equations (3) and (4).

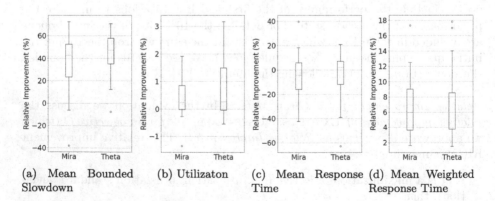

(a) Mean Bounded Slowdown   (b) Utilizaton   (c) Mean Response Time   (d) Mean Weighted Response Time

**Fig. 3.** Relative improvement of EXACT over USER-WALLTIME for different metrics. The subfigures have different scales. Utilization is a maximization objective while the others are minimization objectives.

The quantitative results in Fig. 3 demonstrate the importance of the selection of the objective function. If we study the bounded slowdown, having a perfect estimate of the walltime seems to improve the performance of the Ressources and Job Management Systems (RJMS) by almost 50% which seems remarkable. Utilization-wise, the performance only sees marginal performance improvement (approximately 0.5%). On the contrary, it seems that knowing in advance precisely the runtime of an application can be detrimental to the response time of the machine (approx. 7% decrease of performance for Mira), but it does not hold if we measure the weighted response time.

Going deeper into these figures, we want to talk about the variability of the performance. Indeed, this is particularly important: discussing the mean of an objective when the variability is highly variable is meaningless: it means that the performance is highly influenced by the workload used as input. This is the case for bounded slowdown (Fig. 3a), as well as the response time (Fig. 3c). We believe that this is because these objectives are highly influenced by the number of *small* jobs available in the input workload. **Hence, the mean Bounded slowdown and mean Response Time cannot be used as performance objectives for the evaluation of RJMS.**

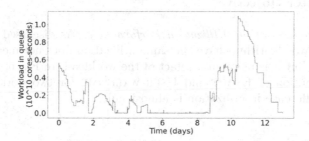

**Fig. 4.** Available work in the waiting queue as a function of time for one of workload sample from Mira when scheduled with the EXACT walltime function. This shows that the availability of jobs is not regular throughout the execution.

With respect to the utilization Fig. 3b, it seems that the improvement is extremely small (about 0.5%). As we explained in Sect. 2.2, this may not be surprising and is an artifact of the non-constant arrival rate (see Fig. 4). When there is a low utilization (and low arrival-rate), all jobs end-up being executed within the measured time-window even with poor packing quality. To demonstrate this, we plot in Fig. 5 the relative improvement of the utilization as a function of the Utilization of USER-WALLTIME.

The measured presented in Fig. 5 confirms our intuition: when the utilization is below 93% there is almost no utilization improvement, while for high-utilization periods (above 95% utilization), EXACT improves the system utilization by 1–2%. Of course above 95% utilization the gap available for improvement is extremely small, and it is hard to use this improvement to quantitatively compare several solutions (different algorithms or in this case the impact of better runtime estimates). This shows the limits of the utilization as an objective to compare two solutions.

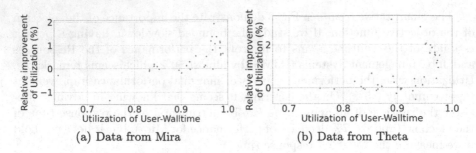

(a) Data from Mira                    (b) Data from Theta

**Fig. 5.** Relative improvement of the Utilization of EXACT over USER-WALLTIME as a function of the Utilization

> These elements underline the fact that simply looking at an objective function without further analysis is risky. We showed that one should not use the average bounded slowdown or average response time as an optimization objective to measure the performance of an HPC batch scheduling algorithm.

## Towards Better Objective

*Qualitative Analysis of the Utilization Performance.* As discussed in Sect. 2.2, the fact that two algorithms have the same utilization does not mean that they are equivalent but it is more an artefact of the workload. In Fig. 6, we show the density distribution of EXACT and USER-WALLTIME for two workloads where the relative difference in utilization is almost null.

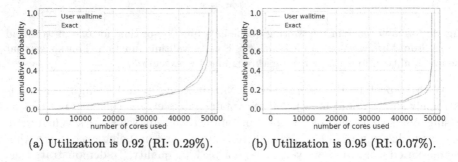

(a) Utilization is 0.92 (RI: 0.29%).     (b) Utilization is 0.95 (RI: 0.07%).

**Fig. 6.** Cumulative distribution functions of the utilization for two selected scenarios from Mira where the difference in utilization between EXACT and USER-WALLTIME is close to 0.

We observe from Fig. 6 that the solution that uses perfect estimation of wall-time functions has more scenarios with extremely low utilization and more with higher utilization. We interpret it as a better management of peaks of submissions, hence that the solution generally performs better job packing. This would be consistent with the fact that the algorithm using EXACT performs better in periods of very dense utilization (> 95%).

As a quantitative objective to be able to compare various algorithms, we propose to measure the standard deviation (std) of utilization. For two algorithm with identical utilization, high standard deviation imply large variation of utilization, that we correlate with more periods of high utilization and more periods of low utilization. We study the standard deviation of utilization in Fig. 7.

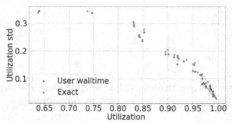

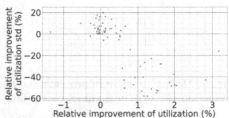

(a) Utilization and its standard deviation of each scenario for both algorithms (Mira Data).

(b) Relative improvement of the standard deviation of the utilization as a function of the relative improvement of the utilization (Mira and Theta data).

**Fig. 7.** Comparison of utilization and standard deviation of the utilization of EXACT and USER-WALLTIME

On Fig. 7, we have plotted the utilization of all workload inputs and their associated standard deviation, even if the ones that are interesting are the ones when the relative improvement of utilization is almost zero. In Fig. 7b we can see that when the relative improvement utilization difference is between $-0.5\%$ and $0.5\%$, the relative difference of the standard deviation of utilization can be up to 20%! This confirms the strong impact of using correct runtime estimates on the utilization of the platform and leaves a lot of room for other solutions.

*Qualitative Analysis of the Response time Performance.* We concluded earlier that the mean response time and mean average bounded slowdown are poor objectives to qualify a schedule because of their high variability. They can however be used to understand the quality of a schedule with respect to fairness to individual jobs: how can we analyze the impact of having a better runtime estimate?

To start this discussion, we remind that when looking at the *mean response time* as an optimization objective, the mean improvement of using a precise runtime estimate was almost null, and that it had high variability. While one could have concluded that improving the runtime estimate led to almost no change, we show how one could study this qualitatively here.

Figures 8, 9a and 9b plot the median relative improvement of response time, function of some job parameters: their execution time, their number of nodes, and the ratio Execution time over user-predicted Walltime ($t_i^{\text{estimate}}$). To create groups of jobs with a similar value for a parameter $A$, we take the interval

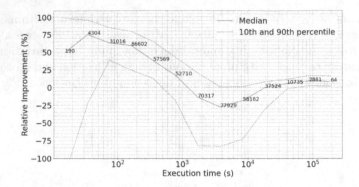

**Fig. 8.** Median Relative Improvement of the response time for Mira and Theta jobs as a function of $t^{\text{real}}$. The numbers on the blue line are the numbers of jobs in each group.

$[\min(A), \max(A)]$ and divide it in 18 subgroups of equal length after scaling, i.e.: when a geometric (resp. linear) scale is used for the x axis, it means that the interval $[\min(A), \max(A)]$ was divided in 18 groups of same size on a geometric (resp. linear) scale. We then only plot results of groups with more than 50 elements.

For example, the first figure splits the set of jobs into 18 groups of jobs with similar execution time (only 16 are displayed because 2 groups contain less than 50 jobs). The blue line corresponds to the median relative improvement of the mean response time over the 70 samples (30 from Mira and 40 from Theta).

The values printed on the blue line are the number of jobs in each group. The green dotted lines correspond to the first and last decile. When computing the median and the deciles, we did not take in account the samples of Mira and Theta for which the group was empty.

In Fig. 8 we observe that the impact of having a correct prediction is highly correlated to the job execution time. Specifically we observe three groups: short jobs, medium-length jobs and long jobs. When switching from USER-WALLTIME to EXACT:

– small jobs have a lower average response time when the precision of their runtime estimate improves EXACT;
– medium-length jobs have an increased average response time;
– longer jobs benefit of a little improvement of their response time.

Again, studying these objectives, one should be concerned about the extremely high variance of the performance.

With these precisions, one then can try to understand the impact of the solution. In this case we suppose that this is because of backfilling: medium-length jobs are less backfilled than they were when the runtime estimate of longer jobs is really wrong. On the contrary, small jobs are easier to backfill in small schedule gaps. Finally long jobs (which are almost never backfilled) benefit from the fact that fewer medium-lengthed take priority over them. We can verify this intuition by measuring the number of jobs that are indeed backfilled.

**Table 1.** Jobs backfilled with USER-WALLTIME and EXACT walltime functions in function of their runtime (Theta data). We removed the first and last 15% jobs as they are not used to compute response time.

|  | All | $Rt < 1e3$ | $1e3 < Rt < 2e4$ | $2e4 < Rt$ |
|---|---|---|---|---|
| Backfilled with USER-WALLTIME | 209230 (75%) | 115998 (82%) | 90357 (71%) | 2845 (26%) |
| Backfilled with EXACT | 199200 (71%) | 117652 (83%) | 80040 (63%) | 1479 (14%) |
| Number of jobs | 279990 | 141903 | 127218 | 10828 |

Table 1 investigates the correlation between jobs runtime and response time by comparing the number of backfilled jobs in the three categories identified on Fig. 8. We consider that a job $J$ is backfilled if and only if there is another job B which has a lower submission time than $J$ and starts after $J$ on at least one of the nodes $J$ used. The impact of EXACT walltime function is to reduce the number of medium and long backfilled jobs. The ratio of backfilled short jobs is almost the same, but the removal of the largest jobs permit the large improvement in response time observed in Fig. 8. Medium runtime jobs are thus negatively impacted by EXACT walltime function. Finally, even if they are twice less backfilled, the response time of long jobs is slightly decreased due to a better packing of EXACT.

Note, we believe that backfilling could also explain the high variance in response time improvement for job response-time: we expect that the $10^{\text{th}}$ percentile of small jobs with $RI < -100\%$ corresponds to jobs that are backfilled with USER-WALLTIME but not backfilled with EXACT. The thorough study of this behavior becomes out of the scope of this work: we try to focus on *how to* analyzing performance via the study of optimization objectives, however, if one was studying the impact of runtime estimates, this variability should be analyzed.

> We have showed that response time could be used to understand qualitatively the performance of a solution. Again, one should be careful about unexplained large variance in performance.

In Fig. 9, we evaluate the relative improvement of the response time as a function of the number of nodes of the jobs and as a function of the ratio execution time over runtime estimate (a ratio of one means that the users have predicted perfectly the length of their jobs, while a ratio of 0 means that they have done an extremely poor prediction).

Again, this figure shows how one can use the response time as a tool for qualitative analysis: in this case it seems that the relative improvement is not correlated to the number of nodes used by the jobs, except for very large jobs. The variability also decreases with larger jobs. However, unsurprisingly we can see that the worse the prediction of the user, the better the relative improvement.

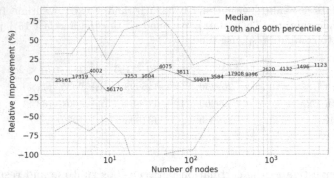

(a) Evolution of response time for jobs as a function of the Number of nodes (only Theta data)

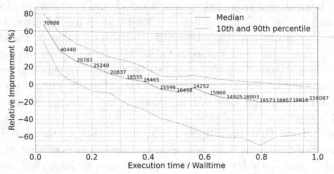

(b) Evolution of response time for jobs as a function of the ratio $t^{\text{real}}/t^{\text{estimate}}$

**Fig. 9.** Relative Improvement of EXACT over USER-WALLTIME of the response time (Mira and Theta data), as a function of some job parameters. The numbers on the blue line are the numbers of jobs in each group. (Color figure online)

---

This qualitative analysis confirms the theoretical limitations that we discussed in Section 2. Response time can be used for qualitative analysis by studying it on specific job parameters. We have also demonstrated how one can use the standard deviation of the utilization to differentiate to solutions that seems to have similar performances.

---

## 4    Related Work

The question of metrics in HPC Batch schedulers is addressed by Goponenko et al. [13]. They focus on the question of packing efficiency and fairness. They consider the metrics of unweighted average bounded slowdown, unweighted average response time, weighted average response time, and a last metric weighted by number of requested nodes that increases with the waiting time. Utilization is not considered as a metric but as a global objective for selecting a good metric.

They conclude in a poor interest of average bounded slowdown and unweighted average response time in terms of efficiency and fairness.

The choice of one or more metrics is driven by some general abstract objective, as quality of packing or fairness between users. Verma et al. [22] compares 4 metrics designed for packing efficiency including utilization. The other metrics are Hole filling, that count the number of unitary jobs that could have been added in holes of the schedule, workload inflation that increases the size of the workload until the limit of pending jobs is reached, and cluster compaction that reduces the number of nodes until the same limit. These metrics are compared for different criteria including accuracy and time for computation of the metric (the two last metrics imply the computation of multiple schedules).

Some other metrics have been used to measure the packing capacity of an algorithm. The loss of capacity is the name of two different metrics used to evaluate idle time while jobs are waiting. Leung et al. [15] use the loss of capacity to measure the capacity of improvement of the utilization, that is the average minimum between the number of nodes requested by pending jobs and the number of available nodes. Zhang et al. [25], use it to measure the average fraction of idle nodes when there are waiting jobs. Some authors [6,18] consider the mean response time and bounded slowdown for different categories of jobs based on their duration and number of requested nodes.

## 5    Conclusion

Evaluating correctly the performance of resource and job management systems is a major question that relies on many dimensions. With the generalization of black-box recommendation systems, being confident in the evaluation is a key research problem.

Tsafrir et al. [20,21] have discussed how one should generate workloads in order to evaluate correctly the impact of runtime estimates. In the line of their work, we discuss the objectives that one should consider in order to evaluate correctly the impact of runtime estimates on job schedulers.

In this work we were able to show that certain average objectives such as the mean bounded slowdown or mean response time should not be used as they are subject to too much variability depending on the input. We have discussed the limitation of the utilization for a given workload to compare different traces. Finally, we introduced a new optimization metric which can help inform about the quality of a schedule: the standard deviation of the utilization.

We used a specific use-case, runtime predictions, to show experimentally the limits of these objectives.

**Acknowledgment.** This work was supported in part by the French National Research Agency (ANR) in the frame of DASH (ANR-17-CE25-0004) and in part by the Inria Exploratory project REPAS.

# References

1. ALCF Public Data. https://reports.alcf.anl.gov/data/. This data was generated from resources of the Argonne Leadership Computing Facility, which is a DOE Office of Science User Facility supported under Contract DE-AC02-06CH11357. Accessed 08 Dec 2022
2. Top500. https://www.top500.org/
3. Bailey Lee, C., Schwartzman, Y., Hardy, J., Snavely, A.: Are user runtime estimates inherently inaccurate? In: Feitelson, D.G., Rudolph, L., Schwiegelshohn, U. (eds.) JSSPP 2004. LNCS, vol. 3277, pp. 253–263. Springer, Heidelberg (2005). https://doi.org/10.1007/11407522_14
4. Carastan-Santos, D., De Camargo, R.Y.: Obtaining dynamic scheduling policies with simulation and machine learning. In: Proceedings of the International Conference for High Performance Computing, Networking, Storage and Analysis, pp. 1–13 (2017)
5. Carastan-Santos, D., De Camargo, R. Y., Trystram, D., Zrigui, S.: One can only gain by replacing easy backfilling: a simple scheduling policies case study. In: 2019 19th IEEE/ACM International Symposium on Cluster, Cloud and Grid Computing (CCGRID), pp. 1–10. IEEE (2019)
6. Chiang, S.-H., Arpaci-Dusseau, A., Vernon, M.K.: The impact of more accurate requested runtimes on production job scheduling performance. In: Feitelson, D.G., Rudolph, L., Schwiegelshohn, U. (eds.) JSSPP 2002. LNCS, vol. 2537, pp. 103–127. Springer, Heidelberg (2002). https://doi.org/10.1007/3-540-36180-4_7
7. Du, Y., Marchal, L., Pallez, G., Robert, Y.: Doing better for jobs that failed: node stealing from a batch scheduler's perspective
8. Dutot, P.-F., Mercier, M., Poquet, M., Richard, O.: Batsim: a Realistic Language-Independent Resources and Jobs Management Systems Simulator. In: 20th Workshop on Job Scheduling Strategies for Parallel Processing (Chicago, United States, May 2016)
9. Fan, Y., et al.: DRAS: deep reinforcement learning for cluster scheduling in high performance computing. IEEE Trans. Parallel Distrib. Syst. **33**(12), 4903–4917 (2022)
10. Fan, Y., Rich, P., Allcock, W.E., Papka, M.E., Lan, Z.: Trade-off between prediction accuracy and underestimation rate in job runtime estimates. In: 2017 IEEE International Conference on Cluster Computing (CLUSTER), pp. 530–540. IEEE (2017)
11. Gainaru, A., Pallez, G.: Making speculative scheduling robust to incomplete data. In: 2019 IEEE/ACM 10th Workshop on Latest Advances in Scalable Algorithms for Large-Scale Systems (ScalA), pp. 62–71. IEEE (2019)
12. Gainaru, A., Pallez, G., Sun, H., Raghavan, P.: Speculative scheduling for stochastic HPC applications. In: Proceedings of the 48th International Conference on Parallel Processing, pp. 1–10 (2019)
13. Goponenko, A.V., Lamar, K., Peterson, C., Allan, B.A., Brandt, J.M., Dechev, D.: Metrics for packing efficiency and fairness of HPC cluster batch job scheduling. In: 2022 IEEE 34th International Symposium on Computer Architecture and High Performance Computing (SBAC-PAD), pp. 241–252 (2022)
14. Legrand, A., Trystram, D., Zrigui, S.: Adapting batch scheduling to workload characteristics: what can we expect from online learning? In: 2019 IEEE International Parallel and Distributed Processing Symposium (IPDPS), pp. 686–695. IEEE (2019)

15. Leung, V.J., Sabin, G., Sadayappan, P.: Parallel job scheduling policies to improve fairness: a case study. In: 2010 39th International Conference on Parallel Processing Workshops, pp. 346–353. IEEE (2010)
16. Mu'alem, A.W., Feitelson, D.G.: Utilization, predictability, workloads, and user runtime estimates in scheduling the IBM SP2 with backfilling. IEEE Trans. Parallel Distrib. Syst. **12**(6), 529–543 (2001)
17. Patel, T., Liu, Z., Kettimuthu, R., Rich, P., Allcock, W., Tiwari, D.: Job characteristics on large-scale systems: long-term analysis, quantification, and implications. In: SC20: International conference for high performance computing, networking, storage and analysis, pp. 1–17. IEEE (2020)
18. Perkovic, D., Keleher, P.J.: Randomization, speculation, and adaptation in batch schedulers. In: SC 2000: Proceedings of the 2000 ACM/IEEE Conference on Supercomputing, pp. 7–7. IEEE (2000)
19. Tang, W., Lan, Z., Desai, N., Buettner, D.: Fault-aware, utility-based job scheduling on Blue, Gene/P systems. In: 2009 IEEE International Conference on Cluster Computing and Workshops, pp. 1–10. IEEE (2009)
20. Tsafrir, D.: Using inaccurate estimates accurately. In: Frachtenberg, E., Schwiegelshohn, U. (eds.) JSSPP 2010. LNCS, vol. 6253, pp. 208–221. Springer, Heidelberg (2010). https://doi.org/10.1007/978-3-642-16505-4_12
21. Tsafrir, D., Etsion, Y., Feitelson, D.G.: Backfilling using system-generated predictions rather than user runtime estimates. IEEE Trans. Parallel Distrib. Syst. **18**(6), 789–803 (2007)
22. Verma, A., Korupolu, M., Wilkes, J.: Evaluating job packing in warehouse-scale computing. In: 2014 IEEE International Conference on Cluster Computing (CLUSTER), pp. 48–56, IEEE (2014)
23. D Zhang, D., Dai, D., He, Y., Bao, F.S., Xie, B.: RLScheduler: an automated HPC batch job scheduler using reinforcement learning. In: SC20: International Conference for High Performance Computing, Networking, Storage and Analysis, pp. 1–15. IEEE (2020)
24. Zhang, D., Dai, D., Xie, B.: SchedInspector: a batch job scheduling inspector using reinforcement learning. In: Proceedings of the 31st International Symposium on High-Performance Parallel and Distributed Computing (New York, NY, USA, 2022), HPDC, pp. 97–109. Association for Computing Machinery (2022)
25. Zhang, Y., Franke, H., Moreira, J.E., Sivasubramaniam, A.: Improving parallel job scheduling by combining gang scheduling and backfilling techniques. In: Proceedings 14th International Parallel and Distributed Processing Symposium. IPDPS 2000, pp. 133–142. IEEE (2000)

# An Experimental Analysis of Regression-Obtained HPC Scheduling Heuristics

Lucas Rosa[1] , Danilo Carastan-Santos[2] , and Alfredo Goldman[1]([⊠])

[1] Institute of Mathematics and Statistics, University of São Paulo, Sao Paulo, Brazil
`roses.lucas@usp.br,gold@ime.usp.br`
[2] University Grenoble Alpes, CNRS, Inria, Grenoble INP, LIG, Grenoble, France
`danilo.carastan-dos-santos@inria.fr`

**Abstract.** Scheduling jobs in High-Performance Computing (HPC) platforms typically involves heuristics consisting of job sorting functions such as First-Come-First-Served or custom (hand-engineered). Linear regression methods are promising for exploiting scheduling data to create simple and transparent heuristics with lesser computational overhead than state-of-the-art learning methods. The drawback is lesser scheduling performance. We experimentally investigated the hypothesis that we could increase the scheduling performance of regression-obtained heuristics by increasing the complexity of the sorting functions and exploiting derivative job features. We used multiple linear regression to develop a factory of scheduling heuristics based on scheduling data. This factory uses general polynomials of the jobs' characteristics as templates for the scheduling heuristics. We defined a set of polynomials with increasing complexity between them, and we used our factory to create scheduling heuristics based on these polynomials. We evaluated the performance of the obtained heuristics with wide-range simulation experiments using real-world traces from 1997 to 2016. Our results show that large-sized polynomials led to unstable scheduling heuristics due to multicollinearity effects in the regression, with small-sized polynomials leading to a stable and efficient scheduling performance. These results conclude that (i) multicollinearity imposes a constraint when one wants to derive new features (i.e., feature engineering) for creating scheduling heuristics with regression, and (ii) regression-obtained scheduling heuristics can be resilient to the long-term evolution of HPC platforms and workloads.

**Keywords:** Scheduling Heuristics · High Performance Computing · Machine Learning · Linear Regression

## 1 Introduction

In many fields of science and industry (climate, health, economics, artificial intelligence, *etc.*), High-Performance Computing (HPC) is an essential element to solve complex problems and to process the ever-increasing amount of data being

© The Author(s), under exclusive license to Springer Nature Switzerland AG 2023
D. Klusáček et al. (Eds.): JSSPP 2023, LNCS 14283, pp. 116–136, 2023.
https://doi.org/10.1007/978-3-031-43943-8_6

generated. Informally, HPC consists of utilizing highly parallel and distributed computing platforms. We have reached an extreme-scale of such platforms, with ranks such as the Top500 [21] listing supercomputers with millions of interconnected processors.

Among the many important problems that arise at such a scale, resource management is a critical problem that needs to be solved efficiently for a proper use of such platforms. Resource management involves assigning when and where HPC applications (hereafter referred to as jobs) will be processed in an HPC platform. HPC platform users (research groups, companies, *etc.*) submit their jobs to be processed at any given point, and limited information about the jobs is available for decision-making. This decision-making typically requires solving instances of a problem called online parallel job scheduling.

Despite the numerous theoretical advancements, the practical solution for online parallel job scheduling is typically based on scheduling heuristics that employ waiting queue sorting algorithms. The widely used algorithm is the First-Come-First-Served (FCFS) job ordering, alongside the utilization of backfilling algorithms [22]. One of possible reasons for this phenomenon is the explainability of the scheduling heuristics, which may be given by their simplicity. Waiting queue sorting heuristics are easy to understand by both the HPC platform maintainers and users, with FCFS ordering arguably being the easiest to understand. Regarding FCFS, this high level of explainability, comes with the drawback of poor scheduling performances [7].

Recent works [6,17] employ Machine Learning (ML) techniques to exploit simulation and platform workload data to create scheduling heuristics, as an attempt to encode scheduling knowledge obtained by ML with explainable and efficient scheduling heuristics. With this regard, regression methods [6] appear as a promising approach, since we can express scheduling knowledge in the form of simple features of the jobs' characteristics. The hypothesis of a trade-off between simplicity/performance is still present. We may need to sacrifice simplicity of the features to obtain better scheduling performances. Another underexplored concern is whether we need to readjust the regression-obtained heuristics as the platforms and jobs characteristics evolve.

Our work is a step towards clarifying this hypothesis by concerning the following research questions: *(i) By using regression methods to create scheduling heuristics, do we gain scheduling performance by using more complex features?* and *(ii) do regression-obtained heuristics provide stable scheduling performance over the evolution of HPC platforms and workloads?*

This work is a step forward from the work of Carastan-Santos and de Camargo [6]. We used the same methodology of exploiting simulations to gather scheduling knowledge, but extended it by creating a collection of scheduling heuristics based on empirical scheduling data. These heuristics rely on general polynomials of job characteristics as templates, which we hypothesize to be both efficient and more explainable in the scheduling context than the functions defined by Carastan-Santos and de Camargo.

We found a surprising result that multicollinearity – a phenomenon intrinsic to regression methods – may drastically degrade the scheduling performance of obtained scheduling heuristics constituted by complex, large-sized polynomials. A functional form constituted by a linear combination of the jobs' characteristics – the simplest and smallest of all polynomials evaluated – presented the best scheduling performances. More specifically, in this paper we present the following contributions:

- We performed an experimental study on how to obtain online parallel job scheduling policies in the form of polynomials of the jobs' characteristics. We adapted simulation and regression methods to evaluate a class of polynomials with increasing degrees of complexity. Our results indicate that multicollinearity effects may happen when using regression methods with high degree polynomials, leading to instability of the coefficients and inefficient scheduling performances.
- We showed experimental evidence that small-sized polynomials – a linear combination of the jobs' characteristics in our example – can lead to efficient scheduling heuristics in terms of the average bounded slowndown performance metric. We also showed that regression-obtained heuristics can be resilient to the long-term evolution of HPC platforms and workloads without needing to be readjusted over time.

We organized the remaining of this paper as follows: in Sect. 2, we present an overview of related works, and in Sect. 3 some preliminary definitions of online parallel job scheduling. We present our methodology in Sect. 4 and our experimental results in Sect. 5. Lastly, in Sect. 6, we present our concluding remarks and future works. The code base for this paper is openly available at a Github repository[1].

## 2   Related Work

**Scheduling in Theory.** The research community studied the parallel job scheduling problem under a general problem called multiple-strip packing problem [4]. Given a set of rectangles (jobs) and set of strips (set of computing resources), the objective is to find a packing of the rectangles into the strips, that minimizes the height among the used strips. Such a problem in the single-strip case is already NP-hard [4]. Many theoretical works [5,16,27,28,30] proposed approximation algorithms and performance bounds, but many of these works relied on analytically tractable objective metrics such as makespan (i.e., the completion time of the last finishing job). Makespan is arguably less relevant in the online case, when compared to metrics such as waiting time or slowdown (see Sect. 4), since we do not have information about a "last job" in an online scheduling configuration.

---

[1] https://github.com/fredgrub/scheduling-simulator.

**Scheduling in Practice: Scheduling Heuristics.** In online parallel job scheduling, many works explore list scheduling [23] based algorithms that rely on waiting queue ordering heuristics. These heuristics can be created by hand-engineering methods [25], and by tuning methods [17,18], that forecast possible outcomes of a certain heuristic.

It is long known [12], however, that most practitioners employ First-Come-First-Served (FCFS) based heuristics with a backfilling [22] mechanism, or arbitrary job prioritization, using for instance multiple queue priorities [24]. A possible explanation for the popularity of FCFS-based heuristics is the fact that FCFS is (i) easily understandable by both practitioners and users and (ii) it offers desirable properties such as no-starvation (i.e., every job will eventually execute).

**Machine Learning in Scheduling.** Machine Learning (ML) is used in the context of online job scheduling mainly in two scenarios: (i) to improve scheduling by predicting the jobs' characteristics [14,19,31], and (ii) to create novel heuristics by using techniques such as non-linear regression [6] and evolutionary [17] strategies. More recently, deep reinforcement learning methods [10,29] are being explored to perform online job scheduling.

Legrand *et al.* [17] explored a larger class of mixed policies by combining various features extracted from the jobs in a linear expression, and by determining optimal weights for each feature. On the other hand, Carastan-Santos and de Camargo [6] introduced regression methods to derive clear and interpretable scheduling heuristics.

Our work goes beyond the approach of Carastan-Santos and de Camargo. While their heuristics relied on features based on terms such as square roots and logarithms, which can be challenging to interpret in the context of scheduling, our work is based on a functional form generation procedure that creates heuristics using simple polynomials of the job characteristics. This approach takes into account increasing levels of complexity and derivative features.

## 3   Background

### 3.1   Online Parallel Job Scheduling

In a usual HPC platform, users submit their applications at any given moment to be processed. The resource and job management system (RJMS) manages both the applications and platform resources [15]. The RJMS registers information about the jobs in a log file, often shared using the *Standard Workload Format* (SWF) [13]. Moreover, the online parallel job scheduling problem is a key issue that the RJMS must address in order to effectively manage platform resources and applications.

The online parallel job scheduling problem involves the decision-making process of determining the optimal time and machine allocation to process parallel jobs, which arrive at any given time, on a set of $n$ homogeneous machines that are connected by an arbitrary interconnection topology. The primary goal of this decision-making process is to maximize performance objective(s) related to the efficient utilization of platform resources.

A job, denoted by $j$, is commonly described as a workload with specific data, including (i) the estimated processing time of the job ($\tilde{p}_j$), typically provided by the user, (ii) the number of processors required to execute the job ($q_j$), and (iii) the time at which the job was submitted to the platform ($r_j$, also known as the release time). This characterization of jobs is often used in scheduling algorithms, where jobs are treated as independent entities requiring fixed amounts of resources for processing.

Another important piece of information that is only available after finishing a job $j$ is its actual processing time ($p_j$). The estimation of the processing time $\tilde{p}_j$ usually works as an upper bound of the actual processing time $p_j$. We also consider that the number of processors $q_j$ is fixed and can not change over time (also referred to as rigid jobs).

## 3.2   Scheduling Policies and Backfilling

The order in which the jobs are submitted for processing is often determined by a *scheduling policy*, which is a crucial component of many online parallel job scheduling heuristics. A scheduling policy typically consists of a job sorting function $f(j)$, that takes as input the characteristics of a job $j$ (e.g., $\tilde{p}_j$, $q_j$, and $r_j$), and outputs a number that quantifies the priority of processing $j$. The lower the value of $f(j)$, the more priority a job $j$ has. Ideally, the decision-making process applies $f(j)$ to all jobs in the waiting queue to set their execution priorities in two events: (i) when a new job arrives in the waiting queue and (ii) when one or more processors are released and become available.

On top of a scheduling policy, often a *backfilling* [22] mechanism is applied. Informally, backfilling mechanisms allow a job $j$ to be selected for processing earlier – and breaking the priority order defined by the scheduling policy – if $j$ does not delay the processing of jobs with higher priority. Backfilling is known to consistently bring positive performance effects, regardless of the scheduling policy [7], and it is widely used by practitioners, in conjunction with the First-Come-First-Served (FCFS, $f(j) = r_j$) scheduling policy.

## 3.3   Scheduling Performance Metric

In this work we adopt the average bounded slowdown (AVGbsld) as the scheduling performance metric. Given a job $j$, its bounded slowdown (bsld) value can be computed as follows

$$\text{bsld}_j = \max \left\{ \frac{w_j + p_j}{\max(p_j, \tau)}, 1 \right\} \tag{1}$$

where $w_j$ is the time that a job waited for processing since its submission and $\tau$ is a constant that is typically set in the order of $10\,\text{s}$, that prevents small jobs from having excessively large slowdown values. The average bounded slowdown takes into account the slowdown average for a set of jobs $J$ and is defined as

$$\text{AVGbsld}(J) = \frac{1}{|J|} \sum_{j \in J} \max \left\{ \frac{w_j + p_j}{\max(p_j, \tau)}, 1 \right\} \qquad (2)$$

AVGbsld is an interesting metric in the sense that it can express the expectation that the waiting time of the jobs should be proportional of their processing time [11], though this metric is more sensible to small jobs (i.e., jobs with small $p$ and $q$ values). AVGbsld is also a hard objective to be treated theoretically in online parallel job scheduling, and it is in practice mainly manageable by heuristics.

## 4    Experimental Procedure

As previously mentioned, we have adapted the method proposed by Carastan-Santos and Camargo [6] in our work. We retained their approach of acquiring scheduling knowledge through simulations of sets of jobs executed under different conditions, represented by an approximate scheduling problem, termed as *proxy scheduling problem*, similar yet simpler than online parallel job scheduling. However, we have made modifications to the models defined in the regression step. We incorporated the knowledge obtained from the simulations into a multiple linear regression model and transformed this knowledge into polynomial functions capable of determining the priority of the jobs in the queue based on their characteristics. Our main hypothesis is that these functions represent effective scheduling policies for the online parallel job scheduling problem.

### 4.1    Simulation Strategy

The proxy scheduling problem differs from the online parallel job scheduling problem (described in Sect. 3) in a few key ways. First, the proxy problem have access to perfect information about the job processing time (i.e., $\tilde{p}_j = p_j$). Second, the proxy problem is an offline scheduling problem, which means that all the information regarding the jobs' characteristics, including $p$, $q$, and $r$, is known in advance. Finally, the number of jobs arriving in the proxy problem is finite. The purpose of defining this simplified scheduling problem is to enable quick simulations that are similar to the target problem.

We define a proxy scheduling problem as the scheduling of a set of jobs $Q$ in an HPC platform with $m$ interconnected processors, while another set of jobs $S$ is currently being processed. This configuration models the waiting queue ($Q$) and the initial state of the platform ($S$). Job sets $S$ and $Q$ are generated from a job log file, or trace, denoted by $N$. A subtrace $M \subset N$, consisting of $|S| + |Q|$ jobs, is randomly selected from $N$, where the first $|S|$ jobs from $M$ belong to $S$ and the remaining $|Q|$ jobs from $M$ belong to $Q$.

For a pair of sets of jobs $(S, Q)$, we start the simulation by submitting the jobs from the set $S$ in FCFS order. When the last job of $S$ is submitted, jobs from $S$ may still be processing in the platform, thus representing a possible initial state. At this point we start branching the simulation, with different branch (also referred in the text as *trials*) representing a possible way to schedule the jobs in $Q$.

We proceed by randomly generating permutations $Q^*$ of the set $Q$, where each $Q^*$ is a simulation branch. For each permutation $Q^*$, we simulate the scheduling of the jobs in $Q$ in the order specified by $Q^*$. It is important to note that the number of possible permutations of $Q$ grows exponentially with the size of $Q$, and the number of sample permutations required to adequately represent the permutation space increases rapidly as well. The use of a proxy scheduling problem, as discussed previously, is necessary to ensure that this simulation branching strategy can be executed within a feasible amount of time for a fixed and small number of jobs in $Q$, as detailed in Sect. 5.

With $\mathcal{P}$ being the set containing all sampled permutations, when the scheduling simulation of all branches end, we compute and assign a score for each job $j \in Q$:

$$score(j) = \frac{\sum_{Q_j^* \in \mathcal{P}(j_0=j)} \text{AVGbsld}(Q_j^*)}{\sum_{Q_k^* \in \mathcal{P}} \text{AVGbsld}(Q_k^*)} \tag{3}$$

The score represents the impact of scheduling a job $j \in Q$ first (represented by $j_0$ in Eq. 3), in terms of the average bounded slowdown of all jobs in $Q$. Jobs with lower *score* values can have a positive impact on the overall average slowdown when they are executed first. We conjecture that with an initial state represented by the scheduling of the jobs in $S$, sorting the jobs in $Q$ in increasing order of score$(j)$ results in an efficient schedule regarding the AVGbsld$(Q)$ (Eq. 2).

To generate a distribution of scores, denoted as $score(p, q, r)$, we replicated the aforementioned simulation strategy with multiple samples of job set pairs $(S, Q)$. This distribution represents the primary outcome of the simulations. The idea is that the scheduler of an HPC system could prioritize a job from the queue with the smallest $score(p, q, r)$ value for the corresponding $(p, q, r)$ values.

## 4.2   Creating Regression-Based Scheduling Heuristics

Regression methods can be employed on the scores distribution to obtain a more generalized and smoother representation. This representation is in the form of functions that can be used to prioritize jobs on an HPC platform. Carastan-Santos and de Camargo's approach utilized features such as square roots and logarithms, which can be difficult to interpret in the context of scheduling. In contrast, the approach proposed in this work explores polynomial-based functions.

Let $J$ denote the set of all jobs present in the scores distribution, and let $score(j)$ be the computed value of score for each job $j \in J$. The problem at hand is to determine functions $f(p_j, q_j, r_j)$ that provide an accurate approximation of the score values for all jobs in $J$. To accomplish this, we have modified the original strategy proposed by Carastan-Santos and de Camargo [6]. Specifically, we have defined a family of functions $\mathcal{F}$, consisting of parametrized functions of the form:

$$f(\theta, \mathbf{x}) = \theta^T \mathbf{x} \qquad (4)$$

where $\theta$ is a parameter vector, and $\mathbf{x}$ is the features vector of the jobs' characteristics $p$, $q$ and $r$.

**Table 1.** Features of the four parametrized functions used in multiple linear regression.

| Vector components | Vector $\mathbf{x}$ | | | |
|---|---|---|---|---|
| | Lin | Qdr | Cub | Qua |
| $(1, p, q, r)$ | ✓ | ✓ | ✓ | ✓ |
| $(p^2, q^2, r^2, pq)$ | | ✓ | ✓ | ✓ |
| $(p^3, q^3, r^3, p^2q, pq^2)$ | | | ✓ | ✓ |
| $(p^4, q^4, r^4, p^3q, p^2q^2, pq^3)$ | | | | ✓ |

We have defined a function family comprising four functions, whose vectors $\mathbf{x}$ are displayed in Table 1. Each function works as a template for deriving the scheduling heuristics, and each element in the vectors (also known as basis functions) are monomials of the jobs' characteristics.

The function Lin is just a linear combination of the jobs' characteristics $p$, $q$ and $r$. The others Qdr, Cub and Qua are functions that progressively increase the degree of the basis functions, and with multiplicative factors related to $pq$, which is often referred in the literature as the area of the jobs. We considered derivative factors that correspond to well-known scheduling policies, notably the First-Come First-Served (FCFS = $r$), Shortest Processing Time first (SPT = $p$), Shortest Number of Processors First (SQF = $q$), and Shortest Area First (SAF = $pq$). We chose these functions for the following reasons:

- Our intention was to avoid possible non-linearity between the parameters, which allows us to use multiple linear regression, in which a least squares minimization algorithm can provide optimal parameters $\theta$ with regards to the sum of squared loss (see Eq. 5).
- We wanted to evaluate the effectiveness of using multiple regression to develop scheduling heuristics for functions of varying complexity. Thus, we have defined a limited collection of polynomials that exhibit significant variation in complexity among them.
- We sought to use more easily understandable terms in the scheduling sense, as opposed to the more complex terms that were used in [6], such as square roots and logarithms. Additionally, we aimed to avoid using job characteristic polynomials with unconventional degrees (such as 0.5 for square root, -0.5 for inverse square root, or 1.5), and combinations of job characteristics that do not correspond to a known scheduling heuristic (such as derivative features of $pr$ or $qr$).

– We wanted to evaluate the effects of derivative features of $p$, $q$ and $r$ and the area (see explanation below) $pq$, with increasing degrees of penalization for their values.

We employ a weighted multiple linear regression [8] procedure, which minimizes the weighted sum of squared loss function:

$$\Sigma_{\text{wL}} = \sum_{j \in J} \left[ (p_j q_j) \cdot (f(\theta, \mathbf{x}) - \text{score}(j)) \right]^2 \tag{5}$$

The weight $(p_j q_j)$ emphasizes that the approximation must perform a good estimation of the score of large area jobs (i.e., jobs with $p$ and $q$ large), as they can end up blocking the execution of small jobs, degrading the overall scheduling performance.

After obtaining the coefficients $\hat{\theta}^f$ from the multiple linear regression approximation for all functions $f(\theta, \mathbf{x}) \in \mathcal{F}$, we can measure the approximation quality through the *Mean Absolute Error* function (MAE, Eq. 6).

$$\text{MAE}(f) = \frac{1}{|J|} \sum_{j \in J} \| f(\hat{\theta}^{\mathbf{f}}, \mathbf{x}) - \text{score}(j) \| \tag{6}$$

## 5    Results and Discussion

In this section, we present the main results of our research. Firstly, we generated three distributions of scores by employing the simulation strategy presented in Sect. 4.1. The traces were derived from one synthetic and two real-world workloads. Subsequently, we performed multiple linear regression to obtain the optimal parameters for the polynomial functions, taking into account the different score distributions. Finally, we analyzed the relationship between the size of the polynomials and the scheduling effectiveness, as well as the robustness of the regression-obtained heuristics over the long term.

### 5.1    Simulation-Based Approach for Extracting Scheduling Knowledge

To generate the scores distribution, we considered an HPC platform composed by homogeneous processors, simulated using the SimGrid [9] simulation framework. The traces used to construct the characteristics of the jobs, both synthetic and real-world, were obtained from the Parallel Workloads Archive [13]. Finally, we employed sets of 16 and 32 jobs for the sets $S$ and $Q$, respectively.

To construct the synthetic workload, we used the Lublin and Feitelson [20] model (with 256 nodes), which is capable of representing the geometry of jobs ($p$ and $q$) as well as including a daily cycle arrival pattern. Additionally, we utilized the Cornell Theory Center (CTC) IBM SP2 log, which contains 11 months of records from the 512-node IBM SP2, and the San Diego Supercomputer Center (SDSC) Blue Horizon log, a 144-node IBM SP covering over two years of production use.

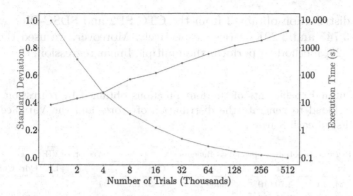

**Fig. 1.** The figure, adapted from [6], shows, in red, the normalized standard deviations of the trial score distributions obtained with different numbers of trials, and in blue, the execution time in the chosen instance in logarithmic scale.

**Table 2.** Mean Absolute Error (MAE) of the functions for the different workloads used in the training step.

| Functions | MAEs | | |
|---|---|---|---|
| | Synthetic | CTC-SP2 | SDSC-Blue |
| Lin | $4.5 \cdot 10^{-3}$ | $3.6 \cdot 10^{-3}$ | $12.1 \cdot 10^{-3}$ |
| Qdr | $4.5 \cdot 10^{-3}$ | $3.7 \cdot 10^{-3}$ | $13.9 \cdot 10^{-3}$ |
| Cub | $5.4 \cdot 10^{-3}$ | $5.9 \cdot 10^{-3}$ | $3.3 \cdot 10^{-3}$ |
| Qua | $7.2 \cdot 10^{-3}$ | $36.2 \cdot 10^{-3}$ | $14.8 \cdot 10^{-3}$ |

The simulations were carried out on an Amazon EC2 instance equipped with a second-generation AMD EPYC 7002 processor that can reach up to 3.3 GHz frequencies, 8 virtual CPU cores, and 16GB of RAM. In obtaining the scores distribution, we had to determine the maximum number of trials we could execute with a pair $(S, Q)$ on this instance. This was necessary to achieve a balance between precision in calculating the scores distributions and efficient execution time.

Figure 1 illustrates the normalized standard deviation of calculating the scores as a function of the number of trials and the corresponding processing times for one pair $(S, Q)$ executed on the instance. After considering these factors, we decided to use 256 thousand trials as it provided accurate calculations of the scores distribution within an acceptable processing time and budget.

## 5.2 Does the Effectiveness of Regression-Based Scheduling Heuristics Increases as a Function of Polynomial Size?

To address this question, we employed multiple linear regression to compute the optimal parameters of the heuristics derived from the model functions for various score distributions. The synthetic score distribution encompasses 14,081 job characteristics linked to their corresponding score values. On the other hand, the distribution obtained from the CTC SP2 and SDSC-Blue workloads comprises 3,745 and 3,201 entries, respectively. Moreover, we used the SciPy's `curve_fit` [26] method to perform the multiple linear regression.

**Table 3.** Optimal coefficients of the four functions obtained by regression using the synthetic workload to generate the distribution of scores and the Variance Inflation Factors (VIFs) of each feature.

| Coefficients | Regression-obtained optimal coefficients | | | | Vector $x$ | VIF | | | |
|---|---|---|---|---|---|---|---|---|---|
| | Lin | Qdr | Cub | Qua | | Lin | Qdr | Cub | Qua |
| $\theta_0$ | $3.24 \cdot 10^{-2}$ | $3.70 \cdot 10^{-2}$ | $3.33 \cdot 10^{-2}$ | $4.83 \cdot 10^{-2}$ | $1$ | – | – | – | – |
| $\theta_1$ | $1.15 \cdot 10^{-7}$ | $2.65 \cdot 10^{-7}$ | $2.83 \cdot 10^{-7}$ | $-6.42 \cdot 10^{-7}$ | $p$ | 1.3 | 3.7 | 12.1 | 36.1 |
| $\theta_2$ | $2.61 \cdot 10^{-5}$ | $-3.05 \cdot 10^{-5}$ | $8.71 \cdot 10^{-5}$ | $-2.40 \cdot 10^{-4}$ | $q$ | 1.3 | 9.6 | 35.5 | 99.0 |
| $\theta_3$ | $-1.57 \cdot 10^{-7}$ | $-3.96 \cdot 10^{-7}$ | $-5.83 \cdot 10^{-7}$ | $-6.50 \cdot 10^{-7}$ | $r$ | 1.2 | 6.0 | 21.8 | 58.6 |
| $\theta_4$ | – | $-3.04 \cdot 10^{-12}$ | $-6.33 \cdot 10^{-14}$ | $1.66 \cdot 10^{-11}$ | $p^2$ | – | 2.6 | 41.8 | 338.5 |
| $\theta_5$ | – | $1.17 \cdot 10^{-7}$ | $-5.06 \cdot 10^{-7}$ | $2.41 \cdot 10^{-6}$ | $q^2$ | – | 8.3 | 275.0 | 2835.5 |
| $\theta_6$ | – | $2.75 \cdot 10^{-12}$ | $6.78 \cdot 10^{-12}$ | $8.81 \cdot 10^{-12}$ | $r^2$ | – | 4.8 | 82.1 | 620.8 |
| $\theta_7$ | – | $6.77 \cdot 10^{-10}$ | $-6.02 \cdot 10^{-10}$ | $1.14 \cdot 10^{-8}$ | $pq$ | – | 3.9 | 49.4 | 295.3 |
| $\theta_8$ | – | – | $-7.55 \cdot 10^{-18}$ | $-2.03 \cdot 10^{-16}$ | $p^3$ | – | – | 20.8 | 961.6 |
| $\theta_9$ | – | – | $7.05 \cdot 10^{-10}$ | $-9.52 \cdot 10^{-9}$ | $q^3$ | – | – | 147.3 | 10491.8 |
| $\theta_{10}$ | – | – | $-2.14 \cdot 10^{-17}$ | $-4.67 \cdot 10^{-17}$ | $r^3$ | – | – | 34.6 | 1387.1 |
| $\theta_{11}$ | – | – | $-2.72 \cdot 10^{-14}$ | $9.29 \cdot 10^{-15}$ | $p^2q$ | – | – | 9.8 | 393.1 |
| $\theta_{12}$ | – | – | $9.52 \cdot 10^{-12}$ | $-7.94 \cdot 10^{-11}$ | $pq^2$ | – | – | 30.1 | 1032.9 |
| $\theta_{13}$ | – | – | – | $9.34 \cdot 10^{-22}$ | $p^4$ | – | – | – | 322.7 |
| $\theta_{14}$ | – | – | – | $1.36 \cdot 10^{-11}$ | $q^4$ | – | – | – | 3572.5 |
| $\theta_{15}$ | – | – | – | $9.84 \cdot 10^{-23}$ | $r^4$ | – | – | – | 373.6 |
| $\theta_{16}$ | – | – | – | $-9.07 \cdot 10^{-19}$ | $p^3q$ | – | – | – | 63.8 |
| $\theta_{17}$ | – | – | – | $1.89 \cdot 10^{-16}$ | $p^2q^2$ | – | – | – | 125.0 |
| $\theta_{18}$ | – | – | – | $1.55 \cdot 10^{-13}$ | $pq^3$ | – | – | – | 457.2 |

The mean absolute error (MAE) values obtained by the multiple linear regression for the heuristics Lin, Qdr, Cub, and Qua are reported in Table 2. It can be observed that the MAE values are relatively small and close to each other for the same function, regardless of the workload used. This shows that the functions appropriately describe the distribution of scores used to build the models.

Furthermore, the optimal coefficients of the heuristics obtained by regression for each of the functions are illustrated in Tables 3, 4 and 5. However, we observed instabilities in the features' coefficients of Qdr, Cub, and Qua. These instabilities were observed through changes in the sign of the coefficients of a particular feature, which carry implications for job scheduling. In the case of synthetic workload, the Lin function prioritizes jobs with lower $q$ values (positive coefficients), whereas the Qdr function prioritizes jobs with higher $q$ values (negative coefficients).

For Lin, the positive coefficient for $q$ is expected to be beneficial for the schedule, as it is associated with the Smaller Number of Processors First (SQF) scheduling policy which has been reported to improve scheduling performance

**Table 4.** Optimal coefficients of the four functions obtained by regression using the CTC-SP2 workload to generate the distribution of scores and the Variance Inflation Factors (VIFs) of each feature.

| Coefficients | Regression-obtained optimal coefficients | | | | Vector $x$ | VIF | | | |
|---|---|---|---|---|---|---|---|---|---|
| | Lin | Qdr | Cub | Qua | | Lin | Qdr | Cub | Qua |
| $\theta_0$ | $3.11 \cdot 10^{-2}$ | $2.86 \cdot 10^{-2}$ | $2.42 \cdot 10^{-2}$ | $6.09 \cdot 10^{-2}$ | 1 | – | – | – | – |
| $\theta_1$ | $3.00 \cdot 10^{-8}$ | $2.00 \cdot 10^{-7}$ | $1.18 \cdot 10^{-6}$ | $-3.13 \cdot 10^{-6}$ | $p$ | 1.3 | 17.2 | 85.7 | 282.4 |
| $\theta_2$ | $5.42 \cdot 10^{-5}$ | $2.27 \cdot 10^{-5}$ | $-1.72 \cdot 10^{-4}$ | $8.73 \cdot 10^{-5}$ | $q$ | 1.1 | 5.5 | 18.6 | 43.2 |
| $\theta_3$ | $-6.41 \cdot 10^{-8}$ | $1.81 \cdot 10^{-7}$ | $-1.37 \cdot 10^{-8}$ | $-2.40 \cdot 10^{-6}$ | $r$ | 1.4 | 9.2 | 31.6 | 79.4 |
| $\theta_4$ | – | $-3.14 \cdot 10^{-12}$ | $-3.50 \cdot 10^{-11}$ | $1.42 \cdot 10^{-10}$ | $p^2$ | – | 15.2 | 483.3 | 5148.2 |
| $\theta_5$ | – | $-2.08 \cdot 10^{-8}$ | $1.66 \cdot 10^{-6}$ | $-8.57 \cdot 10^{-6}$ | $q^2$ | – | 4.1 | 114.1 | 709.1 |
| $\theta_6$ | – | $-4.19 \cdot 10^{-12}$ | $4.57 \cdot 10^{-12}$ | $1.86 \cdot 10^{-10}$ | $r^2$ | – | 7.2 | 141.9 | 972.4 |
| $\theta_7$ | – | $8.50 \cdot 10^{-10}$ | $3.89 \cdot 10^{-9}$ | $1.49 \cdot 10^{-8}$ | $pq$ | – | 1.5 | 23.7 | 215.7 |
| $\theta_8$ | – | – | $2.97 \cdot 10^{-16}$ | $-2.46 \cdot 10^{-15}$ | $p^3$ | – | – | 201.3 | 11733.9 |
| $\theta_9$ | – | – | $-3.91 \cdot 10^{-9}$ | $6.03 \cdot 10^{-8}$ | $q^3$ | – | – | 60.4 | 2059.7 |
| $\theta_{10}$ | – | – | $-1.02 \cdot 10^{-16}$ | $-4.92 \cdot 10^{-15}$ | $r^3$ | – | – | 62.4 | 2016.0 |
| $\theta_{11}$ | – | – | $-3.33 \cdot 10^{-14}$ | $-6.88 \cdot 10^{-13}$ | $p^2q$ | – | – | 16.6 | 844.4 |
| $\theta_{12}$ | – | – | $-6.33 \cdot 10^{-12}$ | $2.37 \cdot 10^{-10}$ | $pq^2$ | – | – | 9.1 | 339.8 |
| $\theta_{13}$ | – | – | – | $1.47 \cdot 10^{-20}$ | $p^4$ | – | – | – | 2784.2 |
| $\theta_{14}$ | – | – | – | $-1.12 \cdot 10^{-10}$ | $q^4$ | – | – | – | 617.3 |
| $\theta_{15}$ | – | – | – | $4.07 \cdot 10^{-20}$ | $r^4$ | – | – | – | 474.2 |
| $\theta_{16}$ | – | – | – | $6.11 \cdot 10^{-18}$ | $p^3q$ | – | – | – | 378.6 |
| $\theta_{17}$ | – | – | – | $-7.14 \cdot 10^{-16}$ | $p^2q^2$ | – | – | – | 99.5 |
| $\theta_{18}$ | – | – | – | $-9.75 \cdot 10^{-13}$ | $pq^3$ | – | – | – | 69.9 |

compared to the First Come First Serve (FCFS) policy [7]. For Qdr, the negative coefficient for $q$ is likely to have a detrimental effect on the scheduling, since it is linked to the Largest Number of Processors First (LQF) policy which has been shown to cause worse scheduling performance than FCFS, and is thus often disregarded in scheduling policy research [7,17].

Figure 2 demonstrates the impact of varying the values of $p$ and $q$ on the normalized *score* values of the functions Lin, Qdr, Cub and Qua, while holding $r$ constant, in order to illustrate these instabilities. Darker regions in the figure indicate higher job priorities. The behavior of all functions is distinct, independent of the type of workload considered. The Lin function prioritizes jobs with lower values of $p$ and $q$, which is similar to the Shortest Area First (SAF) scheduling policy, widely known for its efficiency [7]. The Qdr, Cub, and Qua functions give varying degrees of priority to certain regions that are less interpretable.

To assess the effectiveness of the obtained functions as scheduling policies, we conducted simulations of parallel job scheduling with the same workload used in the score distribution generation, enabling us to gain deeper insights into the capabilities of these functions. From the workloads, we selected a subtrace consisting of a fifteen-day (15) job submission. The output of the scheduling experiments is the average bounded slowdown (Eq. 2). Moreover, to enable a meaningful comparison, we included established scheduling policies, according to Table 6, alongside the obtained functions.

**Table 5.** Optimal coefficients of the four functions obtained by regression using the SDSC-Blue workload to generate the distribution of scores and the Variance Inflation Factors (VIFs) of each feature.

| Coefficients | Regression-obtained optimal coefficients | | | | Vector $x$ | VIF | | | |
| --- | --- | --- | --- | --- | --- | --- | --- | --- | --- |
| | Lin | Qdr | Cub | Qua | | Lin | Qdr | Cub | Qua |
| $\theta_0$ | $1.83 \cdot 10^{-2}$ | $1.39 \cdot 10^{-2}$ | $3.34 \cdot 10^{-2}$ | $2.27 \cdot 10^{-2}$ | $1$ | – | – | – | – |
| $\theta_1$ | $8.88 \cdot 10^{-8}$ | $-1.47 \cdot 10^{-7}$ | $5.97 \cdot 10^{-8}$ | $1.58 \cdot 10^{-6}$ | $p$ | 1.1 | 8.1 | 32.3 | 81.2 |
| $\theta_2$ | $3.05 \cdot 10^{-5}$ | $-8.40 \cdot 10^{-5}$ | $3.09 \cdot 10^{-5}$ | $1.07 \cdot 10^{-4}$ | $q$ | 1.1 | 5.3 | 22.9 | 53.1 |
| $\theta_3$ | $-6.87 \cdot 10^{-8}$ | $-4.02 \cdot 10^{-7}$ | $-4.79 \cdot 10^{-7}$ | $-1.77 \cdot 10^{-6}$ | $r$ | 1.2 | 5.4 | 15.3 | 39.6 |
| $\theta_4$ | – | $5.59 \cdot 10^{-14}$ | $1.79 \cdot 10^{-12}$ | $-4.00 \cdot 10^{-11}$ | $p^2$ | – | 6.7 | 175.1 | 1479.2 |
| $\theta_5$ | – | $6.92 \cdot 10^{-8}$ | $-1.02 \cdot 10^{-7}$ | $-1.91 \cdot 10^{-7}$ | $q^2$ | – | 4.6 | 140.6 | 1109.7 |
| $\theta_6$ | – | $5.77 \cdot 10^{-12}$ | $1.12 \cdot 10^{-11}$ | $1.04 \cdot 10^{-10}$ | $r^2$ | – | 4.6 | 59.1 | 393.1 |
| $\theta_7$ | – | $5.50 \cdot 10^{-10}$ | $-6.67 \cdot 10^{-10}$ | $-6.55 \cdot 10^{-9}$ | $pq$ | – | 1.7 | 28.2 | 164.2 |
| $\theta_8$ | – | – | $-1.51 \cdot 10^{-17}$ | $3.93 \cdot 10^{-16}$ | $p^3$ | – | – | 79.7 | 3719.5 |
| $\theta_9$ | – | – | $7.15 \cdot 10^{-11}$ | $1.21 \cdot 10^{-10}$ | $q^3$ | – | – | 73.6 | 4177.1 |
| $\theta_{10}$ | – | – | $-9.27 \cdot 10^{-17}$ | $-2.26 \cdot 10^{-15}$ | $r^3$ | – | – | 26.3 | 704.1 |
| $\theta_{11}$ | – | – | $-6.38 \cdot 10^{-16}$ | $1.25 \cdot 10^{-13}$ | $p^2 q$ | – | – | 13.1 | 465.1 |
| $\theta_{12}$ | – | – | $1.08 \cdot 10^{-12}$ | $4.03 \cdot 10^{-12}$ | $pq^2$ | – | – | 8.2 | 453.6 |
| $\theta_{13}$ | – | – | – | $-1.28 \cdot 10^{-21}$ | $p^4$ | – | – | – | 987.8 |
| $\theta_{14}$ | – | – | – | $-1.49 \cdot 10^{-14}$ | $q^4$ | – | – | – | 1462.3 |
| $\theta_{15}$ | – | – | – | $1.50 \cdot 10^{-20}$ | $r^4$ | – | – | – | 156.1 |
| $\theta_{16}$ | – | – | – | $-6.68 \cdot 10^{-19}$ | $p^3 q$ | – | – | – | 129.6 |
| $\theta_{17}$ | – | – | – | $-4.72 \cdot 10^{-17}$ | $p^2 q^2$ | – | – | – | 63.7 |
| $\theta_{18}$ | – | – | – | $3.65 \cdot 10^{-16}$ | $pq^3$ | – | – | – | 192.9 |

**Table 6.** Scheduling policies used for comparison. Detailed information regarding WFP3, UNICEF, and F2 policies can be found in [6,25].

| Policy name | Function |
| --- | --- |
| FCFS | $r_j$ |
| SPT | $\tilde{p}_j$ |
| SAF | $\tilde{p}_j \cdot q_j$ |
| WFP3 | $-(w_j/\tilde{p}_j)^3 \cdot q_j$ |
| UNICEF | $-w_j/(\log_2(q_j) \cdot \tilde{p}_j)$ |
| F2 | $\sqrt{\tilde{p}_j} \cdot q_j + 2.56 \times 10^4 \cdot \log_{10}(r_j)$ |

The online scheduling simulation involves jobs arriving at a centralized waiting queue, where a decision-making mechanism reschedules jobs in the queue following a scheduling policy when a new job arrives or a resource becomes available. If the number of processors requested by a job is fewer than the total number of available processors, the scheduling mechanism reserves and makes the required processors inaccessible until the job is completed. If there are insufficient processors available, the decision-making process is delayed until one of the two rescheduling occurrences occurs. Job data such as $\tilde{p}$, $q$, and $r$ are only available to the scheduling mechanism at the time of job arrival.

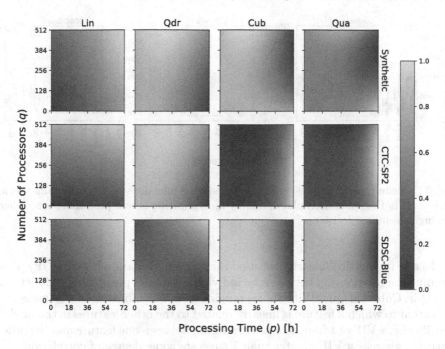

**Fig. 2.** Dependency of the Lin, Qdr, Cub, and Qua functions on the job characteristics $p$ and $q$ ($r = 300$) for the synthetic score distribution, as well as for the CTC SP2 and SDSC-Blue score distributions. (Color figure online)

The average bounded slowdown for all simulations is presented in Fig. 3. The results indicate that the more complex scheduling functions Qdr, Cub, and Qua perform worse than the established scheduling policies regardless of the workload used to generate them. Additionally, the performance of Qdr, Cub and Qua was as inefficient as FCFS and this further cemented the negative effects of their coefficients. Conversely, the Lin function demonstrated better results that are comparable to SAF, a well-known efficient scheduling policy. The reasons for the inefficiency of the Qdr, Cub, and Qua functions will be discussed further in the following section.

**Multicollinearity Results in Poor Scheduling Heuristics.** The instability observed in the coefficients of Qdr, Cub, and Qua implies that these functions may be affected by multicollinearity [2]. Multicollinearity occurs when the features used in a regression analysis are highly correlated with each other, which can lead to unstable and unreliable coefficient estimates. In our case, adding derivative features in combination with the original job characteristics $p$, $q$, and $r$ (such as $q^2$, $q^3$, and $q^4$) may have contributed to multicollinearity. This phenomenon can affect the accuracy of the regression models and make their coefficients less interpretable.

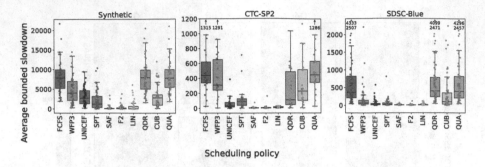

**Fig. 3.** Schedule performance results by scheduling jobs derived from the same workloads used in the simulation phase, and by incorporating actual processing time when making scheduling decisions.

To test for multicollinearity, we used the Variance Inflation Factor (VIF) [1] to examine the relationship between the individual features present in the functions Lin, Qdr, Cub, and Qua. With values ranging from 1 to infinity, the VIF measures the extent to which a feature is linearly related to the other features in the model. Specifically, a VIF of 1 indicates no correlation between one feature and the other features, whereas a VIF greater than 1 suggests some degree of correlation.

VIF's numerical value indicates how much the variance of a specific coefficient is inflated, with a larger VIF indicating a stronger association with other features. For example, a VIF of 1.9 indicates that the variance of a coefficient is 90% larger than expected if there was no multicollinearity with other features. In general, a VIF threshold of 5 or 10 is used to identify features with high multicollinearity, as values above these thresholds suggest that the features may be too closely related to each other to be included in the model.

The calculated Variance Inflation Factor (VIF) values for the functions obtained from three different workloads are presented in Tables 3, 4 and 5. The synthetic workload produced VIF values that were already quite high, particularly for the higher degree functions. However, the VIF values for the CTC-SP2 and SDSC-Blue workloads were even higher, with some functions having values greater than 10,000.

These results suggest that the addition of more derivative features in the models would lead to even larger VIFs, indicating the presence of multicollinearity. This problem might have a substantial influence on model accuracy and stability, potentially leading to overfitting and difficulty in interpreting the coefficients. Hence, it is advisable to carefully evaluate the incorporation of extra features in developing novel scheduling heuristics for HPC platforms.

In the subsequent experiments, our attention was directed solely towards examining the Lin function due to its relatively lower level of multicollinearity when compared to the other functions. As there was no compelling reason to prefer a specific version of the Lin function, we proceeded to conduct the experiments using the version obtained from the synthetic workload.

## 5.3   How Regression-Obtained Scheduling Heuristics Behave in Long Term?

The purpose of the experiments described below was to evaluate the generalizability of regression-obtained scheduling heuristics across a range of different workloads. This was done by comparing them with the policies presented in Table 6, using workload traces obtained from large-scale HPC platforms. The traces, which can be found at the Parallel Workloads Archive [13] and the ALAS Repository [3], were chosen to represent the long-term development of HPC platforms and workloads, covering 19 years from the oldest to the newest traces. The analyzed traces range from an old IBM SP2 machine with a few hundred CPUs to a modern supercomputer with hundreds of thousands of CPUs.

We conducted online scheduling simulations by selecting subtraces consisting of a fifteen-day job submission, in two different scenarios: (i) scheduling using jobs' processing time estimates and (ii) scheduling using processing time estimates along with aggressive backfilling [22]. The second scenario is particularly relevant to a real-world HPC platform situation. It is noteworthy that the SPT, SAF, and Lin policies do not prevent job starvation. Although the F2 policy does prevent starvation, its anti-starvation capacity diminishes over time due to its term $\log_{10}(r)$. We evaluated these policies without any starvation prevention mechanism. However, job starvation can be effectively prevented for any of these policies through a thresholding mechanism, whereby a job is given the highest priority if it passes a certain threshold, such as waiting time or estimated slowdown.

**Scheduling Experiments Based Solely on User-Estimated Processing Times.** The experimental results are depicted in Fig. 4. The linear function exhibited a low average bounded slowdown for varying workloads, with small data dispersion in nearly all cases, ensuring greater stability and predictability. Moreover, the Lin function exhibited one of the three lowest median bounded slowdown averages across all experiments, contending with SAF and F2 policies for these positions.

There were some cases where the average slowdowns were significantly high. This was attributed to the presence of uncommon fifteen-day workloads. One such example is the HPC2N trace, which includes bursts of jobs with large processing time, thereby overloading the platform, irrespective of the policy in place. Despite distinct workload traces, the regression-obtained heuristics were found to be effective scheduling policies for diverse job types.

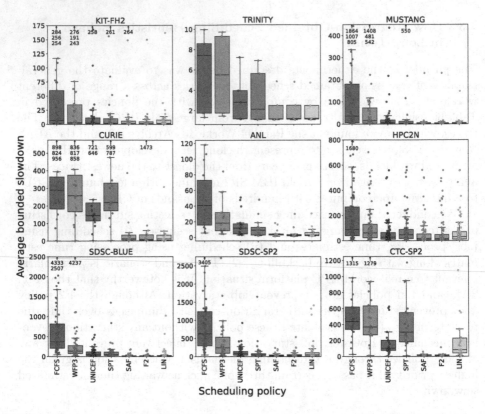

**Fig. 4.** Computed average bounded slowdown for different scheduling policies. Experiments based solely on user-estimated processing times.

**Scheduling Experiments Using Estimated Processing Times and Aggressive Backfilling.** We used an aggressive backfilling technique to reduce the platform's idleness in order to achieve a more realistic scenario. Figure 5 shows that backfilling improves noticeably the performance of suboptimal heuristics like FCFS. Nevertheless, it is not adequate to surpass a superior sorting of the waiting queue, particularly the sorting executed by SAF, F2, and Lin.

Although the Lin function exhibited lower performance levels compared to the F2 and SAF policies, in most cases, it resulted in lower average bounded slowdowns and narrower differences between the extreme quartiles across most workloads. This highlights its favorable scheduling performance, notwithstanding its simplicity.

Moreover, these results show that regression-obtained scheduling heuristics (F2 and Lin) can provide stable and efficient scheduling performances over a wide evolution of HPC platforms and workloads. For instance, the Mustang trace comprises a 5-year workload evolution (from 2011 to 2016), and F2 and Lin performed well in all workloads samples from Mustang. Both F2 and Lin were created once, and they did not need to be readjusted over time to provide efficient scheduling performances.

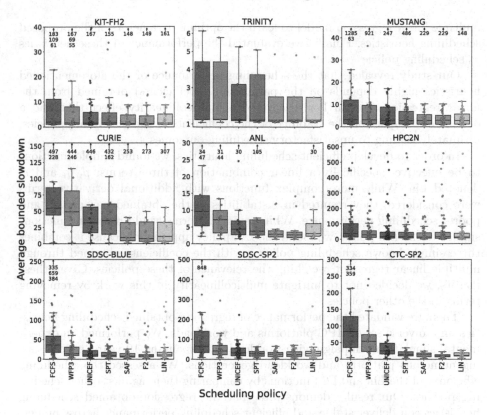

**Fig. 5.** Computed average bounded slowdown for different scheduling policies. Experiments based on user-estimated processing times, with aggressive backfilling algorithm.

## 6    Conclusions and Future Work

The complexity of online parallel scheduling algorithms has always been a negative factor for their deployment in real scenarios. Scheduling heuristics that sorts the jobs in a waiting queue scheduling policies were always the scheduling algorithm of choice in real deployments. This choice is arguably due to the simplicity and interpretability of scheduling heuristics.

Machine learning (ML) methods, particularly regression methods, can be a compelling approach to creating scheduling heuristics that are simple, transparent, and efficient. However, an unexplored aspect of such methods is determining how much scheduling performance can be gained by increasing the complexity of the heuristics. Another uncharted aspect is the long-term stability of these heuristics since both workloads and HPC platforms are constantly changing.

In this work, we conducted an experimental analysis to investigate how the performance of regression-obtained scheduling heuristics can be improved. Initially, three datasets were generated by conducting quick scheduling simulations for various scheduling contexts using a synthetic workload trace and the CTC-SP2 and SDSC-Blue workloads traces. These datasets were then used to train a multiple linear regression model to learn the optimal parameters of the proposed scheduling heuristics. Finally, we evaluated the performance of these heuristics as scheduling policies.

Our study revealed that the scheduling performance of the aforementioned heuristics highly depends on the parameters (coefficients) obtained from the linear regression. We further discovered a multicollinearity effect that had a detrimental impact on the stability of the coefficients of the scheduling policies, ultimately leading to unsatisfactory scheduling outcomes.

In order to develop efficient scheduling heuristics, we found simple functions to be effective, specifically a linear combination of three terms: $p$, $q$, and $r$, denoted Lin. While more complex functions with additional derivative terms were considered, they resulted in instabilities in the obtained parameters and poorer scheduling performance. While removing terms would result in functions similar to the $Lin$ policy, we found the $Lin$ policy appealing because it combines three simple known scheduling policies, with the coefficients obtained through multiple linear regression weighing the relevance of these policies. Given these factors, we decided not to mitigate multicollinearity in this work by removing terms in the other policies.

Then, we validated the performance of regression-obtained scheduling heuristics on a diverse set of HPC platforms and workloads. We performed an experimental simulation campaign with workload data spanning 19 years, encompassing numerous platform and workload generations. We assessed the scheduling efficiency of the Lin and F2 functions by comparing them against other scheduling policies. Our results demonstrate that the regression-obtained scheduling heuristics can deliver stable and efficient scheduling performance across numerous HPC platforms and workloads without the need to readjust their coefficients over time.

We also observed that regression-obtained scheduling heuristics that combine the characteristics $p$, $q$, and $r$ in more unusual ways, like the policy F2 [6], possibly lead to slightly better performances than Lin. This slight performance increase comes with the drawback of lesser interpretability, as it is harder to interpret why the square roots and logarithms in F2 lead to better scheduling. We can obtain better policies than Lin by increasing the complexity of combining $p$, $q$, and $r$, but we do not foresee significant performance gains.

For future work, we plan to enhance the proposed regression method by incorporating new platform and workload features, such as platform utilization, remaining time of processing jobs, and the time of day. We plan to extend the work by searching for possible scheduling heuristics while considering the level of multicollinearity among the features. Moreover, we plan to extend this work to consider the jobs' power demand as a feature, with the objective of reaching similar levels of scheduling performance with the lowest possible overall power consumption of the platform.

**Acknowledgement.** This research was supported by the EuroHPC EU Regale project (g.a. 956560), São Paulo Research Foundation (FAPESP, grants 19/26702-8 and 22/06906-0), and the MIAI Grenoble-Alpes institute (ANR project number 19-P3IA-0003).

# References

1. Akinwande, M.O., Dikko, H.G., Samson, A.: Variance inflation factor: as a condition for the inclusion of suppressor variable(s) in regression analysis. Open J. Stat. **05**, 754–767 (2015). https://doi.org/10.4236/ojs.2015.57075
2. Alin, A.: Multicollinearity. Wiley Interdisc. Rev. Comput. Stat. **2**, 370–374 (2010). https://doi.org/10.1002/wics.84
3. Amvrosiadis, G., et al.: The atlas cluster trace repository. Usenix Mag. **43**(4) (2018)
4. Baker, B.S., Coffman, E.G., Jr., Rivest, R.L.: Orthogonal packings in two dimensions. SIAM J. Comput. **9**(4), 846–855 (1980)
5. Bougeret, M., Dutot, P., Jansen, K., Otte, C., Trystram, D.: Approximation algorithms for multiple strip packing. In: Approximation and Online Algorithms, 7th International Workshop, WAOA 2009, Copenhagen, Denmark, September 10–11, 2009. Revised Papers, pp. 37–48 (2009). https://doi.org/10.1007/978-3-642-12450-1_4
6. Carastan-Santos, D., de Camargo, R.Y.: Obtaining dynamic scheduling policies with simulation and machine learning. In: Proceedings of the International Conference for High Performance Computing, Networking, Storage and Analysis, pp. 32:1–32:13. SC 2017, ACM, New York (2017). https://doi.org/10.1145/3126908.3126955
7. Carastan-Santos, D., De Camargo, R.Y., Trystram, D., Zrigui, S.: One can only gain by replacing easy backfilling: a simple scheduling policies case study. In: 2019 19th IEEE/ACM International Symposium on Cluster, Cloud and Grid Computing (CCGRID), pp. 1–10 (2019). https://doi.org/10.1109/CCGRID.2019.00010
8. Carroll, R., Ruppert, D.: Transformation and Weighting in Regression. Chapman & Hall/CRC Monographs on Statistics & Applied Probability, Taylor & Francis (1988), https://books.google.com.br/books?id=I5rGEPJd57AC
9. Casanova, H., Giersch, A., Legrand, A., Quinson, M., Suter, F.: Versatile, scalable, and accurate simulation of distributed applications and platforms. J. Parallel Distrib. Comput. **74**(10), 2899–2917 (2014)
10. Fan, Y., Lan, Z., Childers, T., Rich, P., Allcock, W., Papka, M.E.: Deep reinforcement agent for scheduling in HPC. In: 2021 IEEE International Parallel and Distributed Processing Symposium (IPDPS), pp. 807–816 (2021). https://doi.org/10.1109/IPDPS49936.2021.00090
11. Feitelson, D.G.: Metrics for parallel job scheduling and their convergence. In: Feitelson, D.G., Rudolph, L. (eds.) JSSPP 2001. LNCS, vol. 2221, pp. 188–205. Springer, Heidelberg (2001). https://doi.org/10.1007/3-540-45540-X_11
12. Feitelson, D.G., Rudolph, L., Schwiegelshohn, U., Sevcik, K.C., Wong, P.: Theory and practice in parallel job scheduling. In: Feitelson, D.G., Rudolph, L. (eds.) JSSPP 1997. LNCS, vol. 1291, pp. 1–34. Springer, Heidelberg (1997). https://doi.org/10.1007/3-540-63574-2_14
13. Feitelson, D.G., Tsafrir, D., Krakov, D.: Experience with using the parallel workloads archive. J. Parallel Distrib. Comput. **74**(10), 2967–2982 (2014)
14. Gaussier, E., Glesser, D., Reis, V., Trystram, D.: Improving backfilling by using machine learning to predict running times. In: Proceedings of the International Conference for High Performance Computing, Networking, Storage and Analysis, pp. 64:1–64:10. SC 2015, ACM, New York (2015). https://doi.org/10.1145/2807591.2807646
15. Georgiou, Y.: Resource and job management in high performance computing, Ph. D. thesis, Joseph Fourier University, France (2010)

16. Hurink, J.L., Paulus, J.J.: Online algorithm for parallel job scheduling and strip packing. In: Kaklamanis, C., Skutella, M. (eds.) WAOA 2007. LNCS, vol. 4927, pp. 67–74. Springer, Heidelberg (2008). https://doi.org/10.1007/978-3-540-77918-6_6

17. Legrand, A., Trystram, D., Zrigui, S.: Adapting batch scheduling to workload characteristics: What can we expect from online learning? In: 2019 IEEE International Parallel and Distributed Processing Symposium (IPDPS), pp. 686–695 (2019). https://doi.org/10.1109/IPDPS.2019.00077

18. Lelong, J., Reis, V., Trystram, D.: Tuning easy-backfilling queues. In: Klusáček, D., Cirne, W., Desai, N. (eds.) JSSPP 2017. LNCS, vol. 10773, pp. 43–61. Springer, Cham (2018). https://doi.org/10.1007/978-3-319-77398-8_3

19. Li, J., Zhang, X., Han, L., Ji, Z., Dong, X., Hu, C.: OKCM: improving parallel task scheduling in high-performance computing systems using online learning. J. Supercomput. **77**(6), 5960–5983 (2021)

20. Lublin, U., Feitelson, D.G.: The workload on parallel supercomputers: modeling the characteristics of rigid jobs. J. Parallel Distrib. Comput. **63**(11), 1105–1122 (2003). https://doi.org/10.1016/S0743-7315(03)00108-4

21. Meuer, H., Strohmaier, E., Dongarra, J., Simon, H., Meuer, M.: TOP500 Supercomputer Sites (2023). https://www.top500.org/. Access 21 Feb 2023

22. Mu'alem, A.W., Feitelson, D.G.: Utilization, predictability, workloads, and user runtime estimates in scheduling the IBM SP2 with backfilling. IEEE Trans. Parallel Distrib. Syst. **12**(6), 529–543 (2001)

23. Pinedo, M.L.: Scheduling: Theory, Algorithms, and Systems. Springer (2016)

24. Rodrigo, G.P., Östberg, P.O., Elmroth, E., Antypas, K., Gerber, R., Ramakrishnan, L.: Towards understanding HPC users and systems: a NERSC case study. J. Parallel Distrib. Comput. **111**, 206–221 (2018)

25. Tang, W., Lan, Z., Desai, N., Buettner, D.: Fault-aware, utility-based job scheduling on BlueGene/P systems. In: Cluster Computing and Workshops, 2009. CLUSTER 2009. IEEE International Conference on, pp. 1–10. IEEE (2009)

26. Virtanen, P., et al.: SciPy 1.0: fundamental algorithms for scientific computing in Python. Nat. Methods **17**(3), 261–272 (2020). https://doi.org/10.1038/s41592-019-0686-2

27. Ye, D., Han, X., Zhang, G.: Online multiple-strip packing. Theoret. Comput. Sci. **412**(3), 233–239 (2011). https://doi.org/10.1016/j.tcs.2009.09.029. http://www.sciencedirect.com/science/article/pii/S0304397509006896

28. Ye, D., Zhang, G.: On-line scheduling of parallel jobs in a list. J. Sched. **10**(6), 407–413 (2007)

29. Zhang, D., Dai, D., He, Y., Bao, F.S., Xie, B.: RLScheduler: an automated HPC batch job scheduler using reinforcement learning. In: SC20: International Conference for High Performance Computing, Networking, Storage and Analysis, pp. 1–15 (2020). https://doi.org/10.1109/SC41405.2020.00035

30. Zhuk, S.: Approximate algorithms to pack rectangles into several strips. Discrete Math. Appl. **16**(1), 73–85 (2006)

31. Zrigui, S., de Camargo, R.Y., Legrand, A., Trystram, D.: Improving the performance of batch schedulers using online job runtime classification. J. Parallel Distrib. Comput. **164**, 83–95 (2022). https://doi.org/10.1016/j.jpdc.2022.01.003. https://www.sciencedirect.com/science/article/pii/S0743731522000090

# An Efficient Approach Based on Graph Neural Networks for Predicting Wait Time in Job Schedulers

Tomoe Kishimoto[✉] and Tomoaki Nakamura

Computing Research Center, High Energy Accelerator Research Organization, KEK,
Oho 1-1, Tsukuba, Japan
tomoe.kishimoto@kek.jp

**Abstract.** The objective of this study is to predict the wait time in job schedulers with high accuracy. Job executions in supercomputers or data centers are typically managed by job schedulers to efficiently utilize computing resources. A possible disadvantage is that, depending on resource availability and scheduling policy, the job waits for a long time before being executed. Therefore, providing the predicted wait time for individual jobs can contribute to the users' research planning. Additionally, the job wait time potentially becomes an important input for the scheduling policy. However, the prediction of the job wait time is a challenging task because the state of the scheduling system changes dynamically by many uncertainty factors. To address this problem, a graph neural network architecture of deep learning, which is a novel approach for processing job information in the scheduler, was employed in this study. Our experiments using real historical logs confirmed that the proposed deep learning model achieved 0.3–7.9% higher prediction accuracy compared to the boosted decision tree and multi-layer perceptron models. An extensive analysis of the proposed deep learning model was performed to improve the explainability of the experimental results. In particular, the visualization of attention weights in the graph neural network expanded our understanding of the behavior of the proposed deep learning model.

**Keywords:** Graph neural network · Job scheduler · Explainability

## 1 Introduction

The scheduling of jobs is an essential task for utilizing computing resources in supercomputers and data centers, where the term "job" indicates a unit of program execution. This type of task is typically managed by a computer application, the so-called job scheduler or batch scheduler, such as Simple Linux Utility for Resource Management (SLURM) [27] or HTCondor [22]. The job scheduler controls the execution of jobs based on resource availability and scheduling policies, such as fair share. Jobs may possibly wait for a long time before being executed when the computer cluster is congested. If users are aware of the expected wait time before the job submission to the scheduler, they can optimize the job

© The Author(s), under exclusive license to Springer Nature Switzerland AG 2023
D. Klusáček et al. (Eds.): JSSPP 2023, LNCS 14283, pp. 137–154, 2023.
https://doi.org/10.1007/978-3-031-43943-8_7

configuration, such as reducing the requested processor cores to increase the chance of being executed. Additionally, the job wait time becomes an important factor when data centers are distributed like a grid computing system [7]. A scheduling policy to decide where to submit a job is required in such the distributed computing. However, the job wait time cannot be obtained straightforwardly because the state of the job scheduler changes dynamically, and there are many uncertainty factors. For example, users can provide an expected execution time (wall time) for the job when its submission as a configuration; this user-provided job wall time will become a piece of important information for estimating the job wait time because the wall time would affect a scheduling policy. However, the user-provided job wall time is known to be inaccurate because users tend to overestimate it to avoid job termination by the time limit [16]. To mitigate such uncertainty factors, deep learning (DL) technology is a promising approach that can learn the complex correlations required for prediction automatically by processing a large amount of historical data. We can assume that the DL model is capable of prediction if there is a common feature between past and current prediction data.

The objective of this study is to predict the job wait time with high accuracy using DL technology. DL has been successfully adapted to many scientific fields, particularly computer vision [13, 20]. The convolutional neural network [17] is one of the breakthroughs in computer vision, which introduces several key functions based on the domain knowledge of images, such as the local receptive field and the translation invariance, to efficiently process image data. Thus, we need to design a DL model to efficiently process our data, that is, the job information in a scheduler. To predict the job wait time, the relationship between other already running and waiting jobs in the computer cluster is important because we can expect the job wait time to be long if many high-priority jobs are already waiting in the scheduler. There are two main difficulties in including such information in the prediction. First, the DL model needs to handle variable length data because the number of waiting and running jobs differs depending on the situation, Second, there is a problem with the order of jobs when preparing input data from multiple waiting and running jobs.

In this study, we employed a graph neural network (GNN) [6] architecture to address these problems, which is a novel approach for processing job information in job schedulers. We constructed a DL model based on the GNN architecture and performed experiments using open data [5], which contain historical workload data provided by many data centers, to examine its performance. The obtained results were compared with existing boosted decision tree (BDT) and simple multi-layer perceptron (MLP) models. An extensive analysis of the proposed DL model was conducted to improve the explainability of the experimental results. The details of the datasets and the proposed model structure are discussed in the following sections.

The remainder of this paper is organized as follows. Section 2 describes the related work, including our novelty. Section 3 presents the datasets used in this study. Section 4 provides the details of the proposed model. Section 5 presents the experimental results. Finally, Sect. 6 summarizes the conclusion of the study.

## 2    Related Work

The estimation of the job wait time is a long-standing concern, and many approaches have been studied and discussed. Approaches that exploit historical workload data, such as our study, are ordinary methods. For instance, the study in [18] reported that similar jobs and resources were discovered from historical data to predict the job wait time with the assumption that similar jobs under similar resources would most likely have a similar job wait time. To process historical workload data more efficiently, machine learning (ML) approaches, such as K-nearest neighbor and BDT algorithms, have also become common and have been confirmed to work for prediction [9,12]. However, these ML approaches are limited to processing a fixed length of data, which results in loss of accurate information about job scheduler conditions. To the best of our knowledge, DL techniques for predicting the job wait time have not been adequately discussed, although there is a report for predicting the remaining run time of jobs using a recurrent neural network [26].

In contrast to the aforementioned studies, the first contribution of our study is that the GNN architecture of DL was employed to efficiently process our data. The GNN architecture enabled the processing of data with variable lengths; it was insensitive to the order of jobs, which enabled the handling of multiple waiting and running jobs as input data. Our experiments confirmed that our model outperformed existing BDT and simple MLP models. Second, experiments were performed to improve the explainability of the DL model. The permutation feature importance (PFI) technique was used to determine the importance of the input variables, and the attention mechanism was employed to visualize the importance of the relation between jobs.

## 3    Datasets

Our experiments were performed using datasets from the Parallel Workloads Archive [5], which ensured reproducibility and allowed us to examine several types of environments. In the Parallel Workloads Archive, the standard workload format [11] was defined, where information for each job, such as the wall-clock time, number of allocated processors, and exit status, was provided based on real workload logs. Table 1 summarizes the datasets used in the experiments. The datasets were selected to examine the different types of job schedulers.

The jobs in the datasets were ordered by their submission time and split into training, validation, and test data with a ratio of 80%: 10%: 10% from the beginning. The validation data were used to determine the hyperparameters of the DL models. The test data were used to evaluate performance without bias from the training and validation data. For instance, the training and test data in the SDSC_BLUE dataset correspond to the periods of "2000–04–30 to 2002–05–30"

**Table 1.** Description of datasets. The number of jobs for each experimental phase is shown. The dates (yyyy-mm-dd) in the brackets indicate the period of time for the corresponding phase. More details of each dataset are provided in [5].

| Name | Job scheduler | Training data | Validation data | Test data |
|------|---------------|---------------|-----------------|-----------|
| SDSC_BLUE | Catalina [1] | 186,050 [2000–04–30 to 2002–05–30] | 23,256 [2002–05–30 to 2002–08–29] | 23,256 [2002–08–29 to 2002–12–30] |
| HPC2N | Maui [4] | 162,297 [2002–08–01 to 2005–04–13] | 20,287 [2005–04–13 to 2005–06–13] | 20,287 [2005–06–13 to 2006–01–16] |
| ANL_Intrepid | Cobalt [2] | 55,150 [2009–01–05 to 2009–07–08] | 6,893 [2009–07–08 to 2009–08–05] | 6,893 [2009–08–05 to 2009–09–01] |
| PIK_IPLEX | LoadLeveler | 583.097 [2009–04–09 to 2012–02–06] | 72,887 [2012–02–06 to 2012–04–25 | 72,887 [2012–04–25 to 2012–07–31 |
| RICC | Custom-built | 358,236 [2010–04–30 to 2010–09–13] | 44,779 [2010–09–13 to 2010–09–18 | 44,779 [2010–09–18 to 2010–09–30 |
| CEA_CURIE | SLURM | 250,262 [2012–02–02 to 2012–09–15] | 31,282 [2012–09–15 to 2012–10–02 | 31,282 [2012–10–02 to 2012–10–13 |

and "2002–08–29 to 2002–12–30", respectively. Therefore, a DL model needs to acquire the capability to predict the job wait time in completely different time ranges.

## 3.1 Prediction Class Definition

The aim of this study is to predict the job wait time, which is the difference between a job's submission time and the time at which it actually begins to run (start time). We defined time ranges for the job wait time, as described in Table 2, and the training was performed to predict this class category as a classification problem. The time ranges were determined so that users can recognize a general situation. For example, a job predicted as class 1 may start within 1 min after submission; moreover, a job predicted as class 5 may wait more than 10 h to start. We were interested in conducting a regression analysis to directly predict the job wait time; however, we focused on this classification approach in this study because it simplified the problem.

Figure 1 presents the distribution of the number of jobs in terms of the prediction class for each dataset. The distributions were divided into training, validation, and test phases. We confirmed that the number of jobs in the datasets

**Table 2.** Definition of prediction class.

| Prediction class index | Definition |
| --- | --- |
| 1 | (Wait time) < 1 min |
| 2 | 1 min ≤ (wait time) < 10 min |
| 3 | 10 min ≤ (wait time) < 1 h |
| 4 | 1 h ≤ (wait time) < 10 h |
| 5 | 10 h ≤ (wait time) |

was unbalanced for the prediction class, with class 1 being the dominant contribution. Thus, the weights for each prediction class ($W_i$) were calculated by using following formula:

$$W_i = \frac{\min\limits_{j \in [1,\cdots,5]} N_j}{N_i},\tag{1}$$

where $i$ and $j$ are the prediction class indeces, and $N$ indicates the number of jobs in the class. The weights were obtained from the training data and are used to calculate the loss values to mitigate the imbalance of classes during DL training.

## 3.2  Input Variables

For predicting the job wait time, the cluster status is important information. For example, we can assume that a job will wait for a long time if the cluster is congested with other jobs. Thus, utilizing information from other jobs, such as already running and waiting jobs, is a key concept of this study, as discussed in the previous sections. A snapshot of when the job was submitted was reconstructed from historical logs in the Parallel Workloads Archive. This snapshot was the unit of input data for the DL models. Snapshots were reconstructed for all jobs in the archive, except for jobs canceled before starting. The canceled jobs were removed because their contribution to the status was unclear. Figure 2 shows an overview of the snapshot. The following four types of jobs were defined in the snapshot:

– **Target job**: The job of interest that we aimed to predict the wait time.
– **Running jobs**: Jobs running in the cluster when the target job was submitted. All running jobs in the cluster were used as inputs for the prediction.
– **Waiting jobs**: Jobs waiting in the cluster when the target job was submitted. All waiting jobs in the cluster were used as inputs for the prediction.
– **Finished jobs**: Jobs finished within the last 5 d from the time the target job was submitted. Only 20 finished jobs were used as inputs in order for the latest finished time to reduce the size of the inputs.

Table 3 summarizes the definitions of the input variables for each job. Many of the input variables used the original values from the standard workload format.

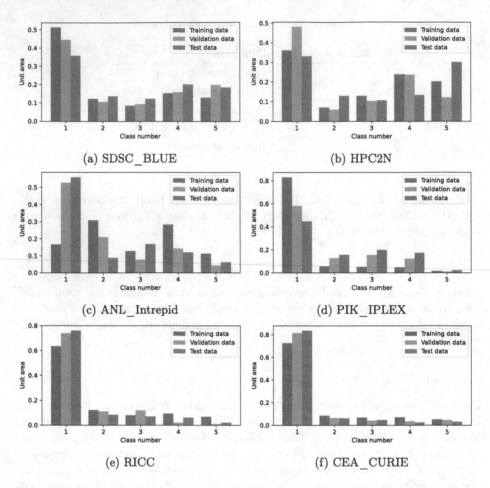

**Fig. 1.** Distribution of prediction classes for each dataset and phase. The area of each histogram is normalized to 1.

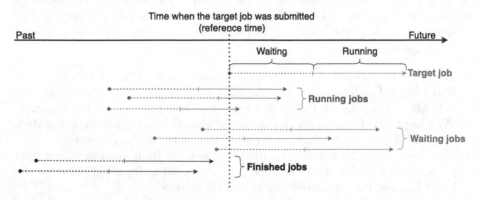

**Fig. 2.** Overview of the snapshot. Each arrow represents a job in the Parallel Workloads Archive. The dashed and solid lines indicate the wait time and run time, respectively.

Input variables that were not available at the time the target job was submitted in a real situation, such as RUN_TIME of the waiting jobs, were masked with 0 or modified with limited information to avoid leaking future information. Log transformation was applied to all input variables to fit the values within a reasonable range. As an example of the input size, if there were 10 jobs in the snapshot, the total number of input variables was 10 (the number of jobs) × 21 (the number of input variables) = 210.

## 4    Proposed DL Model

Figure 3 shows an overview of the proposed DL model. In our model, a graph structure composed of nodes and edges was built for each snapshot. Each node in the graph corresponds to a job in the study. Thus, job features (summarized in Table 3) were assigned to the node attributes in the initial inputs. Edges were prepared between the target job and other jobs as bidirectional graphs. The self-loop of the target job was also included. Edge attributes were empty in the initial inputs.

The model consisted of two parts, that is, a feature module and a classifier module. The feature module was aimed at extracting global features of the snapshot by exchanging information between the target job and other jobs along the edges. The feature module consisted of a stack of blocks, where each block consisted of a graph attention network (GAT) layer [8], batch normalization (BN) layer [14], and the ReLU activation function. The GAT was a key component in our study that introduced the attention mechanism [24] with the GNN architecture. The GAT learned the importance of node relations as edge attributes (attention weights). For instance, if the relation between the target job and the latest finished job was more important than other relations, the attention weight for information exchange obtained a large value. Thus, the attention weights in the GAT layer were considered to improve the learning efficiency and were also useful for visualizing the relation between the jobs (this will be discussed in Sect. 5.2). Another important aspect of the GAT is that it worked with a variable number of jobs and was permutation-invariant because trainable parameters existed only in node-wise and edge-wise computations. This feature overcame the problems of the existing ML approaches discussed in Sect. 2.

The outputs of each block in the feature module were processed by average pooling, which averaged the node attributes, and was then fed into the classifier module. The classifier module was aimed to predict the wait time class, as described in Sect. 3.1. The global feature was obtained by concatenating the outputs of the feature module; then, they were processed by a fully connected (linear) layer, BN, ReLU, and linear layers, as shown in Fig. 4. The dropout function [21] was also introduced before the last layer to mitigate overlearning.

**Table 3.** Definition of input variables for each job. The asterisks indicate that the original values from the standard workload format were used. "reference time" is the time that the target job was submitted.

| ID | Name | Description |
|---|---|---|
| 1 | JOB_NUMBER* | A job identifier indicated by an integer |
| 2 | SUBMIT_TIME | The difference between the job's submission time and the reference time (in seconds) |
| 3 | WAIT_TIME | The running and finished jobs: the difference between the job's submission time and the start time (in seconds). The waiting jobs: the difference between the job's submission time and the reference time (in seconds). The target job: 0 is filled because this is the value of interest |
| 4 | RUN_TIME | The finished jobs: the wall clock time of the job (in seconds). The running jobs: the difference between the job's start time and the reference time (in seconds). The waiting jobs and the target job: 0 is filled |
| 5 | ALLOCATE_CORE* | The number of allocated processors |
| 6 | REQUEST_CORE* | The number of requested processors |
| 7 | REQUEST_TIME* | The requested time (in seconds) |
| 8 | REQUEST_MEMORY* | The requested memory size (in KB) |
| 9 | STATUS | The target job: 0 is filled. The running jobs: 1 is filled. The waiting jobs: 2 is filled. The finished jobs: the original value from the standard workload format + 3 is filled |
| 10 | USER_ID* | A user identifier indicated by an integer |
| 11 | GROUP_ID* | A group identifier indicated by an integer |
| 12 | APPLICATION_NUMBER* | An application identifier indicated by an integer. This might represent a script file used to run jobs. |
| 13 | QUEUE_NUMBER* | A queue identifier indicated by an integer |
| 14 | PARTITION_NUMBER* | A partition identifier indicated by an integer |
| 15 | SUBMIT_WEEKDAY | A weekday identifier $[0, \cdots, 6]$ when the job was submitted |
| 16 | SUBMIT_HOUR | Hour $[0, \cdots, 23]$ when the job was submitted |
| 17 | WAIT_JOB | The number of waiting jobs in the queue at the reference time |
| 18 | RUN_JOB | The number of running jobs in the queue at the reference time |
| 19 | WAIT_CORE | The total number of requested cores of the waiting jobs in the queue at the reference time |
| 20 | RUN_CORE | The total number of requested cores of the running jobs in the queue at the reference time |
| 21 | USER_TIME | A total CPU time consumed by the user during the last 5 days from the reference time |
| 22 | USER_WAIT_TIME | The average wait time of two preceding jobs by the user |

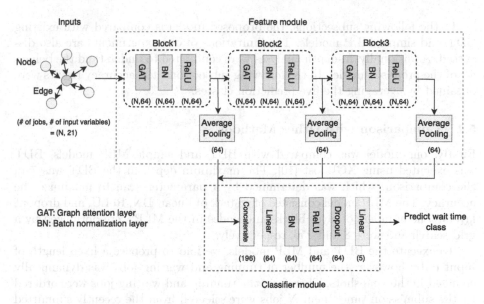

**Fig. 3.** Overview of proposed DL model. The numbers in the brackets indicate output shapes.

# 5    Results and Discussion

The proposed model for this experiment was implemented using the DL libraries: PyTorch [19] and DGL [25], and is available in [3]. All executions used a local cluster of NVIDIA Tesla A100 graphics cards.

The cross-entropy loss between the true and predicted class with sample weights (as discussed in Sect. 3.1) was used as the loss function for training. The best epoch for the validation data was used as the final model parameters after training for up to 30 epochs. We observed that an epoch less than 10 tended to show the best performance owing to overlearning. This indicates that obtaining the generalization between different periods of data is difficult. The Adam [15] algorithm was used as an optimizer with a learning rate of 0.001. The batch size was fixed at 128. Other hyperparameters, such as the number of nodes in the GAT layer and the number of blocks in the feature module, were optimized by a grid search using the SDSC_BLUE dataset.

Figure 4 shows the accuracy of the test data represented in a confusion matrix format. As a global trend, the prediction classes 1 and 5, which are for job wait times of less than 1 min and greater than 10 h, show better accuracies than the other classes. This observation is consistent with a previous study using the BDT [12] and our initial assumption that the intermediate situations are more difficult to predict than clusters that are extremely empty or congested. Another possible reason for the better accuracy in class 1 is that the prediction of class 1 is more robust than that of other classes because the class 1 has more data, as shown in Fig. 1.

In the following subsections, the proposed model is compared with existing BDT and simple MLP models. The limitations of our experiments are also discussed. Additionally, in-depth analyses were conducted to understand the behavior of the proposed model. In the following subsections, the accuracy results were obtained by averaging the five prediction classes.

## 5.1    Comparison with Other Methods

Firstly, our model was compared with BDT and simple MLP models. BDT was executed using XGBoost [10]. The maximum depth in the BDT was 7 in the comparison, which was determined by a parameter scan to maximize the accuracy. The MLP model consisted of a stack of linear, BN, ReLU, and dropout layers. The numbers of layer blocks and nodes in the MLP were optimized by a grid search and were 8 and 256, respectively.

To execute the BDT and MLP models, we had to prepare a fixed length of input data; however, the number of running and waiting jobs was dynamically changed in the snapshots. Therefore, the running and waiting jobs were ordered by the submission time; then, $N$ jobs were selected from the recently submitted jobs. The recently submitted jobs were selected because the attention weights indicated that they were more important than the old jobs (which will be discussed in Sect. 5.3). For instance, if $N$ was 10, the length of the input data was (1 (the number of target jobs) + 10 (the number of running jobs) + 10 (the number of waiting jobs) + 20 (the number of finished jobs)) × 21 (the number of input variables) = 861. Although there were input data that did not include all running and waiting jobs because of the limitation of the fixed length in the BDT and MLP, the global information of clusters was still available via the input variables of WAIT_JOB, RUN_JOB, WAIT_CORE, RUN_CORE, and USER_TIME. If the number of running or waiting jobs was less than $N$, 0 was filled to obtain a fixed length.

Table 4 summarizes the accuracies obtained for each experimental condition and dataset, where the cases of N=10 and 50 were executed for the BDT and MLP models. The results of N=50 tend to show worse accuracy than that of N=10 due to overlearning. Table 4 also includes the results of a simple approach without the ML techniques (average method). The average method, which was proposed in [23], just averages the wait times of two previous jobs by the same user, and uses this averaged value as the prediction. Table 4 confirms that our model shows higher average prediction accuracies for all datasets, which are ranging from 0.3 to 7.9% improvements on top of other approaches. Only the PIK_IPLEX dataset shows the consistent accuracy with the MLP model (N=10) within the error. Therefore, we consider that the proposed model can extract features more effectively based on the GNN architecture than the BDT and simple MLP models.

Our study has the following limitations. The training of our model was significantly slower than that of the MLP model, which was approximately 60 batch/s (our model) and 320 batch/s (MLP model) using SDSC_BLUE dataset. Moreover, the BDT and average method require much lower computational costs

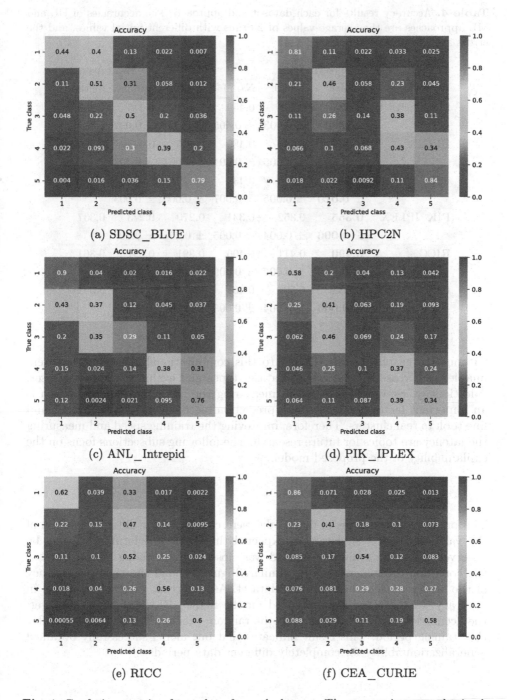

(a) SDSC_BLUE

(b) HPC2N

(c) ANL_Intrepid

(d) PIK_IPLEX

(e) RICC

(f) CEA_CURIE

**Fig. 4.** Confusion matrix of test data for each dataset. The accuracies were obtained by averaging 20 runs with different initial values.

**Table 4.** Accuracy results for each dataset and approach. The accuracies of DL and ML approaches are the average values of 20 runs with different initial values, and the errors are one standard error.

| Dataset | Proposed model | MLP | | BDT | | Average method |
|---------|----------------|-----|-----|-----|-----|----------------|
| | | N=10 | N=50 | N=10 | N=50 | |
| SDSC_BLUE | **0.524** | 0.468 | 0.459 | 0.461 | 0.446 | 0.409 |
| | **± 0.004** | ± 0.003 | ± 0.005 | ± 0.002 | ± 0.002 | |
| HPC2N | **0.537** | 0.495 | 0.489 | 0.465 | 0.448 | 0.380 |
| | **± 0.006** | ± 0.005 | ± 0.004 | ± 0.004 | ± 0.003 | |
| ANL_Intrepid | **0.540** | 0.475 | 0.439 | 0.429 | 0.455 | 0.527 |
| | **± 0.010** | ± 0.005 | ± 0.007 | ± 0.005 | ± 0.003 | |
| PIK_IPLEX | **0.355** | 0.352 | 0.331 | 0.270 | 0.273 | 0.337 |
| | **± 0.006** | ± 0.004 | ± 0.005 | ± 0.005 | ± 0.003 | |
| RICC | **0.490** | 0.411 | 0.406 | 0.391 | 0.397 | 0.361 |
| | **± 0.010** | ± 0.007 | ± 0.009 | ± 0.006 | ± 0.008 | |
| CEA_CURIE | **0.535** | 0.506 | 0.461 | 0.471 | 0.468 | 0.381 |
| | **± 0.006** | ± 0.004 | ± 0.005 | ± 0.004 | ± 0.003 | |

without the graphics cards. Owing to this computational constraint, we were unable to increase the number of dataset types and evaluate a larger dataset. Additionally, we were interested in measuring the prediction latency, which is an important factor for deploying a prediction mechanism, such as a command line tool, to real clusters. Therefore, improving the training speed and measuring the latency are topics for future research. The following subsections focus on the explainability of the proposed model.

## 5.2 Time Dependency

The prediction accuracies of our model were calculated for different periods of the validation and test data. We expected that better performance would be observed when the evaluation period was close to the training period because the condition of clusters may be similar. Figure 5 shows the time dependency of the observed accuracies for each dataset. As expected, a decreasing trend in accuracy was observed if we focused on the SDSC_BLUE dataset. However, the accuracies were still better than the random prediction even 10 weeks after the training period. This result indicates that our model successfully obtained generalization ability for completely different data periods.

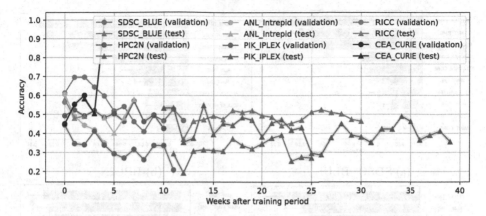

**Fig. 5.** Time dependencies of observed accuracies for each dataset. The proposed model was used. The x-axis represents weeks elapsed since the period of training data. Each point represents the accuracy of the validation or test data within a week. The accuracy is the average value of 20 runs with different initial values, and the errors are one standard error.

## 5.3   Importance of Input Variables

The PFI technique was used to understand the importance of input variables. In the PFI technique, each input variable was randomly shuffled within the dataset during the prediction phase; then, the difference in accuracy from the nominal value ($PFI_i$) was obtained as follows:

$$PFI_i = ACC_{nominal} - ACC_i, \tag{2}$$

where $ACC_{nominal}$ and $ACC_i$ are the accuracies when all input variables are available and variable $i$ is shuffled, respectively. Thus, we can consider that the contribution of variable $i$ to the prediction is large if the $PFI_i$ has a larger value. Figure 6 summarizes the PFI values for each dataset. As global observations, SUBMIT_TIME, WAIT_TIME, and RUN_TIME show larger contributions. We can confirm that our model utilizes the information from the running, waiting, and finished jobs in the snapshot because these input variables were masked in the target job. In Table 4, the PIK_IPLEX dataset shows the lowest accuracy of our proposed model, and a limited improvement compared to the other approaches. One of the reasons is that REQEST_CORE and REQUEST_TIME were not available in the Parallel Workloads Archive of this dataset, which show large contributions in the other datasets.

## 5.4   Visualization of Attention Weights

Figure 7 shows the observed attention weights for the five selected snapshots in the SDSC_BLUE dataset. Each point in the figure indicates the target job (red), running job (blue), waiting job (green), and finished job (black). The arrows with

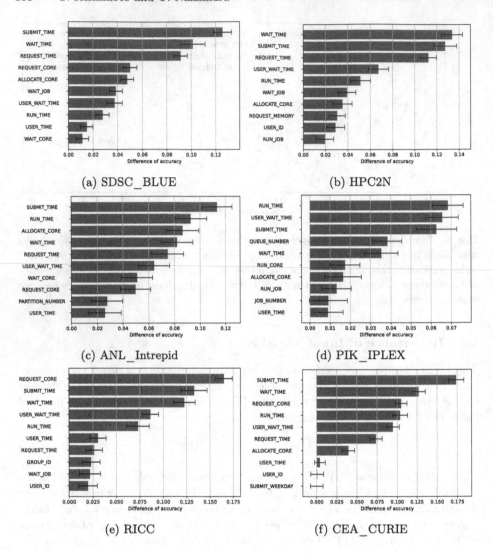

**Fig. 6.** Top 10 PFI values of test data for each dataset. The proposed model was used. The accuracy is the average value of 20 runs with different initial values, and the errors are one standard error.

a color gradient represent the attention weight values between the target job and other jobs, where only the direction to the target job is shown. The distance ($D$) between the target job and the other jobs in the figures was calculated from the difference between the reference time and the submission time for each job, that is, SUBMIT_TIME in Table 3. Log transformation was applied to $D$ to fit the distance within a reasonable range. Thus, a job close to the target job in the figure indicates that it was recently submitted. In addition, the jobs submitted by the same user were clustered so that they were positioned near each other.

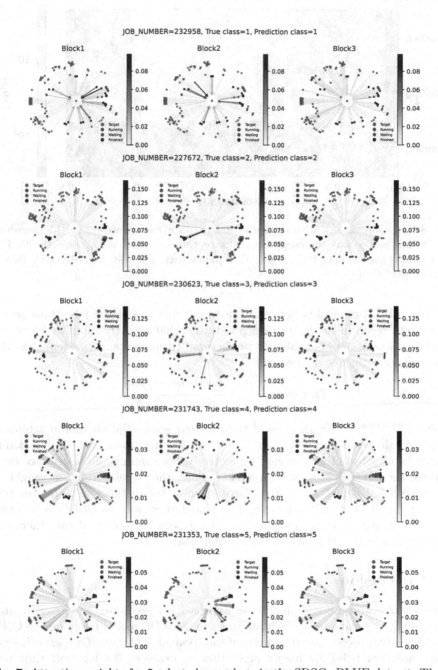

**Fig. 7.** Attention weights for 5 selected snapshots in the SDSC_BLUE dataset. The 5 snapshots, one from each prediction class, are shown from top to bottom. The attention weights for 3 blocks in the feature module are shown from left to right for each snapshot. The snapshots were selected from the test data. (Color figure online)

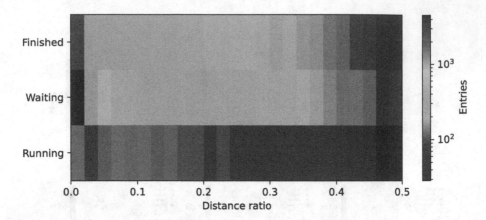

**Fig. 8.** Two-dimensional distribution of maximum attention weight in the snapshot. The x-axis and y-axis represent the distance ratio and job type, respectively. The definition of the distance ratio is described in the text. The test data of SDSC_BLUE dataset were used.

The attention weights between the target job and closer jobs show larger values as a trend in the figure, which indicates that recently submitted jobs are more important than old jobs for prediction. To understand this more clearly, the distance ratio was defined as follows:

$$\text{Distance ratio} = \frac{D^{\text{attention}} - D^{\text{min}}}{D^{\text{max}} - D^{\text{min}}}, \tag{3}$$

where $D^{\text{attention}}$ is the distance of the job that shows the maximum attention weight in the snapshot; $D^{\text{max}}$ and $D^{\text{min}}$ are the maximum and minimum distances for all jobs in the snapshot, respectively. For example, if the distance ratio is zero, the job closest to the target job shows the largest attention weight in the snapshot. Figure 8 shows the distribution of the distance ratio for the test data of the SDSC_BLUE dataset. The distribution was divided by job types, that is, running, waiting, and finished jobs. It can be confirmed that there are large entries in the first bins of the distance ratio = 0.

## 6    Conclusions

In this study, we proposed an efficient approach for predicting the job wait time using a GNN architecture. We built and trained a DL model based on the GNN to efficiently process the dynamic information of job data. Our experiments confirmed that 0.3–7.9% higher prediction accuracy of the job wait time was achieved compared to the BDT and MLP models. An in-depth analysis was conducted to improve the explainability of the proposed model. In particular, the visualization of the attention weights expanded our understanding of the behavior of the DL model, which indicated that the information of recently submitted jobs is important for prediction.

We also identified the limitations of the proposed approach during our experiments. Overlearning is the main concern for improving accuracy. The transfer learning technique seems to be a feasible approach to obtain robustness for different state of clusters. We can train the model using a dataset; subsequently, it can be used as the initial weight parameters for the training of other datasets. The data augmentation technique for our data is also required to suppress overlearning. The prediction latency was not measured in our experiments, and is a topic for future research.

# References

1. Catalina scheduler. https://www.sdsc.edu/catalina/. Accessed 30 Nov 2022
2. Cobalt scheduler. https://trac.mcs.anl.gov/projects/cobalt/. Accessed 30 Nov 2022
3. Deepbatch. https://github.com/ktomoe/deepbatch/. Accessed 16 Dec 2022
4. Maui scheduler. http://docs.adaptivecomputing.com/maui/. Accessed 30 Nov 2022
5. Parallel workloads archive. https://www.cs.huji.ac.il/labs/parallel/workload/index.html. Accessed 30 Nov 2022
6. Battaglia, P.W., et al.: Relational inductive biases, deep learning, and graph networks (2018). https://doi.org/10.48550/ARXIV.1806.01261, https://arxiv.org/abs/1806.01261
7. Bos, K., et al.: LHC computing grid: technical design report. version 1.06 (20 Jun 2005), Technical design report, LCG, CERN, Geneva (2005). http://cds.cern.ch/record/840543
8. Brody, S., Alon, U., Yahav, E.: How Attentive are Graph Attention Networks? In: International Conference on Learning Representations (2022). https://openreview.net/forum?id=F72ximsx7C1
9. Brown, N., Gibb, G., Belikov, E., Nash, R.: Predicting batch queue job wait times for informed scheduling of urgent HPC workloads (2022). https://doi.org/10.48550/ARXIV.2204.13543, https://arxiv.org/abs/2204.13543
10. Chen, T., Guestrin, C.: XGBoost: a scalable tree boosting system. In: Proceedings of the 22nd ACM SIGKDD International Conference on Knowledge Discovery and Data Mining, pp. 785–794. KDD 2016, ACM, New York (2016). https://doi.org/10.1145/2939672.2939785
11. Feitelson, D.G., Tsafrir, D., Krakov, D.: Experience with using the parallel workloads archive. J. Parallel Distrib. Comput. **74**(10), 2967–2982 (2014). https://doi.org/10.1016/j.jpdc.2014.06.013. www.sciencedirect.com/science/article/pii/S0743731514001154
12. Gombert, L., Suter, F.: Learning-based approaches to estimate job wait time in HTC datacenters. In: Klusáček, D., Cirne, W., Rodrigo, G. (eds.) 24th Workshop on Job Scheduling Strategies for Parallel Processing. Job Scheduling Strategies for Parallel Processing. JSSPP 2021, vol. 12985, pp. 101–125. Portland, United States (2021). https://doi.org/10.1007/978-3-030-88224-2_6, https://hal.archives-ouvertes.fr/hal-03357129
13. He, K., Zhang, X., Ren, S., Sun, J.: Deep residual learning for image recognition (2015). https://doi.org/10.48550/ARXIV.1512.03385, https://arxiv.org/abs/1512.03385
14. Ioffe, S., Szegedy, C.: Batch normalization: accelerating deep network training by reducing internal covariate shift. In: Proceedings of the 32nd International Conference on International Conference on Machine Learning - Volume 37, p. 448–456. ICML 2015, JMLR.org (2015)

15. Kingma, D.P., Ba, J.: Adam: a method for stochastic optimization. arXiv preprint arXiv:1412.6980 (2017)
16. Klusáček, D., Chlumský, V.: Evaluating the impact of soft walltimes on job scheduling performance. In: Klusáček, D., Cirne, W., Desai, N. (eds.) Job Scheduling Strategies for Parallel Processing, pp. 15–38. Springer International Publishing, Cham (2019)
17. Krizhevsky, A., Sutskever, I., Hinton, G.E.: ImageNet classification with deep convolutional neural networks. Commun. ACM **60**(6), 84–90 (2017). https://doi.org/10.1145/3065386
18. Li, H., Groep, D., Wolters, L.: Efficient response time predictions by exploiting application and resource state similarities. In: The 6th IEEE/ACM International Workshop on Grid Computing, p. 8 (2005). https://doi.org/10.1109/GRID.2005.1542747
19. Paszke, A., et al.: Pytorch: an imperative style, high-performance deep learning library. In: Wallach, H., Larochelle, H., Beygelzimer, A., d'Alché-Buc, F., Fox, E., Garnett, R. (eds.) Advances in Neural Information Processing Systems, vol.32, pp. 8024–8035. Curran Associates, Inc. (2019). http://papers.neurips.cc/paper/9015-pytorch-an-imperative-style-high-performance-deep-learning-library.pdf
20. Simonyan, K., Zisserman, A.: Very deep convolutional networks for large-scale image recognition (2014). https://doi.org/10.48550/ARXIV.1409.1556, https://arxiv.org/abs/1409.1556
21. Srivastava, N., Hinton, G., Krizhevsky, A., Sutskever, I., Salakhutdinov, R.: Dropout: a simple way to prevent neural networks from overfitting. J. Mach. Learn. Res. **15**(56), 1929–1958 (2014). http://jmlr.org/papers/v15/srivastava14a.html
22. Thain, D., Tannenbaum, T., Livny, M.: Distributed computing in practice: the condor experience. Concurrency Pract. Experience **17**(2–4), 323–356 (2005)
23. Tsafrir, D., Etsion, Y., Feitelson, D.G.: Backfilling using system-generated predictions rather than user runtime estimates. IEEE Trans. Parallel Distrib. Syst. **18**(6), 789–803 (2007). https://doi.org/10.1109/TPDS.2007.70606
24. Vaswani, A., et al.: Attention is all you need. In: Guyon, I., (eds.) Advances in Neural Information Processing Systems, vol. 30. Curran Associates, Inc. (2017). https://proceedings.neurips.cc/paper/2017/file/3f5ee243547dee91fbd053c1c4a845aa-Paper.pdf
25. Wang, M., et al.: Deep graph library: a graph-centric, highly-performant package for graph neural networks. arXiv preprint arXiv:1909.01315 (2019)
26. Wang, Q., Zhang, H., Qu, C., Shen, Y., Liu, X., Li, J.: RLSchert: an HPC job scheduler using deep reinforcement learning and remaining time prediction. Appl. Sci. **11**(20), 9448 (2021). https://doi.org/10.3390/app11209448. https://www.mdpi.com/2076-3417/11/20/9448
27. Yoo, A.B., Jette, M.A., Grondona, M.: Slurm: simple Linux utility for resource management. In: Feitelson, D., Rudolph, L., Schwiegelshohn, U. (eds.) Job Scheduling Strategies for Parallel Processing, pp. 44–60. Springer, Berlin Heidelberg, Berlin, Heidelberg (2003)

# Evaluating the Potential of Coscheduling on High-Performance Computing Systems

Jason Hall[1], Arjun Lathi[2], David K. Lowenthal[3], and Tapasya Patki[4(✉)]

[1] iBoss, Inc., Boston, USA
[2] Expedia, Inc., Seattle, USA
[3] Department of Computer Science, The University of Arizona, Tucson, USA
[4] Lawrence Livermore National Laboratory, Livermore, USA
patki1@llnl.gov

**Abstract.** Modern high-performance computing (HPC) system designs have converged to heavyweight nodes with growing numbers of processors. If schedulers on these systems allocate nodes in an exclusive and dedicated manner, many HPC applications and scientific workflows will be unable to fully utilize and benefit from such hardware. This is because at such extreme scale, it will be difficult for modern HPC applications to utilize all of the node-level resources on these systems.

In this paper, we investigate the potential of moving away from dedicated node allocation and instead using *intelligent coscheduling*—where multiple jobs can share node-level resources—to improve node utilization and therefore job turnaround time. We design and implement a coscheduling simulator, and, using traces from a high-end HPC cluster with 100K jobs and 1158 nodes, demonstrate that coscheduling can improve average turnaround times by up to 18% when compared to easy backfilling. Our results indicate that coscheduling has the potential to be a more efficient way to schedule jobs on high-end machines in both turnaround time and system and component utilization.

**Keywords:** coscheduling · high-performance computing

## 1 Introduction

Modern high-performance computing (HPC) system designs have converged to *heavyweight* nodes with growing numbers of CPUs that are supported by accelerators such as GPUs. Several top supercomputers [23], such as Frontier, Lumi, Leonardo, Sierra, and Summit, have tens of CPU cores and multiple GPUs on each node. These designs have many advantages, including better scaling [42], reduced power and network switch costs, and decreased network interference [36].

The heavyweight node trend should motivate the HPC community to rethink scheduling policies that allocate a set of dedicated nodes to each job. Dedicated node allocation is the most common policy on high-end systems and provides predictable performance and efficient execution when nodes have modest resources.

© The Author(s), under exclusive license to Springer Nature Switzerland AG 2023
D. Klusáček et al. (Eds.): JSSPP 2023, LNCS 14283, pp. 155–172, 2023.
https://doi.org/10.1007/978-3-031-43943-8_8

However, with modern systems, dedicated node allocation will often cause unten-able levels of internal fragmentation of *multiple* node resources, including CPUs, GPUs, memory capacity, memory bandwidth, and network capacity—leading to significant underutilization of available resources.

Cloud installations, including scheduling infrastructures in Mesos [16], Kubernetes [31], and YARN [41], provide infrastructure for scheduling multi-ple jobs onto a node or nodes (to increase profit), but not in a way appropriate for HPC applications. Specifically, the HPC user base has more stringent perfor-mance expectations than cloud users and will not tolerate arbitrary performance degradation for their applications.

This paper studies the potential of *intelligent coscheduling* on modern HPC systems. We define intelligent coscheduing as scheduling multiple jobs, con-currently, onto overlapping nodes such that average job turnaround time is decreased and performance degradation for most jobs is at most modest. Such an approach accepts (some) intra-node interference between jobs rather than rigidly avoiding it via dedicated node allocations. Doing so will make a greater fraction of a system's resources available to jobs. Intelligent coscheduling will lower aver-age turnaround time by decreasing the average time a job spends waiting to execute. This in turn will improve overall system utilization and throughput.

In particular, this paper is focused on studying and understanding the decrease in average turnaround time when using coscheduling compared to backfilling, which is generally the de-facto scheduling approach on high-end HPC installations. This paper focuses only on sharing nodes (and their mem-ory) in multi-node applications. We describe our design and implementation of coscheduling and backfilling and provide results that show that coscheduling leads to lower average turnaround times: up to 18% compared to backfilling and over 80% compared to first-come, first-served. The downside is that some indi-vidual applications take longer to execute (once started), but the substantial decrease in wait time still leads to an average decrease in turnaround time.

The rest of this paper is organized as follows. Section 2 provides an overview of HPC scheduling and provides our assumptions made in this paper. Section 3 describes our implementation of backfilling and coscheduling. Section 4 explains our experimental setup, and Sect. 5 provides the experimental results. Finally, Sect. 6 discusses related work and Sect. 7 summarizes the paper.

## 2    Background and Assumptions

In this paper, we assume a high-performance computing system with a total of $N$ nodes. Each node contains $C$ cores. This section first reviews briefly the basics of HPC scheduling, and then proceeds to discuss our job submission assumptions and coscheduling.

### 2.1    Traditional HPC Job Scheduling

With traditional HPC job scheduling, each application submitted for execution on the system requests $n$ nodes, where $1 \leq n \leq N$. The job also specifies an estimated runtime. When the scheduler has $n$ nodes available and the job is at the front of the queue, the job is scheduled. The job is assigned all $C$ cores, but actually uses $c$ cores, where $1 \leq c \leq C$. (There may be a performance benefit to using fewer than $C$ cores because of a decrease in memory contention.) The estimated runtime is used to set a deadline for the job, and the job is terminated if it exceeds this deadline.

Traditional HPC systems typically use dedicated node allocation (often called *space sharing* or *space slicing* [10]). Here, every node in the system is assigned to at most one job. This policy provides high system utilization, and, equally importantly, relatively predictable performance. In particular, it reserves all the memory on each of the $n$ nodes for a single application. This avoids competition between multiple competing applications for memory, which can potentially cause thrashing (if the system is paged) or worse, a system crash in non-paged systems if the aggregate memory demand between the applications exceeds the size of physical memory.

## 2.2   Evaluating Scheduling Policies

There are many ways to evaluate different scheduling policies, including job throughput, system utilization, and average job turnaround time. Job throughput is defined as the number of jobs completed per unit time. System utilization is defined as the average fraction of nodes that are busy. Finally, the average job turnaround time across all jobs is simply the average wallclock time it takes from the time a job is submitted until the time it is completed.

It is well known that a typical first-come, first served (FCFS) scheduling policy will fall short in all three of these dimensions. If a job in an FCFS scheduling system cannot be scheduled because there are not enough nodes, the job *and* all jobs behind it on the queue are blocked, leading to a convoy effect.

## 2.3   Backfilling

The typical way HPC systems improve all of throughput, utilization, and turnaround time is to use *backfilling* [18, 21, 24, 35]. A backfilling policy addresses the convoy effect caused by FCFS by executing smaller jobs out of order on idle nodes so that utilization is improved—in turn reducing the overall average turnaround time. Backfilling is available in modern resource managers such as SLURM [2] or Flux [3].

However, backfilling is a strategy that is incentivized by utilization being defined as the number of busy nodes, rather than the number of busy *components* of nodes. With modern nodes containing large values of $C$ along with on-board accelerators, this definition of utilization is outdated—a node can be busy, but its components may be ill-utilized. Accordingly, we look to an alternative scheme—coscheduling—to improve all three of throughput, utilization, and turnaround time. However, this requires relaxing job requirements.

## 2.4   Job Configuration Assumptions

In this work, we assume a more flexible job submission scheme. We assume that jobs are *malleable*, meaning they adapt to the number of nodes actually assigned to them [9]. Specifically, applications can be run with (i.e., assigned) *many* different values of $n$ (nodes) and $c$ (cores per node). We denote $(n \times c)$ as a *configuration*, and the set of all configurations in which the application can be executed as $\mathcal{S}$. The user submits a job with $\mathcal{S}$, which asserts to the job scheduler that the application can be executed with any configuration in $\mathcal{S}$. The user also specifies one of these configurations as the *base configuration*, denoted $B$.

We assume that configurations cannot have more total cores than the number used in $B$. As an example, assume that $B$ for a job is $(n \times c)$. In this case, the user might include configurations $(2n \times c/2)$ and $(n/2 \times c)$ in $\mathcal{S}$. Configurations are not limited to ones with $n \times c$ cores; for example, we term the aforementioned $(n/2 \times c)$ as a *degraded* configuration because the number of total cores is less than that in the base configuration. The incentive for a user submitting a job with many configurations, including degraded ones, is potentially lower turnaround time via coscheduling. (Moreover, as discussed later, using configurations such as $(2n \times c/2)$ potentially benefit a job by decreasing memory pressure.)

# 3   Implementation

This section describes our implementations of backfilling and coscheduling.

## 3.1   Backfilling

Backfilling has two primary variants: *easy* and *conservative*. Easy backfilling allows short jobs to execute out of order as long as they do not delay the *first* queued job. Conservative backfilling, on the other hand, only allows short jobs move ahead if they do not delay *any* queued job. Easy backfilling performs better for most workloads [24]. In addition, backfilling algorithms frequently use a greedy algorithm that picks the *first-fit* from the set of available jobs in the job queue. The *first-fit* might not always be the *best-fit*, and a job further down the queue may fit the backfilled hole better. Finding the *best-fit* involves scanning the entire job queue, which increases job scheduling overhead significantly [34].

We use an Easy backfilling algorithm with first-fit. Our implementation skips over the first job at the head of the queue, in the case that (a) that job cannot be run given the currently available resources and has to wait until other jobs finish and (b) there exists a job that satisfies backfill constraints. We allow up to 150 jobs in the backfilling window, and when we backfill, the job at the head of the queue receives a reservation.

## 3.2   Coscheduling

As with FCFS, our coscheduling algorithm considers jobs in order on the submission queue. For each job at the head of the queue, our coscheduler either places the job on the system (and the job commences execution), or it blocks and no job can execute. The fundamental difference with our coscheduler is that a job can be placed on nodes that are already (partially) occupied by another job.

**Coscheduling Benefits and Penalties.** There are a number of things to consider with a coscheduling implementation.

- A job that uses fewer cores per node will potentially achieve a speedup due to an increase in available memory bandwidth. We denote this as *memorySpeedup*.
- A job that is coscheduled on a node will potentially have a penalty due to a decrease in effective memory bandwidth. We denote this as *memorySlowdown*.
- A job that uses more (fewer) nodes will potentially have a remote communication penalty (benefit) due to an increase (decrease) in internode communication. We denote this as *communicationSlowdown*.
- A job that uses fewer cores than its base configuration will have a slowdown penalty. We denote this as *degradationSlowdown*.

We assume that we know (or can derive from known quantities) all of *memorySpeedup*, *memorySlowdown*, *communicationSlowdown*, and *degradationSlowdown*. Section 4 provides further details.

**Coscheduling Implementation.** We found that with coscheduling, a first-fit approach produces poor results because it fails to (1) take advantage of the memory benefit when spreading a job out and (2) consider all configurations. Our coscheduler instead provides a modified best-fit approach.

Our modified best-fit coscheduling procedure is shown in Algorithm 1. For each job $J$ at the head of the queue, we execute function PlaceJob. This function iterates through all possible configurations, and for each one we find the best placement. In this context, *best* means the placement that leads to the fastest execution for the job; i.e., we do not consider potential changes in execution time of other jobs sharing nodes with $J$. (Hence, our best-fit algorithm is greedy in the sense that it focuses only on $J$, and it also will allocate [completely] unoccupied nodes if possible. Another option, which we leave for future work, is to allow a job to specify a maximum slowdown it is willing to incur; such an approach has been used in other contexts [28].)

Function GetBestPlacement finds the best placement for a set of nodes and a given configuration used by $J$. First, we calculate the potential speedup due to memory effects (function GetMemoryBenefit) for the given configuration. Then, for each node in the system that is usable (determined by function CanSchedule), we determine the memory slowdown (and therefore the relative node performance) for $J$. To make this determination, we take into account the memory slowdown that occurs due to other jobs already executing on the node; the memory sensitivity of $J$ is used in this calculation. A node is usable if it has a

**Algorithm 1.** Sketch of coscheduling algorithm.
___
**function** PLACEJOB(*job*)
    **for** config in Configurations **do**
        bestPlacement = None
        bestRunTime = Infinity
        (placement, relNodePerf) = GetBestPlacement(job, config)
        runTime = EstimateRunTime(config, relNodePerf)
        **if** runTime < bestTime **then**
            bestRunTime = runTime
            bestPlacement = placement
    **return** bestPlacement

**function** GETBESTPLACEMENT(job, config)
    memSpeedup = GetMemoryBenefit(config)
    allocatedNodes = {}
    **for** node in Nodes **do**
        **if** CanSchedule(node) **then**
            memSlowdown = DetermineMemorySlowdown(job.sensitivity, node)
            #relNodePerf is the relative node performance; can be faster or slower,
            #depending on which of memSpeedup and memSlowdown is larger
            relNodePerf = GetNodeSlowdown(memSpeedup, memSlowdown, node)
            **if** len(allocatedNodes) < config.nodes **then**
                allocatedNodes.insertSorted(node, relNodePerf)
            **else if** tail(allocatedNodes).relNodePerf > relNodePerf **then**
                allocatedNodes.remove(tail(allocatedNodes))
                allocatedNodes.insertSorted(node, relNodePerf)
    **if** len(allocatedNodes) == config.nodes **then**
        **return** (allocatedNodes, tail(allocatedNodes).relNodePerf)
    **else**
        **return** ([], -1)

**function** DETERMINEMEMORYSLOWDOWN(sensitivity, node)
    **for** each other job $J'$ on this node **do**
        determine and add in slowdown due to effect on $J$ by $J'$
    **return** memSlowdown

**function** ESTIMATERUNTIME(config, relNodePerf)
    **if** config.isDegraded **then**
        computationTime = config.baseRunTime * degradationSlowdown
    computationTime = computationTime * relNodePerf
    communicationTime = config.communicationTime * communicationSlowdown
    runTime = computationTime + communicationTime
    **return** runTime

**function** GETMEMORYBENEFIT(config)
    fractionCores = config.coresPerNode / systemCoresPerNode
    **return** improvement[fractionCores]

**function** CANSCHEDULE(node)
    **return** node.freeCores >= config.numCores and within coscheduling limit
___

sufficient number of free cores to accommodate the configuration. (Optionally, our implementation allows for hard limits on the number of jobs that can be coscheduled on a node.)

Function `GetBestPlacement` adds the node to the allocation for $J$ if either (1) we do not yet have the target number of nodes needed by the configuration, or (2) the slowdown for $J$ will decrease if the node replaces a node that currently is part of the allocation. Note that the slowdown for the job is the maximum slowdown over all nodes in $J$.

Function `PlaceJob` iterates through all configurations (and all nodes in each configuration)[1]. If an allocation is found with a sufficient number of nodes, then the runtime (relative to the base configuration) of $J$ is computed. If the runtime is better than the best known runtime, this placement is marked as the current best. As some configurations use more nodes and fewer cores/node, jobs have the potential to have *lower* execution time than would be possible in a strict FCFS (or backfilled) scheduler.

Our implementation has hooks to allow several variations within our modified best-fit algorithm. The variations are all based on restricting what jobs can be coscheduled on the same nodes. One such variation is preventing two jobs that have high memory sensitivity from executing on the same node, which avoids a large penalty due to memory interference. Section 5 provides results of using these variations.

## 4    Experimental Setup

We next describe our experimental infrastructure and evaluation setup. Our simulator is written in python and allows us to run experiments with different cluster sizes and numbers of jobs. The simulator takes as input a trace that contains, for each job, an entry that contains a unique id, arrival time, execution time, and number of nodes used. It also contains the coscheduling benefits and penalties described in the previous section. The way the benefits and penalties are chosen is discussed below.

The particular trace used is from Cab [12], a (now decommissioned) cluster at Lawrence Livermore National Laboratory that had 1296 nodes, but commonly operated with 1158 nodes in the batch partition. While the Cab trace has nearly 700,000 jobs, to keep simulation time manageable we used subsets of 100,000 jobs taken from this trace for each experiment. The first job was selected after job number 50,000 to avoid any anomalies having to do with machine bootup; we experimented with four traces in all, each having a unique, non-overlapping set of jobs.

The simulator can handle arbitrary numbers of nodes and cores per node, but as Cab had 1158 nodes and 16 cores per node, we used this configuration for all experiments except the one that studies varying the number of nodes. (Other

---

[1] This paper is focused on studying the viability of coscheduling, so we trade off scheduling time (traversing all nodes) for potentially better decisions. There are many ways to improve search time, including ordering the nodes by free cores.

Cab features, such as a Sandy Bridge node architecture, are irrelevant for our study.) The base configuration for a job is therefore $(n \times 16)$. For our backfilling experiments, we used EASY backfilling with a window size of 150.

While our simulator is not optimized for speed of simulation, it is important to ensure that coscheduling does not take an unreasonably long time to place jobs. The average time for placing a job is less than 5ms for coscheduling, 4ms for easy backfilling, and 400us for FCFS. Notably, coscheduling and backfilling are reasonably comparable, and both are, as expected, much slower than FCFS.

For coscheduling experiments, it is necessary to add job-level information. The coscheduling benefits and penalties are chosen from a uniform random distribution with the following endpoints:

- Memory sensitivity: not sensitive (denoted "low"), somewhat sensitive (denoted "moderate"), or very sensitive (denoted "high");
- Percentage of total time spent in communication: chosen between 1% and 20%;
- Communication penalty: chosen between 0% and 40% (applied only to the communication portion); and,
- Degradation penalty: chosen between a slowdown of 1.5 and 2 each time the number of cores is halved.

Each of these (randomized) values is added to the entry of each job in the trace. In general it would be necessary to automatically generate this information; for example, Tang et. al [38] used a database to store application performance data that could be used if the job were executed again. While we envision a different approach to gathering such information, as this paper is a study to determine the potential extent of the benefits of coscheduling, we assume that this information is known and stored in the job file on a per-job basis.

We note that determining memory sensitivity in a clear and concise form in general is a challenging problem. This paper is focused on evaluating the potential of coscheduling. There are a number of ways to estimate memory sensitivity, including the aforementioned keeping of a database of prior program executions [38], executing a so-called skeleton version of the code to infer behavior, and taking input from the user through program annotations or other interface. (The last approach has the potential problem of dishonest users.) However, handling discovery and representation of memory sensitivity of programs falls outside the scope of this paper, and we leave this for future work.

Given that we are assuming 16-core nodes, our prototype considers these configurations for every job: $(4n \times 4)$, $(2n \times 8)$, $(n \times 16)$, $(2n \times 4)$, $(n \times 8)$, $(n/2 \times 16)$, $(n/2 \times 8)$, where the base configuration is $(n \times 16)$, and the last four are degraded configurations as they use less than $n \times 16$ cores. We ran experiments with additional configurations (e.g., $(8n \times 2)$), but they did not perform as well. Similarly, we set a maximum number of coscheduled jobs per node of three; with the configurations considered, the hard limit is four, but we found that led to inferior results.

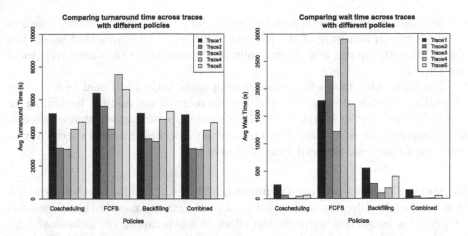

**Fig. 1.** Comparing Coscheduling, FCFS, Backfilling, and Coscheduling with Backfilling ("Combined") on Trace1 through Trace5. The left graph shows turnaround time, and the right graph shows wait time. For readability, the y-axis ranges are different in the two graphs.

## 5 Results

This section presents our results. We begin by discussing turnaround times for coscheduling, backfilling, and FCFS. Next, we discuss the impact of coscheduling on job execution times. The following two subsections discuss varying the number of nodes and coscheduling restrictions. Finally, we provide a short discussion of the implications of our results.

### 5.1 Turnaround Time Results

**Average Turnaround Time Results.** Figure 1 (left) shows average turnaround times for coscheduling, FCFS, FCFS with easy backfilling (hereafter denoted as just "backfilling"), and coscheduling with backfilling. These tests are conducted using different 100K sections (and so 100K jobs) of the Cab trace file (denoted Trace1, Trace2, Trace3, Trace4, and Trace5). When using coscheduling, for each trace, we ran five experiments, and each used a different random seed; the result shown is the one with the median average turnaround time. For our traces, the coefficient of variation was as low as 0.15% and as high as 1.09%. When using FCFS or backfilling, there is no randomness, so we only ran one experiment per trace.

Coscheduling results in turnaround times up to 18% lower than backfilling and over 80% lower than FCFS, due to smaller average wait times (shown in the right part of the figure). Not surprisingly, the performance is trace dependent. Coscheduling has lower average turnaround time than backfilling for all five traces (by between 1% [Trace1] and the aforementioned 18% [Trace2]), with four of the five traces showing a difference of 14% or more. The reason for the smaller gain on Trace1 is in part because of larger average wait time, which in turn is likely an attribute of the job mix in Trace1. This shows that scheduling algorithm performance is at least somewhat dependent on the characteristics of the job mix.

The figure also shows that coscheduling gains little additional benefit from backfilling; in our five traces, the improvement from adding backfilling to coscheduling is always less than 3%. This is not surprising, given that coscheduling is aggressively scheduling jobs onto partially occupied nodes, specifically to lower wait time—so, the wait time is *already* low.

**Impact on Individual Job Turnaround Times.** The above results establish that coscheduling decreases *average* turnaround time compared to backfilling and FCFS. This subsection explores the effect of coscheduling on *individual* jobs; i.e., does the decrease in average turnaround time come at the cost of greatly increasing the turnaround time of specific jobs? (All results from here to the end of Sect. 5 use Trace1, because this is the trace where backfilling was most competitive with coscheduling.)

In Fig. 2, we show three comparisons across the 100K jobs from Trace1. The vertical axis on these graphs represents the ratio of turnaround times of the policies being compared, in a manner that allows the reader to visualize when a certain policy results in better turnaround times than another. We begin by taking the ratio of turnaround times between two policies for each job. If this ratio is greater than one, we know that the second policy had a better overall turnaround time than the first policy. We plot these values as-is. If the ratio is less than one, we know that the first policy had a better overall turnaround time on the job, and we negate and invert this ratio for better readability. As a result, in the subgraphs shown in Fig. 2, a value less than zero shows that the first policy had better turnaround time for a certain job and by what factor. Similarly, a value greater than zero indicates that the second policy did better and shows its associated improvement.

The first subgraph in Fig. 2 compares coscheduling to backfilling. The key point is that at the extreme right on the x-axis, turnaround times for coscheduling are

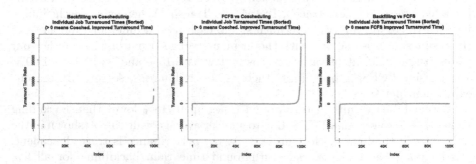

**Fig. 2.** Job Turnaround Time comparison across the three policies for Trace1.

much better (over 5000x) than backfilling; the opposite is true at the extreme left on the x-axis. These extreme points are dominated by wait time; both coscheduling and backfilling encounter situations where the cluster is full or nearly full and a job incurs significant wait time—coscheduling just has that occur for different jobs than for backfilling. Given that which jobs end up incurring the large wait times is arbitrary for each of coscheduling and backfilling, coscheduling achieves its decrease in average turnaround time *without* significantly increasing worst-case wait times for individual jobs.

The second subgraph in Fig. 2 shows the same job-level comparison for coscheduling compared to FCFS. The shape of the graph is similar, but as expected, there are many more large wait times for FCFS because of the convoy effect. Accordingly, coscheduling is better in average turnaround time and has fewer large wait times. For comparison, the third subgraph shows the job-level comparison for backfilling and FCFS. As can be seen, backfilling does not have any large job wait times compared to FCFS—in particular, no job in FCFS is more than 89% slower than backfilling. This does not mean than backfilling does not have jobs with large wait times—but rather that those jobs have even larger wait times with FCFS.

Because the data points in the middle are not easily readable on these subgraphs (due to the scale), Table 1 depicts the quartile data for the distributions. Note that the negative values in the table indicate the negation and inversion explained earlier.

**Table 1.** Quartiles of Turnaround Time Ratios for Policies

| Policies | 0% | 25% | 50% | 75% | 100% |
|---|---|---|---|---|---|
| Backfilling vs FCFS | −16187 | −1.0900 | 1.0000 | 1.0000 | 1.8900 |
| FCFS vs Coscheduling | −9799.0 | −1.0080 | 1.0900 | 1.6800 | 29805 |
| Backfilling vs Coscheduling | −10856 | −1.0200 | 1.0500 | 1.3400 | 6631.6 |

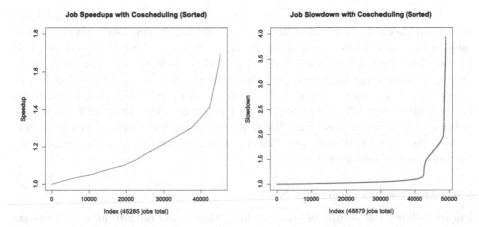

**Fig. 3.** Job Execution Time Speedup and Slowdown distributions (sorted) from Trace1

## 5.2   Impact on Individual Job Execution Times

This subsection explores the effect of coscheduling on individual job *execution* times. Figure 3 shows this effect. Depending on the configuration that an incoming job is assigned at allocation time and the other jobs it shares its allocation with, the incoming job may experience a speedup in execution time (due to reduced memory contention), no change in execution time, or a slowdown in execution time (due to decreased memory bandwidth, communication penalty, or degraded configuration, as described in Sect. 3.2). Note that the execution time of a job only experiences a change with the coscheduling policy—both FCFS and backfilling use the original execution time from the job trace and do not modify individual job execution times.

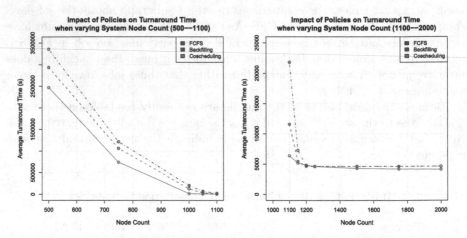

**Fig. 4.** Varying node count. Because of the large range of average turnaround times, two graphs are shown with different ranges of node count for better readability. Results use Trace1.

We analyzed one of the traces of 100K jobs (Trace1), where 45,285 jobs had decreased execution time (speedup), 48,879 jobs had increased execution time (slowdown), and 5,836 jobs had no change in execution time. The left graph in Fig. 3 shows the sorted distribution of jobs that sped up, and the right graph shows the sorted distribution of jobs that slowed down. We observed that for the 48.8% jobs that slowed down, most did not experience a significant slowdown. Only a little over 6% of the jobs slowed down by more than 20% in Trace1. Additionally, with coscheduling, the number of jobs that slowed down by factors of two, three, and four were 588, 226, and one, respectively. No job slowed down by more than a factor of five.

## 5.3   Differing Numbers of Nodes

Figure 4 shows the results of coscheduling, FCFS, and backfilling as the system node count varies from 500 to 2000. Two graphs are used for readability; please note that the x-axis of the left graph starts at 500 and goes to 1100, and the x-axis of the right graph starts at 1100 and goes to 2000. As with the previous results, coscheduling consistently leads to the lowest average turnaround time. The job trace we use is for a system of 1158 nodes, so when we use relatively small system node counts (e.g., 500), the average turnaround time is extremely high (as expected). Coscheduling leads to the best average turnaround time because wait time dominates this scenario (and coscheduling is designed to decrease wait time at the expense of execution time). When the node count is sufficiently large (1400 and above), all algorithms converge to a single value because there are enough nodes to avoid any waiting (again, the trace is for a system of 1158 nodes). Coscheduling converges to a lower average turnaround time because it leverages the additional nodes to spread out a larger number of jobs, achieving a memory bandwidth benefit on such jobs.

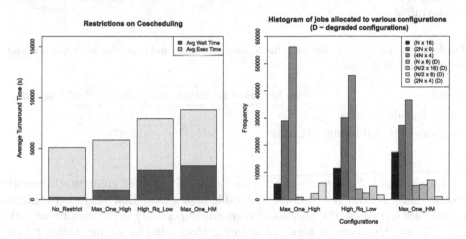

**Fig. 5.** Restricted coscheduling. The left graph shows four scenarios, from no restrictions (No_Restrict) to allowing only one high *or* medium sensitivity job on a node (Max_One_HM). The middle two bars are, in turn, allowing at most one high sensitivity job on a node (Max_One_High) and any high sensitivity job on a node requiring all other jobs on the node to be low sensitivity (High_Rq_Low). The right graph shows the distribution of configurations for the experiment. Results use Trace1.

## 5.4   Restricting Coscheduling

Our coscheduling algorithm places no restrictions on which types of jobs (low, moderate, high) can be coscheduled. An alternative coscheduling design attempts to limit coscheduling overhead due to memory contention by restricting coscheduling possibilities. Figure 5 shows the effect of doing so on Trace1.

In the left graph, each bar shows turnaround time, broken down into wait time and execution time. The leftmost bars show results of our base coscheduling algorithm (No_Restrict), which has no restrictions. Proceeding rightward, the next bar shows results if we restrict coscheduling to at most one high sensitivity job

(`Max_One_High`). The third bar further restricts coscheduling to require a high sensitivity job to be coscheduled only with low sensitivity jobs (`High_Rq_Low`). Finally, the fourth bar requires that coscheduling occur with at most one high *or* moderate sensitivity job (`Max_One_HM`).

The figure shows that restrictions lead to higher turnaround times. Unsurprisingly, placing restrictions on which types of jobs can be coscheduled leads to higher wait times. Counterintuitively, restrictions also lead to higher execution times. The reason for this (see the right graph in the figure) is that the higher wait times cause degraded configurations to be used more often (to avoid increasing wait times even more). The number of degraded configurations with `No_Restrict` is 6,106; in turn, that number is 9,121 for `Max_One_High`, 12,880 for `High_Rq_Low`, and 18,825 for `Max_One_HM`. Obviously, if average wait and average execution time both increase, so does average turnaround time. Fundamentally, one is generally better off just using FCFS than placing restrictions on coscheduling.

**Table 2.** Number of jobs blocked, due to fragmentation and capacity, with and without degraded configurations.

| Version | Num blocked (fragmentation) | Num blocked (capacity) |
| --- | --- | --- |
| With degraded configs | 5,805 | 7,595 |
| Without degraded configs | 41,664 | 25,671 |

Finally, Table 2 shows the effect, specifically, of degraded configurations with coscheduling *without* restrictions. The table makes clear that degraded configurations are critical to the success of coscheduling as they avoid significant wait time. This is true both in terms of avoiding blocks due to fragmentation (there are sufficient total resources, but not in usable form) and capacity (there are insufficient total resources). Avoiding wait time in exchange for slightly slower execution time is a tradeoff that is clearly better.

## 6    Related Work

Allocating dedicated nodes has a long history at HPC centers because it prevents inter-job interference (especially due to cache/memory) on a node. However, it does not eliminate sharing the interconnect, and it does not prevent CPU interrupts on a node. CPU interrupts can be quite damaging to performance [29,40]. For example, if a noise event occurs on just one out of $N$ cores running identical code, for large $N$, the next global synchronization point will suffer a delay equal to the duration of the noise event [7,14,29]. Even if synchronization is local, this can still result in so-called cascading effects [11,17]. The community has responded with many techniques to avoid problems due to core context switching. These include core specialization [2], lightweight operating systems [19], and zero-noise operating systems [1,39].

Some of the work on coscheduling comes from the HPC scheduling community. For example, paired gang scheduling [44] had the goal of modifying gang scheduling to execute two jobs on a node, one CPU bound and the other I/O bound. In addition, virtualization often leads to consolidation of applications (often done to conserve power), which is a form of coscheduling [43].

A significant amount of work on coscheduling comes from cloud installations, where the primary goal is the profit of the cloud provider. Kubernetes [31] and YARN [41] provide infrastructure for scheduling multiple jobs onto a node or nodes; application degradation is only limited by the service-level agreement. HPC schedulers for these frameworks only schedule individual applications to Cloud nodes [33], and cloud schedulers that gang-schedule processes generally implement only simple scheduling algorithms [27]. None of these approaches improves system-wide utilization and turnaround time for multiple, diverse HPC applications.

Two recent related papers have used coscheduling. Tang et al. [38] use coscheduling that results in jobs being spread out, similar to our technique. This work fixes the number of cores, whereas our approach considered degraded configurations. Saba et al. [32] use coscheduling to tackle the specific problem of CPU-GPU applications. They formulate an optimization problem and use machine learning to do the partitioning. Theoretical aspects of coscheduling for HPC with a focus on memory and resilience have also been explored in Pottier's dissertation [30].

Modern batch schedulers for HPC systems such as SLURM [2] and FLUX [3] support the assignment of multiple jobs to a node in the sense that one *could* use them to coschedule. However, they typically allocate dedicated nodes in practice to avoid performance penalties that can arise from sharing caches, main memory, network interfaces, or any other node-level resource [8,15,22,25]. In addition, there is an inter-node penalty when multiple jobs share a node in that more pressure may be put on network links, resulting in network interference. Other scheduling policies other than allocating dedicated nodes exist, such as time-sharing, gang scheduling [13], or implicit coscheduling [5]. Gang scheduling and implicit coscheduling are ways to try to get all nodes of a job active at the same time, without resorting to space sharing. Using gang scheduling with admission control to avoid paging and thrashing has also been studied [6].

## 7   Summary

This paper has presented a coscheduling approach on a high-performance computing system and evaluated its effectiveness compared to FCFS and backfilling. While coscheduling may increase execution time, its decrease in wait time generally makes it a superior approach in situations where average job turnaround time is most important. Combining backfilling and coscheduling can further reduce wait times, albeit marginally.

There are still many aspects of this problem to be studied. For example, we assumed we knew job characteristics, such as memory sensitivity or communication patterns, but in general such information must be discovered through historical data analysis of job traces or through performance counter based models. Similarly, many HPC systems include multiple GPUs per node, and application kernels can share a GPU [20,37]. We did not study the impact of determining which application kernels work well together in a shared GPU environment, or how AI/ML workflows with GPUs would fare. We focused on average turnaround times and hence, job throughput, and we did not address system or component utilization. Modeling component utilization (such as cores, GPUs, memory) or flow resource utilization (such as power, network, or I/O bandwidth)—as well as identifying what occupancy or idleness means for each of these resources— is crucial to conduct a tradeoff analysis of utilization versus throughput when comparing backfilling and coscheduling. For GPUs, occupancy and utilization metrics are provided through vendor interfaces, such as the NVML or ROCm libraries [4,26]. Designing a model to determine core occupancy or memory occupancy, or power utilization, however, is an area of future research. These are just a few of the avenues we will pursue, given the results here that coscheduling— applied judiciously—can improve the efficiency of HPC systems.

**Acknowledgments.** This work was performed in part under the auspices of the U.S. Department of Energy by Lawrence Livermore National Laboratory under Contract DE-AC52-07NA27344 (LLNL-CONF-844869). In addition, this material is based upon work supported by the National Science Foundation under Grant No. 2103511. This research used resources of the National Energy Research Scientific Computing Center, a DOE Office of Science User Facility supported by the Office of Science of the U.S. Department of Energy under Contract No. DE-AC02-05CH11231. We would also like to thank the anonymous reviewers for their helpful suggestions.

# References

1. Mckernel. https://www.pccluster.org/en/mckernel/download.html
2. Slurm workload manager. https://slurm.schedmd.com/core_spec.html
3. Ahn, D.H., Garlick, J., Grondona, M., Lipari, D., Springmeyer, B., Schulz, M.: Flux: A next-generation resource management framework for large HPC centers. In: Workshop on Scheduling and Resource Management for Parallel and Distributed Systems (September 2014)
4. AMD: AMD ROCm Platform Reference. https://cgmb-rocm-docs.readthedocs.io/en/latest/index.html
5. Arpaci-Dusseau, A.C.: Implicit coscheduling: coordinated scheduling with implicit information in distributed systems. ACM Trans. Comput. Syst. **19**(3), 283–331 (2001)
6. Batat, A., Feitelson, D.: Gang scheduling with memory considerations. In: International Parallel and Distributed Processing Symposium, pp. 109–114 (2000)
7. Beckman, P., Iskra, K., Yoshii, K., Coghlan, S.: The influence of operating systems on the performance of collective operations at extreme scale. In: International Conference on Cluster Computing (Sep 2006)
8. Delimitrou, C., Kozyrakis, C.: Paragon: QoS-aware scheduling for heterogeneous datacenters. SIGPLAN Not. **48**(4), 77–88 (2013)

9. Fan, Y., Lan, Z., Rich, P., Allcock, W.E., Papka, M.E.: Hybrid workload scheduling on HPC systems. In: 2022 IEEE International Parallel and Distributed Processing Symposium (IPDPS) (2022)

10. Feitelson, D.G., Rudolph, L.: Parallel job scheduling: issues and approaches. In: Workshop on Job Scheduling Strategies for Parallel Processing (1995)

11. Ferreira, K.B., Bridges, P., Brightwell, R.: Characterizing application sensitivity to OS interference using kernel-level noise injection. In: SC 2008: Proceedings of the 2008 ACM/IEEE Conference on Supercomputing (Supercomputing) (Nov 2008)

12. Flux Framework Team: 2014 Cab supercomputer job scheduling traces (2020)

13. Franke, H., Pattnaik, P., Rudolph, L.: Gang scheduling for highly efficient, distributed multiprocessor systems. In: Proceedings of the 6th Symposium on the Frontiers of Massively Parallel Computation (1996)

14. Garg, R., De, P.: Impact of noise on scaling of collectives: an empirical evaluation. In: International Conference on High Performance Computing (Dec 2006)

15. Govindan, S., Liu, J., Kansal, A., Sivasubramaniam, A.: Cuanta: quantifying effects of shared on-chip resource interference for consolidated virtual machines. In: ACM Symposium on Cloud Computing (2011)

16. Hindman, B., et al.: Mesos: a platform for fine-grained resource sharing in the data center. In: Networked Systems Design and Implementation (2011)

17. Hoefler, T., Schneider, T., Lumsdaine, A.: Characterizing the influence of system noise on large-scale applications by simulation. In: Proceedings of the 2010 ACM/IEEE Conference on Supercomputing (Supercomputing) (Nov 2010)

18. Jackson, D., Snell, Q., Clement, M.: Core Algorithms of the Maui Scheduler. In: Job Scheduling Strategies for Parallel Processing (2001)

19. Lange, J., et al.: Palacios and Kitten: new high performance operating systems for scalable virtualized and native supercomputing. In: Proceedings of the 24th IEEE International Parallel and Distributed Processing Symposium (April 2010)

20. Li, B., Patel, T., Samsi, S., Gadepally, V., Tiwari, D.: MISO: Exploiting multi-instance GPU capability on multi-tenant GPU clusters. In: Proceedings of the 13th Symposium on Cloud Computing (2022)

21. Lifka, D.: The ANL/IBM SP Scheduling System. In: Job Scheduling Strategies for Parallel Processing. vol. 949, pp. 295–303 (1995)

22. Mars, J., Tang, L., Hundt, R., Skadron, K., Soffa, M.L.: Bubble-up: increasing utilization in modern warehouse scale computers via sensible co-locations. In: IEEE/ACM International Symposium on Microarchitecture (2011)

23. Meuer, H., Strohmaier, E., Dongarra, J., Simon, H.: Top500 Supercomputer Sites (2022). http://www.top500.org

24. Mu'alem, A.W., Feitelson, D.: Utilization, predictability, workloads, and user runtime estimates in scheduling the IBM SP2 with backfilling. IEEE Trans. Parallel Distrib. Syst. **12**(6), 529–543 (2001)

25. Nathuji, R., Kansal, A., Ghaffarkhah, A.: Q-clouds: managing performance interference effects for QoS-aware clouds. In: Proceedings of the 5th European Conference on Computer Systems (EuroSys) (2010)

26. NVIDIA Corp.: NVML API Reference Guide. https://docs.nvidia.com/deploy/nvml-api/index.html

27. Palantir, I.: Spark scheduling in kubernetes (May 2019). https://medium.com/palantir/spark-scheduling-in-kubernetes-4976333235f3

28. Patki, T., et al.: Practical resource management in power-constrained. high-performance distributed computing In: High Performance Computing (Jun 2015)

29. Petrini, F., Kerbyson, D.J., Pakin, S.: The case of the missing supercomputer performance: Achieving optimal performance on the 8,192 processors of ASCI Q. In: SC 2003: Proceedings of the 2003 ACM/IEEE Conference on Supercomputing (Supercomputing) (2003)

30. Pottier, L.: Co-scheduling for large-scale applications : memory and resilience. Ph.D. thesis, Université de Lyon (2018) https://theses.hal.science/tel-01892395/

31. Rensin, D.K.: Kubernetes - Scheduling the Future at Cloud Scale. 1005 Gravenstein Highway North Sebastopol, CA 95472 (2015). http://www.oreilly.com/webops-perf/free/kubernetes.csp

32. Saba, I., Arima, E., Liu, D., Schulz, M.: Orchestrated co-scheduling, resource partitioning, and power capping on CPU-GPU heterogeneous systems via machine learning. In: Architecture of Computing Systems (2022)

33. Saha, P., Beltre, A., Govindaraju, M.: Scylla: A Mesos framework for container based MPI jobs. CoRR abs/1905.08386 (2019). http://arxiv.org/abs/1905.08386

34. Shmueli, E., Feitelson, D.G.: Backfilling with lookahead to optimize the performance of parallel job scheduling. In: Feitelson, D., Rudolph, L., Schwiegelshohn, U. (eds.) JSSPP 2003. LNCS, vol. 2862, pp. 228–251. Springer, Heidelberg (2003). https://doi.org/10.1007/10968987_12

35. Skovira, J., Chan, W., Zhou, H., Lifka, D.: The EASY — LoadLeveler API project. In: Feitelson, D.G., Rudolph, L. (eds.) JSSPP 1996. LNCS, vol. 1162, pp. 41–47. Springer, Heidelberg (1996). https://doi.org/10.1007/BFb0022286

36. Smith, S.A., et al.: Mitigating inter-job interference using adaptive flow-aware routing. In: Supercomputing (Nov 2018)

37. Rennich, S.: CUDA C/C++ Streams and Concurrency. https://developer.download.nvidia.com/CUDA/training/StreamsAndConcurrencyWebinar.pdf

38. Tang, X., et al.: Spread-n-share: Improving application performance and cluster throughput with resource-aware job placement. In: Supercomputing (2019)

39. The BlueGene/L Team: An overview of the BlueGene/L supercomputer. In: Proceedings of the 2002 ACM/IEEE Conference on Supercomputing (SC 2002) (2002)

40. Tsafrir, D., Etsion, Y., Feitelson, D., Kirkpatrick, S.: System noise, OS clock ticks, and fine-grained parallel applications. In: International Conference on Supercomputing (Jun 2005)

41. Vavilapalli, V.K., et al.: Apache hadoop YARN: yet another resource negotiator. In: Proceedings of the 4th Annual Symposium on Cloud Computing (2013)

42. Vazhkudai, S.S., et al.: The Design, Deployment, and Evaluation of the CORAL Pre-Exascale Systems. In: Supercomputing (November 2018)

43. Verma, A., Ahuja, P., Neogi, A.: Power-aware dynamic placement of HPC applications. In: International Conference on Supercomputing (2008)

44. Wiseman, Y., Feitelson, D.: Paired gang scheduling. IEEE Trans. Parallel Distrib. Syst. **14**(6), 581–592 (2003)

# Scaling Optimal Allocation of Cloud Resources Using Lagrange Relaxation

Luis de la Torre[1]([✉]) and Mahantesh Halappanavar[1,2]

[1] Washington State University, Pullman, WA, USA
`luis.delatorre@wsu.edu`
[2] Pacific Northwest National Laboratory, Richland, WA, USA
`hala@pnnl.gov`

**Abstract.** The rapid growth of Cloud Computing (CC) has increased the variety of computing resources, storage, and communication services that pose significant new challenges for the efficient use of cloud resources. The cost-efficient allocation of cloud resources has become a decisive premise for the adoption of CC services. The cost-efficient selection and scheduling of these resources to meet the demands of a scientific workflow is a challenging problem that is exacerbated by the inclusion of multiple CC providers. In this paper, we present a new strategy for the cost-efficient selection of CC resources using Lagrange relaxation. Our approach is based on preselection of resources and demand decomposition to create a series of smaller sub-problems, which allow the estimation of the best cost-structures and selection of CC service providers for a subset of the time period of the planning horizon. Decomposition of the demand is achieved through the boundary analysis of a continuous relaxation of the problem. Using the metrics defined in terms of the cost and time of completion, we demonstrate excellent performance with respect to optimal solutions. Our method reduced the computational time from hours to seconds for a representative 36-month problem and provided high-quality solutions ($<0.05\%$ relative error). Given the importance of selecting resources and scheduling complex scientific workflows, we believe that this novel strategy will be beneficial for many researchers and users of cloud computing resources.

**Keywords:** Cloud Computing · Cost-efficient Selection · Cost Model

## 1 Introduction

The computational demands of modern applications have increased considerably [13], especially for data-intensive applications such as high-energy physics workflows that are conventionally executed on dedicated computing resources. However, these applications are increasingly being executed on geographically distributed opportunistic resources such as Cloud Computing Resources (CCR) [8]. Such special configurations pose a tremendous challenge for efficiently using computing resources. To reduce the total computing cost, it is

© The Author(s), under exclusive license to Springer Nature Switzerland AG 2023
D. Klusáček et al. (Eds.): JSSPP 2023, LNCS 14283, pp. 173–192, 2023.
https://doi.org/10.1007/978-3-031-43943-8_9

necessary to implement energy-efficient power management and techniques to allocate tasks to appropriate computing resources optimally. Further, the operating overhead cost of traditional dedicated resources is a significant fraction of the total computational cost [3]. Consequently, opportunistic resources provide a cost-efficient alternative with reduced infrastructure costs and lower energy consumption while providing compute and storage capacity on demand. While there are several CCR providers, we limit our study to two main providers as representative examples: Amazon AWS and Google Cloud. These providers have different cost models based on consumption. Example models include On-Demand, Savings Plans, Reserved Instances (No Upfront, Partial Upfront, Total Upfront), Sustained Usage, and Spot Instances. Further, the computing power for each resource is estimated by a specific metric, for example, Elastic Compute Unit (ECU) for Amazon AWS and Google Compute Engine Unit (GCEU) for Google Cloud.

Although there are many research papers on cloud resource allocation [9,14], there is a dearth of work on the analytical comparison of different cost models that exist for CCR. Further, existing studies do not address forecasted demands that are longer than one year in duration. In this paper, *we present a computationally efficient approximation algorithm using Lagrange relaxation for optimal resource allocation on the cloud.* Our study is motivated by the complex workflow from the Belle II experiments, a high-energy physics experiment designed to probe the interactions of the most fundamental constituents of our universe. Belle II is expected to generate about 25 petabytes ($25 \times 10^{15}$ bytes) of raw data per year with expected total storage to reach over 350 petabytes [1,6]. The data is generated from the physical experiment through the Belle II detector, from Monte Carlo simulations, and user analysis. This data is processed and reprocessed through a complex set of operations, which is followed by analysis in a collaborative manner. Users, data, storage, and compute resources are geographically distributed across the globe, offering a complex data-intensive workflow as a case study, and providing an excellent case study to test the efficacy of the proposed approach.

One of the key problems in these cloud computing scenarios is the selection of cloud resources that can meet the predicted demand in a cost-efficient manner for a given period of time. In order to solve this problem in an efficient manner, the analogy of the *unit commitment* problem in electric power grids (Sect. 3) has been used. This analogy was shown to be successful in formulating and solving the resource selection problem using a mixed-integer linear program (MILP) [5], and later using genetic algorithms [2]. Although successful, these methods do not scale for larger problem sizes. Therefore, our goal in this paper is to scale this approach using *Lagrange relaxation* (Sect. 4). We employ Lagrange relaxation to explore the solution space and create a list of subintervals of the planning horizon that can describe the entire space and produce a series of small subproblems with a reduced number of resources. We detail the mathematical formulation and the boundary analysis in Sect. 4. Boundary condition analysis enables the computation of *normalized average cost value*, which is a good estimator for the specific average cost for each resource in terms of the period of its utilization. We provide an illustrative case study based on a carefully designed synthetic workflow inspired by the Belle II experiment (Sect. 6). We demonstrate the proximity and quality of the proposed solution by comparing with optimal solutions that are computed using integer linear programming. This method, on average, is almost negligibly higher (in cost) than the optimal solutions, and the completion time significantly reduces from hours to seconds to compute a solution for an allocation problem spanning a 36-month period.

### Contributions

We make the following key contributions:

- Building on the unit commitment framework of Halappanavar *et al.* [5], we present a novel Integer Linear Program formulation for efficient allocation of cloud resources (Sect. 3);
- Present a Lagrange relaxation-based approach to scale computation (Sect. 4), and a novel strategy and approximation algorithms based on a low boundary approach to decompose the forecast demand into a set of smaller sub-demand problems (Sect. 5 and Sect. 6); and
- Using a representative problem, we demonstrate performance speedups up to **9×** for 16-machine configuration and **1412×** for 162-machine configuration, relative to the optimal solution – from hours to seconds. We show that the relative error is negligible, less than 0.05% for all cases (Sect. 7).

To the best of our knowledge, this is the first effort to analyze the Lagrange relaxation to scale cloud resource allocation problem in complex scientific workflows formulated as a unit commitment problem.

## 2  Background: Cloud Computing Model

In the context of large-scale scientific workflows, the demand for computation and storage varies significantly over time. The demand needs to be satisfied from a heterogeneous set of resources that comprise dedicated and shared high performance computing (HPC) resources, and cloud services from several commercial and non-commercial vendors. Effective solutions to identify the cost-efficient subset of resources to meet a forecasted demand should consider the operating costs emerging from computation, data movement, and storage. However, current solutions, such as DIRAC in the case of Belle II [5], only consider computational aspects of available resources. The demand for resources can be roughly estimated through historical data and performance modeling approaches. For example, several Monte Carlo campaigns are conducted in Belle II with the predicted number of events to be simulated over a given period of time ($P_d$). The forecasted demand can be satisfied through a combination of shared and dedicated HPC resources, and cloud computing resources.

Two broad categories of cost models for cloud computing are: (*i*) on-demand subscription, and (*ii*) reservation-based subscription. We briefly describe these two models in the following discussion.

*On-demand Subscription:* The *"pay-as-you-go"* model is the simplest pricing model. This approach is designed to pay just for the machines that are in use. In other words, the customer pays only for the resources used during a specific period of time and is supported by many providers including Amazon AWS, Google Cloud, and Windows Azure. The model is better suited for situations with short bursts of infrequent and unpredictable use. As an exception, Google Cloud offers special discounts for *sustained usage* with up to 30% discounts for workloads that run for a significant portion of a billing month. Further, *"spot pricing"* is a particular on-demand model, where the price varies according to the demand and supply for resources at a given point in time.

*Reservation-Based Subscription:* Another common pricing model is "subscription" or "committed use discounts." In this model, a customer pays or commits to use specific resources in advance for a predefined period of time, independent of the actual use of the resources. Amazon AWS is one of the leading companies using this model. A few variants of the subscription model are as follows:

- *No Upfront* model is designed to reserve resources for a fixed period of time without a subscription cost but full payment for the amount of resources used.
- *Partial Upfront* model enables reservation in advance for a fixed period of time with an initial cost and a discounted payment for the amount of resources used.
- *Total Upfront* model charges the customer a one-time fixed payment for using specific resources, usually in time units measured by years. This model provides the most cost-effective means for sustained yearlong use of specific resources.
- *Committed-Use Discounts* model is offered by Google Cloud services, where the user agrees to purchase a "committed-use contract" for a usage term of 1 year or 3 years. In this model the user receives up to 57% discount no normal prices.

As an illustration, we present a sample of different cost plans as advertised by Amazon EC2 and Google Cloud in Table 1. The table lists only a small set of possible cost plans for three machine types: T2, C4, and n1-standard. The third column, **CPU**, provides an estimated value for the processing power of a given machine instance. The CPU values provided for the first four machines (marked by an asterisk) are estimated by a standard Linux benchmark "sysbench" running on 128 threads to find 50,000 prime numbers. The results are compared with regular Amazon ECU values using the following equation: $ECU = 1925/t$, where $t$ is the benchmark makespan time. The fourth column (**Tm**) represents the subscription time for the machine under a specific subscription plan. The fifth column (**s**) represents the fixed subscription cost (in dollars) for the period specified in the fourth column. The sixth column (**c**) represents the monthly usage cost (in dollars per month).

**Table 1.** Representative subscription costs for Amazon EC2 and Google Cloud resources. This information was accessed on 5/10/2022. *Values estimated based on "sysbench" benchmark and the CPU burst minutes, the price includes the monthly use discount.

| Cost plan | Machine type | CPU | Tm ($m$) | $s$ ($\$$) | $c$ ($\$$/month) |
|---|---|---|---|---|---|
| On-Demand | n1 standard 1 | 3.3* | 1 | 0 | 24.27 |
| On-Demand | n1 standard 2 | 6.6* | 1 | 0 | 48.54 |
| On-Demand | n1 highcpu 2 | 6.7* | 1 | 0 | 36.20 |
| On-Demand | n1 highcpu 4 | 13.4* | 1 | 0 | 72.41 |
| No-Upfront | T2 Nano | 0.2 | 12 | 0 | 2.63 |
| No-Upfront | T2 Micro | 0.4 | 12 | 0 | 5.26 |
| No-Upfront | T2 Small | 0.8 | 12 | 0 | 13.14 |
| Partial Upfront 3 year | C4 Large | 8 | 36 | 539 | 15.33 |
| Total Upfront 3 year | C4 Large | 8 | 36 | 1013 | 0 |
| Partial Upfront 3 year | C4 Xlarge | 16 | 36 | 1091 | 30.66 |
| Total Upfront 3 year | C4 Xlarge | 16 | 36 | 2050 | 0 |
| Partial Upfront 3 year | C4 2XLarge | 31 | 36 | 2168 | 59.86 |

# 3    Problem Formulation

A general problem in cloud computing that arises for many users can be expressed as: *Given an estimated (or forecasted) demand for computing resources for a given period of time, what is the specific subset (configuration) of cloud resources that can meet the predicted demand at a minimum cost.* We consider the problem in a batched context, where we bundle the demand for a given time period to make the decisions. However, the time period can be relaxed accordingly. In order to solve this problem in an efficient manner, we use the analogy of the *unit commitment problem* in electric power grids, proposed by Halappanavar *et al.* [5], where a set of power generators are determined to meet the predicted demand for a certain period of time. At present, cloud computing platforms do not provide any tools for optimal selection of resources to satisfy the given computational demand over a certain period of time. However, such a tool becomes necessary for heterogeneous high-performance computing and cloud-based computational resources with varying degrees of usage costs. Consequently, the question that needs to be answered is: *Given an estimated (forecasted) demand, what is the most cost-efficient allocation of resources?* This question becomes especially important when cloud computing services are used as the primary source of resources. In some cases, this question also enables decisions for choosing a particular subset of cloud computing services.

## 3.1  Unit Commitment Problem

The unit commitment problem in the context of resource allocation in cloud computing can be stated as: Given a set of computing resources with different subscriptions and usage costs and forecasted demand, the objective of the solution is to determine the *schedule* to identify the set of computing resources that must be reserved and the amount of each resource needed to meet the forecasted demand at a minimum cost. In order to address this problem, we use a Lagrange relaxation based approach (described in Sect. 4) inspired from the unit commitment problem [12]. A key difference in our approach is the use of comparative analysis of different computing cost models to solve the problem.

Building on the notation of Brittany [16], the unit commitment problem in electric power grids can be formally expressed as follows:

$$\min_{P,u,x} F = \sum_{t=1}^{T} \sum_{j=1}^{N} [C_j(P_j(t)) + S_j(x_j(t), u_j(t))] \tag{1}$$

$$s.t. \sum_{j=1}^{N} P_j(t) = P_d(t) \qquad \forall t = 1, ..., T \tag{2}$$

$$\sum_{j=1}^{N} r_j(x_j(t), P_j(t)) \geq P_r(t) \; \forall t = 1, ..., T \tag{3}$$

where $F$ is the total system cost for $N$ power generators over $T$ time units with operating (fuel) cost function $C_j$ and start-up cost function $S_j$ to generate $P_j$ units of power. The variable $x_j$ represents the number of time units (for example, hours) that a given generator is on (positive) or off (negative). Similarly, the variable $u_j$ represents the state of a generator at a given time unit $t + 1$. It is positive $(+1)$ if the state is up and negative $(-1)$ if the state is down. The constraints enforce that the demand, $P_d(t)$ at time $t$, is satisfied. Further, the system is also required to meet a certain additional (reserve) unanticipated demand $P_r$, and $r_j$ is the reserve function available from generator $j$ for the time unit $t$. The total time period under consideration is $T$. The complete set of restrictions is presented in [16].

The Cloud Computing problem (from the user perspective) has several similarities with this problem. However, it is necessary to carefully define the meaning of the functions $C_j(P_j(t))$ and $S_j(x_j(t), u_j(t))$ in the context of cloud computing, which we present in the following discussion.

## 3.2  Integer Linear Program Formulation

We now present an Integer Linear Program (ILP) formulation of the cloud computing resource (CCR) selection problem. The objective is to compute a minimum-cost allocation of resources to satisfy the forecasted demand using available resources. We define the following variables and parameters. Let $F$ denote the total operating costs attributed to the use of $N$ resources for a total of $T$ time units, where $T$ represents the total time period under consideration. Let $P_d(t)$ represent the predicted demand in CPU units and $P_j(t)$ represent the number of resources used of type $j$ at time unit $t$. The function $S_j(u)$ represents the subscription cost for the use of resource $u$ of type $j$, and $CPU_j$ represents the number of standard computational units for a specific resource type $j$.

The variable $u_j(t)$ represents the number of subscriptions for resource type $j$ at a given time unit $t$. Now, we define $C_j(x)$ and $S_j(u)$ as follows: let $C_j(p) = c_j p$ be the cost of using $p$ units of machine type $j$, and $S_j(u) = s_j u$ be the cost to subscribe $u$ number of machines of type $j$, where $s_j$ is payed once for a continuous interval of time, $Tm_j$. In our formulation, the variable $u_j(t)$ is used as a non-negative integer variable representing the number of resources of a specific type that are subscribed to complete a specific demand, and $P_j^{max}$ represents the maximum number of machines available for every type. Specific numbers can be computed similarly to the work of Singer et al. [14]. Our objective is to minimize the total subscription cost as well as the operating costs while satisfying the demand over the planning horizon. Notations used in this paper are summarized in Table 2. Adapting the unit commitment for cloud computing, we reformulate the power grid-related Eqs. (1–3) as follows:

$$\min_{u,P} F = \sum_{t=1}^{T} \sum_{j=1}^{N} c_j P_j(t) + s_j u_j(t) \tag{4}$$

$$s.t. \sum_{j=1}^{N} CPU_j P_j(t) \geq P_d(t) \qquad \forall t = 1, ..., T \tag{5}$$

$$\sum_{i=max\{1, t-Tm_j\}}^{t} u_j(i) \geq P_j(t), \quad \forall j = 1, ..., N, \ \forall t = 1, ..., T \tag{6}$$

$$0 \leq P_j(t) \leq P_j^{max} \qquad \forall j = 1, ..., N, \ \forall t = 1, ..., T \tag{7}$$

$$u_j(t) \geq 0 \qquad \forall j = 1, ..., N, \ \forall t = 1, ..., T \tag{8}$$

The notation $T$ represents the total planning horizon to allocate the resources to meet the forecasted demand. Equation 5 enforces that the demand, $Pd(t)$ at time t, is met or exceeded. Equation 8 ensures that the total resources used at any time $t$ is less than or equal to the maximum machines available at $t$.

A potential approach to solve the cloud unit commitment problem is to assign integer values to variable $P_j(t)$, which results in its formulation as a *mixed-integer linear programming problem* (MILP). We develop strategies to relax the problem to enable the computation of lower-bound approximate solutions quickly. We then use the approximate solution to compute a feasible close-to-the-optimal integer solution in pseudo-polynomial time (Sect. 4).

## 4   Lagrange Relaxation

In this section, we present an approximate solution to the cloud unit commitment problem (Sect. 3) using Lagrange relaxation. Lagrange relaxation enables us to

**Table 2.** A summary of key notations

| Notation | Description |
|---|---|
| Sets | |
| $J$ | Set of machines, $j \in J$ |
| Parameters | |
| $N$ | No. of machines |
| $P_d^t$ | Demand at period $t$ |
| $s_j$ | Subscription cost for machine $j$ over $Tm_j$ periods |
| $c_j$ | Operating cost of machine $j$ for a single period |
| $T$ | Total planning horizon |
| $\lambda(t)$ | Lagrange multipliers for every time unit $t$ |
| $CPU_j$ | Computing power of machine $j$ |
| $P_j^{max}$ | Maximum machines $j$ available. |
| Variables | |
| $u_j(t)$ | No. of machine $j$ subscribed in the period $t$ |
| $P_j(t)$ | No. of machine of type $j$ used at period $t$ |

explore the solution space efficiently and create a series of smaller sub-problems that can be solved quickly. We start the discussion in this section on the boundary analysis and then proceed to discuss the normalized average cost analysis of the proposed solution.

### 4.1  Boundary Analysis

We formulate the relaxed variants of the resource selection problem where the demand constraint (Eq. 5) is included in the objective function (Eq. 4) using Lagrange multipliers $\lambda(t)$ for every time unit $t$. A new formulation of the objective function can be expressed as follows (Eq. 9):

$$L(u,p,\lambda) = \sum_{t=1}^{T} \left[ \sum_{j=1}^{N} (c_j P_j(t) + s_j u_j(t)) + \lambda(t)\left(P_d(t) - \sum_{j=1}^{N} CPU_j P_j(t)\right) \right]. \quad (9)$$

In this reformulation, the primal problem is converted into a new optimization problem where the penalty terms $\lambda(t)$ become a set of additional variables. The constraint in Eq. 7 is not included in the new formulation since it is only a restriction on the number of machines used.

With the reformulation, the problem now becomes a *max-min* problem where the variables $u$ and $p$ are for the minimization and variables $\lambda(t)$ are for the maximization of the objective function. The problem can be reformulated as:

$$\max_{\lambda \geq 0} \min_{u,p} L(u,p,\lambda), \quad (10)$$

subject to the remaining restrictions. In order to develop a lower boundary for the set of solutions, it is necessary to estimate particular values of the Lagrange multipliers $\lambda(t)$.

## Analytical Solution with Fixed Subscriptions

We develop an analytical solution for the problem when the subscription $\{u_j(t)\}$ is given. The relaxed problem can be decomposed into one sub-problem for each time unit $t$. The objective function for the smallest problem is given by Eq. 11:

$$L_t(\lambda, P) = \sum_{j=1}^{N} (c_j - \lambda CPU_j) P_j(t) + \sum_{j=1}^{N} s_j u_j(t) + \lambda P_d(t). \qquad (11)$$

If enough resources are available to meet the demand, then the minimal values are achieved when the best machines are selected at full capacity and the gap to complete the demand is supplied by the remaining machines with the best values. In other words, machines are selected at the limits imposed by the subscription restrictions in Eq. 6, and the maximum number of machines for a given type, $P_j^{max}$ (cloud providers define the maximum values). If needed, one of the remaining machines is selected partially to satisfy the demand $P_d(t)$.

Based on this consideration, an optimal solution will be one where the machines selected must be such that the fraction $\frac{c_j}{CPU_j}$ is less than $\lambda$ values, which means $(c_j - \lambda CPU_j) \leq 0$. Similarly, the value for $\lambda$ must be large enough to include the machines with $(c_j - \lambda CPU_j) \leq 0$ in a solution set $J$ such that $\sum_{j \in J} CPU_j P_j^* \leq P_d(t)$, where the value is given by

$$P_j^* = \min\{P_j^{max}, \sum_{i=\max\{1, t-Tm_j\}}^{t} u_j(i)\}.$$

Now, let $k$ represent the machines with $\frac{c_k}{CPU_k}$ close to $\lambda$ and,

$$P_k^* = \frac{P_d(t) - \sum_{j \in J} CPU_j P_j^*}{CPU_k}.$$

The optimal values for $L_t(\lambda, P)$ are given by the following equation:

$$L_t(\lambda, P) = \sum_{j \in J} \left( \frac{c_j CPU_k + c_k CPU_j}{CPU_k} \right) P_k^* + \sum_{i=1}^{N} s_j u_j(t). \qquad (12)$$

In this solution, the set of machines $J$ represents the first $k-1$ available ("subscribed" or "on demand") resources in non-decreasing order of $\frac{c_j}{CPU_j}$ values such that $\sum_{j \in J} CPU_j P_j^* \leq P_d(t)$. Variable $k$ is an index to the leading machines when the demand is oversupplied, which means the machines with the best possible values for $\lambda$ is $\lambda^* = \frac{c_k}{CPU_k}$.

## Analytical Boundary with Non-predetermine Subscriptions

In order to determine the best strategy for the problems when subscription $u_j$ is not fixed, we decompose the problem as a set of $N$ low-level minimization problems, one for each resource. If the Lagrangian multipliers $\lambda(t)$ are fixed, the objective function for every lower level problem can be expressed as:

$$L_j(P, u) = \sum_{t=1}^{T} \left( c_j - \lambda(t)CPU_j \right) P_j(t) + \sum_{t=1}^{T} s_j u_j(t). \tag{13}$$

The minimization sub-problems are also subject to the same constraints as maximization problems (Eq. 5).

For every sub-problem, if $(c_j - \lambda(t) \times CPU_j) \leq 0$, then the value of $P_j(t) > 0$. Consequently, the optimal values for $L_j(P, u)$ are expected to be a negative values. Therefore, it is necessary to select the best available machines, i.e., machines with lower $L_j(P, u)$ values. By using the same $\lambda^*$ values for all time units, $\lambda(t) = \lambda^*$, it is possible to create an upper boundary condition for the minimization problem. This is given by Eq. 14. Let $L_j^*(P)$ be the new value when $\lambda(t) = \lambda^*$ then,

$$\max_{\lambda \geq 0} \min_{u,p} L \leq \sum_{j=1}^{N} L_j^*(P) + \sum_{t=1}^{T} \lambda^* P_d(t). \tag{14}$$

The upper bound is useful to estimate the critical values to select a single machine to meet the demand. The critical limit happens when $L_j^*(P) \to 0$. This means that the minimum possible values for any $\lambda(t)$ in order to select one resource $j$ is represented in Eq. 15 as follows:

$$\lambda_j^* = \frac{\sum_{t \in M} \left[ s_j u_j(t) + c_j P_j(t) \right]}{CPU_j \sum_{t \in M} P_j(t)}, \tag{15}$$

where $M$ is the set that contains all the time intervals where machine $j$ is used, $c_j - \lambda(t)CPU_j \leq 0$. Equation 15 can then be interpreted as the *normalized average* CPU cost per unit of time.

### 4.2   Normalized Average Cost Analysis

The formula presented in Eq. 15, is a good estimator for the specific average cost for each resource in terms of how long the resource has been used. In Fig. 1, we present a graphical representation of the cumulative cost $\sum_{t \in M} \left[ s_j u_j(t) + c_j P_j(t) \right]$ for different combinations of $s_j$ and $c_j$ (different cost models), and the average cost per CPU, $\lambda_j^*$ (computed using Eq. 15). We present the information representing the number of time intervals included in set $M$. For this example, we assume that the machines are used for an entire month. The solid lines in Fig. 1 represent the values for the minimum cost by aggregated months in different computing configurations: Amazon AWS initial account, and a combination of Amazon AWS and Google Cloud. On the other hand, the dashed line represents

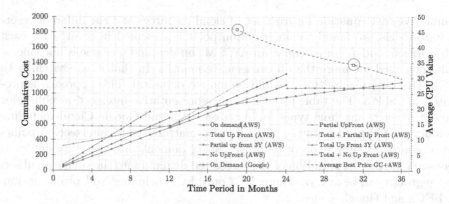

**Fig. 1.** Cumulative and normalized average cost by month.

the normalized average cost over the accumulated months for the best possible configurations computed using Eq. 15. It is possible to compute the best possible combinations by splitting the demand curve into several portions as represented by the red circles in Fig. 1.

**Table 3.** Interception points of accumulated costs (from Fig. 1) for possible machine type configurations.

| Types | On Demand | No Upfront | PU 1 year | TU 1 year | AU+ On-De | PU 3 years | TU 3 years |
|---|---|---|---|---|---|---|---|
| T2 | 6.9 | 11 | 11.51 | 12 | 16.59 | 31 | 36 |
| M3 | 4.97 | 9.8 | 11.51 | 12 | 16.88 | 31 | 36 |
| M4 | 4.97 | 9.7 | 11.51 | 12 | 16.88 | 31 | 36 |
| C3 | 4.97 | 9.7 | 11.51 | 12 | 16.50 | 31 | 36 |
| C4 | 4.97 | 9.8 | 11.51 | 12 | 16.70 | 31 | 36 |
| GCloud | – | – | – | – | – | 19 | 24 |

**Table 4.** Optimal interval for decomposition of the demand curve

| TIntervals | 1-6 | 7-10 | 11 | 12 | 13-17 | 19 | 20-31 | 32-36 |
|---|---|---|---|---|---|---|---|---|
| EC2 | | | | | | | | |
| EC2NU | | | | | | | | |
| EC2NU+GC | | | | | | | | |

In order to decompose the problem into smaller chunks, it is possible to create a list of subsets of resources for the problem under consideration. Using the cumulative cost equation for each set of cloud resources and the different reservation models, we found the intersection point represented in months for each subscription model. For example, an AWS M2 on-demand machine is uneconomical when used for more than 5 consecutive months. In that case, switching to a "No Upfront" Commitment would be more economical. This approach is presented in Table 3. The table lists the most representative intersection points for the entire set of machine types for Amazon AWS and Google Cloud including Memory (MX) and computing (CX) focused machines. The intersection points are measured in time units of months. Table 4 demonstrates the time intervals necessary for the classification of the forecasted demand into the smallest subset. Three groups can be analyzed here: EC2 only, EC2 including No Upfront option, and EC2 and Google Cloud.

# 5    Decomposition of Forecasted Demand

We presented a Lagrange relaxation based method in Sect. 4 as a means to scale the resource selection problem. In this section, we present a heuristic to first decompose the demand curve into partitions (sub-problems), and then present an algorithm to efficiently solve the sub-problems using an integer linear program solver. We present the algorithm for demand decomposition in Algorithm 1, and the ILP-based solution in Algorithm 2.

---

**Algorithm 1** *"Decomp"*, Algorithm to decompose of the demand curve

---

**Input:** $DCurve$[months], $TISet$
**Output:** $DPart$

1: $SD \leftarrow$ SortDemand($DCurve$)
2: $DSets \leftarrow$ initialSet($TISet$)
3: **for** $D$ in SD **do**
4:     $subD \leftarrow$ partialDemand(D,DCurve)
5:     $i \leftarrow$ SelectIIndex($subD, TISet$)
6:     $DPartition[i]$.aggrDemand($subD$)
7: **end for**
8: **return** $DPartition$

---

The results from Table 4 induce a partition in the forecasted demand. This partitioning is created by grouping the demands with the number of active months in the same time interval of forecasted computational needs (CPU hours). For example, there are three intervals for EC2 GH+GC: 1–19, 20–31, and 32–36. Let us denote the intervals with variable $TISet$. We present our method to decompose a given demand curve in Algorithm 1.

Algorithm 1 begins by ordering the demand per month in a non-decreasing order of values to produce a set $SD$ (Line 1). We then create a group of empty sets $DSets$, where each set represents one of the time intervals $TISet$ as shown in

---

**Algorithm 2.** Decomposition Based Approximation Algorithm

---

**Input:** $R, DCurve[months], TISet$
**Output:** TotalCost,$P$,$u$
  1: $DPart \leftarrow$ Decomp($DCurve, TISet$)
  2: $S' \leftarrow \emptyset$
  3: **for** $d$ in $DPartition$ **do**
  4:     **if** $S' \neq \emptyset$ **then**
  5:        $d$.updateDemand($S'$)
  6:     **end if**
  7:     **if** $d.types$ != "OD" **then**
  8:        $S' \leftarrow$ solveILP($R$, $d$)
  9:     **end if**
10:     $S[d.I] \leftarrow S'$
11: **end for**
12: $demand \leftarrow DPartition["OD"]$
13: **for** $t \in T$ **do**
14:     $S[d.I][t] \leftarrow$ solveILP($R, d$.getM($t$))
15: **end for**
16: $Cost \leftarrow$ computeCost($R, S$)
17: **return** $\{Cost, S.P, S.u\}$

---

Table 4. We then construct a vector $subD$ for every value of $D \in SD$. The vector $subD$ contains one value for each time unit (month) and represents the fraction of the demand $D_t$ that remains to be satisfied from the previous time interval, but less than the current time interval. In other words, the value between two intervals in $TISet$ for each time unit (month). This action is represented on Line 4 in Algorithm 1 by the function `partialDemand()`. Scalar variable $i$ represents the index of the time interval based on the number of non-zero values in $subDemand$. Variable $i$ will indicate one particular value in $TIntervalsSet$. Further, the time interval is also important for full and partial upfront subscription schemes. Therefore, the variable $i$ will also depend on the range of active months between non-zero values in $subD$. Variable $i$ is computed by the function `SelectIIndex()`. Finally, we aggregate all the $subD$ values in the same interval. Thus, at the end of the execution, we will have one vector of length equal to the number of time units (months) for each interval representing the cumulative demand that needs to be satisfied for a given month. Thus each $demandPartition$ for a given interval becomes an independent sub-problem that needs to be solved using Algorithm 2.

The underlying intuition of the solution is to precompute the values of normalized average cost to decompose the problem into easily solvable sub-problems. We present a method to efficiently solve sub-problems in Sect. 5.1.

## 5.1  Decomposition Based Approximation Algorithm

Our approximation algorithm uses the demand decomposition method to create a set of small problems, then we use an integer linear program (ILP) to solve each of the sub-problems. Algorithm 2 illustrates the proposed method to compute the machine configurations that need to be purchased to meet the given demand. The algorithm begins by decomposing the given demand (Line 1) using the method described in Algorithm 1. We process the set *DPartition* in an order based on the decreasing value of the number of months in the interval. For example, we process the interval 32–36 before processing the interval 20–31 in Table 4.

The variable $S$ is a two-dimensional matrix consisting of $N$ rows and $T$ columns. Each row represents a machine and each column represents a time unit (month). A given value, $S[t][j] = P_j(t)$, will represent the number machines of type $j$ used at time unit $t$. The variable $S'$ is defined similarly, but holds the temporary solutions that get accumulated in $S$. Algorithm 2 proceeds by processing each demand in a loop (Lines 3–11). If *d.types* != "OD", OD (On-Demand) then we solve the problem using an integer linear program that we will describe in the following paragraphs. The computed solution from the function `solveILP()` is stored in the temporary variable $S'$. In the subsequent iterations of the for loop, $S'$ will be used to update the next demand (Lines 4 and 5). The temporary values are updated in the solution matrix $S$ (Line 10). Since "On-Demand" part of the composition is not processed in the for loop, we process it separately for each time unit (month) (Lines 13–15). Finally, the total cost of the solution is computed on the function *computeCost* using Eq. 1 and the information from the Cloud providers resources $R$ listed on Table 1.

The `solveILP()` function solves an integer linear programming problem using a pseudo-polynomial time algorithm [11], which is known as the inverse Knapsack problem. The problem can be formulated as:

$$
\begin{aligned}
\underset{P}{\text{minimize}} \quad & \sum_{j \in d.J} c_j P_j(t) \\
\text{subject to} \quad & \sum_{j \in d.J} CPU_j P_j(t) \geq d.getM(t).
\end{aligned}
\tag{16}
$$

Note that the problem is solved once for each sub-problem (Line 8), and for at most $T$ times for decisions on "On-Demand" allocations (Line 14). The function $d.getM(t)$ represents the demand for every time step $t \in T$ when called for "On-Demand" allocations, and it represents the maximum demand otherwise. $d.J$ represents the set of "On-Demand" preselect resources. We conclude this section with an observation that the solution computed by the approximation algorithm provides a set of cost-efficient resources that can meet the demand for any given period of time.

## 6  An Illustrative Case Study

As an illustrative case study, we provide a small example inspired by the Belle-II experiments and using representative data obtained from Amazon and Google

Cloud Services. The key information is summarized in Table 1. We use a 36-month demand curve presented in Fig. 2 for this example. The synthetic demand represents a time period $T$ of three years, and the total committed resource for each time period (one month) is the constraint and needs to be satisfied for that period. The horizontal axis in Fig. 2 represents the time periods in months, and the vertical axis represents the demand in CPUs units. For example, the $11^{th}$ month has a total demand of 137 CPU units.

The optimal solution for this problem is computed using the MILP formulation using $P_j(t)$ and $u_j(t)$ as integer values. The solution was computed using the complete set of available machines with the following price models: On-demand, No Upfront, Partial Upfront, and All Upfront.

**Fig. 2.** The Base-forecasted demand curve for an example with a 36-month period.

We computed the optimal solution on an IBM NEOS Solver with CPLEX. We further note that the computation of solutions using this type of solvers is time-consuming, especially when the number of resources used is large. It took more than one hour, using ten threads (CPU cores) to find the optimal solution Table 6. A single optimal approximate solution is presented in Table 5 which illustrates that only a subset of available resources is sufficient to meet the demand for a given period of time under consideration. This side-by-side comparison shows some excellent similitude, the approximation solution put more effort into the C4 Large machines compared with the optimal solution. Also, the optimal solution is more efficient in finding the minimal set of machines to supply the demand, this is beneficial for implementation logistics. We present a possible graphical representation of an optimal solution in Fig. 3. Each bar in the figure represents the computing power provided by the selected resources for each month. The black line, as before, represents the forecasted demand. Different colors in the bars (green, blue, and pink) represent specific resources selected to satisfy the demand by an optimal solution computed using MILP formulation. In Table 5, we present the resources used to supply the demand for the entire three-year period. This optimal solution uses a combination of "Total-Upfront 3 year C4 large" machines, "Partial-Upfront 3 year C4 large" machines,

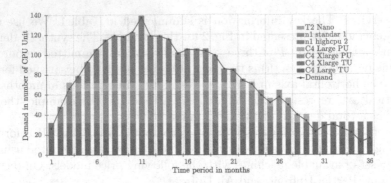

**Fig. 3.** Illustration of an optimal solution using the MILP-based solution. (Color figure online)

**Table 5.** Optimal and approximation solution machine selection sets.

| Machine Type | Type | Optimal | | Aproximation | |
|---|---|---|---|---|---|
| | | Machines | Months | Machines | Months |
| C4 Xlarge | PU 3 year | | | 2 | 49 |
| C4 Large | TU 3 year | 4 | 144 | 4 | 142 |
| C4 Large | PU 3 year | 5 | 123 | 1 | 25 |
| T2 Micro | No-Upfront | | | 2 | 3 |
| T2 Nano | No-Upfront | 4 | 9 | 1 | 3 |
| n1 highcpu 8 | Lower-Price | | | 1 | 1 |
| n1 highcpu 4 | Lower-Price | | | 3 | 7 |
| n1 highcpu 2 | Lower-Price | 10 | 93 | 10 | 75 |
| n1 standar 1 | Lower-Price | 1 | 5 | 1 | 5 |
| | **Total Cost** | | $12,144.21 | | $12,170.29 |

"T2 Nano" from AWS, and "n1 highcpu 2" machines, and one "n1 standard 1" machine from Google Cloud. These machines are used month by month to supply the demand and cost a total of $12,144.21 for the optimal solution. The solution computed by the unit commitment-based formulation provides a set of cost-efficient resources that can meet the predicted demand for a given period of time. However, this solution does not specify how the tasks themselves are assigned to resources. While we do not consider the problem of task assignment in this paper, we refer you to our prior work using combinatorial optimization for energy-efficient assignment of tasks to resources [5]. We discuss the idea of demand decomposition for the efficient computation of solutions next.

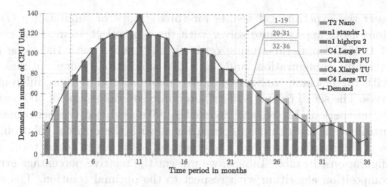

**Fig. 4.** Illustration of a possible solution and decomposition. (Color figure online)

## 6.1 Decomposition of the Forecasted Demand

As described before the Algorithm 1 is used to construct the *DPartition*, which is represented by the red, blue, and green color on the Fig. 4, its colors represent the subdemand (*DPartition*) for each interval 1–19, 20–31, and 32–36 respectively. This decomposition of demand is computed as follows:

- **(1–19)** is the top partition of the demand curve (red color in Fig. 4). This sub-demand is obtained by selecting all parts of the demand with at most 19 months of total used in the entire 36 months span. The demand is satisfied using only the "On Demand Google Cloud" machines type (max 67 CPUs units).
- **(20–31)** is the second partition of the demand curve. This sub-demand is obtained by selecting the demand with at least 20 months of sustained use of the machines and maximum 31 months of sustained used. The optimal solution to satisfy this sub-demand is in blue color (max 40 CPUs units) using only the "Partial Upfront" subscription model.
- **(32–36)** is the third partition of the demand curve shown in green color. The optimal solution fills this part of the demand (up to a maximum of 32 CPUs unit) using only an "All Upfront" subscription model. This particular part of the solution uses these machines for cases where it is required to use more than 32 months of sustained use.

Subsequently, the Algorithm 2 is used to determine the total number of resources used in each step, as described in Table 5. When we compare the cost of the approximate solution it is negligibly higher, which means that quick computation approximated solutions are a promising idea for the forecast problem. For an initial evaluation of the approximation algorithm, we propose a minimal set of experiments in the next section.

## 7    Experimental Results and Discussion

We evaluated the proposed approximation algorithm using a set of distinct scenarios created by adding random variations induced by a distribution function.

We present the experimental results for three groups of simulations: ($i$) 1500 simulations using approximate solver with the a preselect 16-machine configuration, ($ii$) 1500 simulations using optimal (ILP) solver with the same preselect 16-machine configuration, and ($iii$) 1500 simulations using optimal (ILP) solver with 162-machine configuration. We create a total of 1500 different random curves. The set of curves is distributed into several groups of 500-scenarios for each time period (12, 24, and 36 months). We analyzed the performance of the approximation algorithm by comparing it with the optimal solution, both in terms of the running time and the quality of solutions in terms total cost of the configurations. In table Table 6, we present the relative percentage error for the decomposition algorithm with respect to the optimal solution. The results are presented for three time periods (12, 24, and 36 months). The experiment is designed to quantify the accuracy lost by the approximation solutions, which we observe to be negligible with respect to the optimal solutions, less than 0.05% for all cases.

**Table 6.** *Relative Performance:* For Belle II (500) use case with three time periods (12, 24, and 36 months), the columns list relative percentage error for the decomposition algorithm with respect to the optimal solution, and the average completion time in seconds for Approximate, Optimal with 16-machines configuration, and Optimal with 162-machines configuration.

| Period | Relative Error | Approx. (s) | 16-MILP (s) | 162-MILP (s) |
|--------|----------------|-------------|-------------|--------------|
| 12     | 0%             | 1.1         | 8.2         | 909.5        |
| 24     | 0.036%         | 2.7         | 12.4        | 1956.4       |
| 36     | 0.048%         | 2.8         | 26.5        | 3956.2       |

Table 6 also summarizes the average completion time for three approaches: Approximate, Optimal with 16-machine configuration, and Optimal with 162-machine configuration. We observe that the time to compute the Approximate solution, ranging from 1.4 to 2.8 s, is orders of magnitude smaller. The average improvement in performance relative to the optimal solution is 9× for 16 machine-configuration, and 1412× for 162-machine configurations. The approximate method also scales across the forecasted time periods (12, 24, 36). Thus, demonstrating superior performance in quality vs compute time.

## 8    Related Work

Efficient scheduling of computational tasks is a classical problem that has been studied extensively. The minimum makespan scheduling problem on independent machines has also been studied extensively [4]. Given a set of tasks and a set of resources, the objective is to assign tasks to resources such that the load on each resource is balanced. In particular, the maximum load of any resource is minimized. A relaxed variant of this problem has been solved using the semi-matching formulation by several researchers [7]. Scheduling of tasks on heterogeneous resources with different energy consumption patterns is an emerging topic of research [15], that employs mathematical programming for computing efficient solutions. The novelty of our scheduling work comes from employing scalable approaches to solve computationally challenging optimization problems. Preselection of resources in a cost-efficient manner allows us to formulate and solve the complex problem at multiple levels. The unit commitment analogy enables us to build from a large body of work on efficient optimization approaches [10]. However, to the best of our knowledge, we believe this is the first work that employs an analysis of the Lagrange relaxation for the unit commitment-based formulation of cloud resource allocation for complex scientific workflows.

## 9   Summary and Future Work

We presented a computationally efficient approximation algorithm using Lagrange relaxation for the optimal allocation of cloud resources using demand decomposition as a heuristic. We presented a detailed description of mathematical formulation and intuition for employing the Lagrange relaxation-based technique for solving the integer programming problem. We supported the efficiency of the proposed approach using a representative case study and a small set of experiments inspired by the Belle-II experiment and representative cloud computing resources.

In the near future, we plan to conduct an extensive empirical evaluation of the proposed approach using a variety of demand scenarios. We also plan to integrate the solution for Belle-II workflows that can exploit dedicated HPC resources as well as cloud computing resources. We also plan to develop a continuous optimization formulation of the problem that can be used in a continuous setting for resource allocation. We believe that a fast solution to this problem can be beneficial for future applications that are intended to test multiple variations of the forecast demand almost in real-time.

**Acknowledgment.** The research is supported in part by the U.S. DOE Exascale Computing Project's (ECP) (17-SC-20-SC) ExaGraph codesign center and Laboratory Directed Research and Development Program at Pacific Northwest National Laboratory (PNNL).

## References

1. Asner, D.M., Dart, E., Hara, T.: Belle II: experiment network and computing. Technical report arXiv:1308.0672. PNNL-SA-97204, August 2013. Contributed to CSS2013 (Snowmass)
2. Friese, R.D., Halappanavar, M., Sathanur, A.V., Schram, M., Kerbyson, D.J., de la Torre, L.: Towards efficient resource allocation for distributed workflows under demand uncertainties. In: Proceedings of the 21st Workshop on Job Scheduling Strategies for Parallel Processing (2015)

3. Gao, P.X., Curtis, A.R., Wong, B., Keshav, S.: It's not easy being green. ACM SIGCOMM Comput. Commun. Rev. **42**(4), 211–222 (2012)
4. Graham, R.L., Lawler, E.L., Lenstra, J.K., Rinnooy Kan, A.H.G.: Optimization and approximation in deterministic sequencing and scheduling: a survey. Ann. Discret. Math. **5**(2), 287–326 (1979)
5. Halappanavar, M., Schram, M., de la Torre, L., Barker, K., Tallent, N.R., Kerbyson, D.J.: Towards efficient scheduling of data intensive high energy physics workflows. In: Proceedings of the 10th Workshop on Workflows in Support of Large-Scale Science. WORKS '15, pp. 3:1–3:9. ACM, New York, NY, USA (2015)
6. Hara, T.: Belle II: computing and network requirements. In: Proceedings of the Asia-Pacific Advanced Network, pp. 115–122 (2014)
7. Harvey, N.J.A., Ladner, R.E., Lovász, L., Tamir, T.: Semi-matchings for bipartite graphs and load balancing. J. Algorithms **59**(1), 53–78 (2006)
8. Juve, G., Deelman, E.: Scientific workflows and clouds. XRDS **16**(3), 14–18 (2010). https://doi.org/10.1145/1734160.1734166
9. Kamiński, B., Szufel, P.: On optimization of simulation execution on amazon ec2 spot market. Simul. Model. Pract. Theory **58**, 172–187 (2015)
10. Mallipeddi, R., Suganthan, P.N.: Unit commitment - a survey and comparison of conventional and nature inspired algorithms. Int. J. Bio-Inspired Comput. **6**(2), 71–90 (2014). https://doi.org/10.1504/IJBIC.2014.060609
11. Roland, J., Figueira, J.R., De Smet, Y.: The inverse 0,1-knapsack problem: theory, algorithms and computational experiments. Discret. Optim. **10**(2), 181–192 (2013). https://doi.org/10.1016/j.disopt.2013.03.001, https://www.sciencedirect.com/science/article/pii/S1572528613000066
12. Saravanan, B., Das, S., Sikri, S., Kothari, D.P.: A solution to the unit commitment problem–a review. Front. Energy **7**(2), 223–236 (2013)
13. Schwartz, R., Dodge, J., Smith, N.A., Etzioni, O.: Green AI. Commun. ACM **63**(12), 54–63 (2020). https://doi.org/10.1145/3381831
14. Singer, G., Livenson, I., Dumas, M., Srirama, S.N., Norbisrath, U.: Towards a model for cloud computing cost estimation with reserved instances. In: Proceedings of 2nd International ICST Conference on Cloud Computing, CloudComp 2010 (2010)
15. Tarplee, K.M., Friese, R., Maciejewski, A.A., Siegel, H.J.: Efficient and scalable pareto front generation for energy and makespan in heterogeneous computing systems. In: Fidanova, S. (ed.) Recent Advances in Computational Optimization. SCI, vol. 580, pp. 161–180. Springer, Cham (2015). https://doi.org/10.1007/978-3-319-12631-9_10
16. Wright, B.: A review of unit commitment. ELENE4511, 28 May 2013

# Author Index

© The Editor(s) (if applicable) and The Author(s), under exclusive license
to Springer Nature Switzerland AG 2023
D. Klusáček et al. (Eds.): JSSPP 2023, LNCS 14283, p. 193, 2023.
https://doi.org/10.1007/978-3-031-43943-8

Printed in the United States
by Baker & Taylor Publisher Services